Critical Acclaim for *The World Atlas of Beer*

"A sweeping, illustrated overview of beer's bubbly path from history to the present day . . . It's the beer book I'd like to find under the tree."
—EVAN BENN, *ESQUIRE*

"A world tour of the best craft beer you have not heard of—yet."
—JOSHUA M. BERNSTEIN, FOOD REPUBLIC

"What a treasure trove! . . . This book is great for those just beginning to appreciate the popular drink, but it certainly doesn't stop there. . . . In addition to the vast amounts of useful and interesting information . . . this book is stunning. Featuring images of hard-working brewers, charming pubs, and gorgeous fields where barley, wheat, and hops are grown, the eye is satisfied as much as the mind. . . . Perfect for every beer aficionado. Both novices and those already well versed in the art of craft brewing will find this book fascinating, beautiful, and useful."
—SAN FRANCISCO BOOK REVIEW

"Nicely illustrated . . . a coffee table book you'll want to curl up with, favorite brew in hand."
—NEW JERSEY STAR LEDGER

"Light and accessible . . . Something of a landmark . . . Webb and Beaumont have done an excellent job."
—TORONTO SUN

"Beer fans will want this oversized and glossy tome."
—LIQUOR.COM

"If you're a beer devotee traveling around the world—or just from one U.S. state to another—it might be a good idea to pack in your luggage *The World Atlas of Beer*. . . . It's a one-volume beer encyclopedia, and a fun read. . . . The prose flows like a good brew and the authors don't hold back on their opinions, making it a delightful book to read, as well as a reference book."
—HUNTINGTON NEWS

"The coverage of each country, as they say, is like a skirt: long enough to cover the subject, but short enough to keep it interesting. . . . The book comes in the most handy as a guide for the beer traveler. All the information necessary to track down the highlights of a beer-brewing country are included. . . . It will be a good addition to any collection of beer books, and it will also make a great gift for the beer lover in your life. . . . Just be sure to have a beer handy as you leaf through, though, because you will get thirsty reading this book."
—IN SEARCH OF BEER

"*The World Atlas of Beer* has authority, the credentials of its authors ensure that, but it also has visual appeal. . . . Ten minutes with this book in your hand and you're not just gagging to open a few bottles but you're actually starting to think about booking a trip and seeing what the fuss is about for yourself."
—INSIDE BEER

"Comprehensive . . . Webb and Beaumont have made beer easily approachable and understandable while still covering the depth and breadth of the world of beer. . . . A timely and valuable addition to any beer enthusiast's bookshelf. . . . An invaluable and entertaining reference."
—WHISKED FOODIE

"A great read and a beautiful book . . . An enjoyable read and a reference that can be looked back on and read again and again. Grab one for yourself or a friend."
—CRAFT BEER TIME

"Essential to your drinking library."
—GRUB STREET

"A sumptuous snapshot of the world of beer as it is today . . . the *Atlas* gives new insights into how beer is changing and how things are right now. . . . Beaumont and Webb achieve a completeness of information by being concise, informative, and current. Their style is direct and simple. . . . It's an omniscient approach that's carefully selected, and the information they give us is delivered in a way which makes it easy to understand, but it's also truth-worthy and authoritative. . . . Everyone who likes beer should buy it."
—PENCIL AND SPOON

"A full-service guide to the beer across the globe, from fermentation to intoxication . . . easily one of the most comprehensive, clearest, and interesting guides. . . . The book is hopslammed with maps, pictures, and labels as well as plenty of information about the people and places pumping out some of the best beer on Earth."
—BRO BIBLE

"A comprehensive and fascinating volume that any beer drinker will appreciate, especially one who likes to try beers from different parts of the world. Whether you sip from its pages from time to time, or imbibe its contents in one long gulp, *The World Atlas of Beer* is filled with flavor."
—BOOKLOONS

THE
WORLD
ATLAS
OF
BEER

The Essential Guide to the
Beers of the World

Revised and Expanded Edition

TIM WEBB and STEPHEN BEAUMONT

STERLING EPICURE
New York

Dedication

From Tim Webb: Um die fehlenden Engel.
From Stephen Beaumont: For Maggie, with love and gratitude.

STERLING EPICURE
New York

An Imprint of Sterling Publishing Co., Inc.
1166 Avenue of the Americas
New York, NY 10036

ISBN 978-1-4549-2217-9

Distributed in Canada by Sterling Publishing Co., Inc.
c/o Canadian Manda Group, 664 Annette Street
Toronto, Ontario, M6S 2C8, Canada

For information about custom editions, special sales, and premium and corporate purchases, please contact Sterling Special Sales at 800-805-5489 or specialsales@ sterlingpublishing.com.

Manufactured in China

10 9 8 7 6 5 4 3 2 1

www.sterlingpublishing.com

See page 265 for image credits.

A Note About Alcohol Content

The authors believe in the importance of knowing the strength of the beer you drink and have thus listed the alcohol contents for each beer reviewed. Readers should be aware, however, that the allowable margin for error in different countries varies such that the strength listed on the label and that measurable in a lab can vary up to 1 percent and, occasionally, even more.

Confusing matters further, breweries sometimes change the strength of a beer, both in terms of general production and from country to country. So a beer well known as a 6% alcohol by volume pale ale, for example, can unexpectedly morph into a 5.5% or 6.5% brew, or be produced at 6% in its home country but rise to 7.5% for export.

As a result, while the alcohol contents listed in this book were, to the best of the authors' knowledge, accurate at the time of going to press, they may not remain consistent with every consumer's experience.

Contents

A Note About Anheuser-Busch InBev and SABMiller

In 2015, the world's largest brewing company, Anheuser-Busch InBev (AB InBev), proposed a buy-out of the second largest, SABMiller. As we wrote the last pages of this book during the first half of 2016, however, this merger has yet to be approved by competition watchdogs around the world, and neither has a name for the merged entity been proposed. As such, we have left references to the two companies under their individual names and advise the reader that they may have, by the time of reading, become as one.

The spill-over effects of this merger seem likely to include the MillerCoors combination in the United States being sold off to Molson Coors, the proprietorship of Grolsch (NL), Peroni (IT), and Meantime (UK) brands all falling to Asahi, and the full ownership of Snow (CH) being assumed by existing partner-owner China Resources. There would doubtless be other repercussions, as well.

Foreword

I first treated beer seriously in 1974, when I was taken by the efforts of a gathering band, self-dubbed the Campaign for Real Ale, to save "traditional British beer." While the shiny but plain industrial brands starred in the TV advertisements of the day, the superiority of those slower brews, served mainly in Britain's more authentic, time-worn pubs, was easy to taste.

Success seemed unlikely, but against the odds, small victories were won—and in their triumph these helped to foster an extraordinary consumer U-turn. A global industry built on sound business principles discovered that its assumptions displeased many of its customers: a first lesson in consumer relevance, which some in the detached boardrooms of today's global companies have yet to grasp.

Over the millennia, beer has at different times played the roles of intoxicating nutrient, protector from infection, emollient of workforces, provider of revenues, and the basis of huge fortunes. Only in the past 20 years has it become a drink to be explored and enjoyed in its own

right, perhaps because we came close to losing it altogether through the impact of wars, prohibitionists, and corporate narrow-mindedness.

In the past five decades better-tasting beer has been recovered, revived, and—for many countries—created afresh in ways that not even my most zealous contemporaries could have predicted.

It is as if some organic driving force is pushing beer back to what it is supposed to be, after a bizarre century of ill-judged pursuits.

Where our first atlas aimed to provide the curious with an introduction to the best of modern brewing, and aficionados with a framework within which to understand the unprecedented changes that occurred during the first decade of the twenty-first century, our second edition begins to describe the characteristics of a more confident new world of beer.

My own journey to research this edition took me to the world's southernmost brewery in the Argentine part of Tierra del Fuego, gateway to the Antarctic, and to the northernmost, at Longyearbyen on Norway's Svalbard archipelago, the current extremities of craft brewing's reach. This is an atlas, after all.

On my way I was privileged to meet with hundreds of individuals, mostly strangers to one another, all of whom have made a significant personal contribution to this most unlikely of revolutions. They included brewers, hop growers, and maltsters; advocates, educators, and writers; scientists, politicians, and legislators; owners, entrepreneurs, and the odd icon—just some of the people who have taken beer's inexorable drift from rural craft to global business and begun to reverse it.

The impact of this shift was, until a decade ago, barely measurable. If it continues its current course, by 2017 the move in annual global spending away from industrial brands and into craft beers is likely to reach a trillion dollars, euros, or pounds.

Our greatest challenge has been to present and explain the different types of ale, lager, lambic, and mixed-fermentation beers that populate a beer market liberated from the constraints of uniformity. We have tried to absorb and relate this evolution without whooping for passing fads or descending into stylistic pedantry. If enthusiasm breaks through our reportage occasionally, we ask your forgiveness.

Tim Webb
Bristol, UK

Left: Beer in the early twenty-first century—the ultimate consumer U-turn.

Opposite: At the Kasteelhof, atop Mont Cassel in northern France, it is the wide range of locally brewed ales that draws in an enthusiastic crowd of visitors from near and far.

Introduction

In the first edition of this book, I wrote that the world has never seen such an enormous range of brewing activity across all continents. To which I will add for this edition, "until now."

Truly, a lot has happened since this atlas was first published. In the United States—otherwise known as the global poster child for craft beer—the number of breweries has swelled from 2,401 to well in excess of 4,200: the most in the nation's history. The United Kingdom in general and the city of London in particular have witnessed similarly audacious growth, as have Canada, the Netherlands, much of Scandinavia, Czechia, and South Africa.

In other brewing countries, the numbers might be less impressive, but other factors appear just as remarkable. In 2016, Germany celebrated the 500th anniversary of the *Reinheitsgebot* (literally "Purity Order") while witnessing an unprecedented surge in the number of German-brewed IPAs and other decidedly un-German styles. At the same time, iconoclastic Belgium has become only more so, adding ultrahoppy beer styles to its considerable arsenal of diverse and eccentric ales.

Even more extraordinary is what has been going on in countries we would not so readily associate with beer. European wine lands such as Italy and France now boast hundreds of breweries scattered across every *regione* and *département*, with Spain, Greece, and Portugal rushing to join them. Japan can now lay claim to the most mature beer market in Asia, but South Korea and Vietnam may soon have something to say about that. Australia and New Zealand, as geographically isolated as they are, threaten to influence the global brewing industry in ways we are only just beginning to fathom.

In 2012, while our scope was global, our focus rested squarely upon the roughly 30 countries that were actively engaged in beginning, reviving, or growing their national beer cultures. Today, we cast our gaze upon twice that number, including Switzerland and Poland, China and Israel—nations that previously merited but a sentence or two and now boast their own sections. We will risk no predictions as to how this number might grow in the future.

Repeat readers will note that with this edition we have done away with the beer reviews that populated the bottom quarter to a third of most pages. This too comes as a result of the extraordinary growth in global brewing, to the point that even the 500+ reviews we offered previously are woefully unrepresentative of the marketplace as a whole.

We have likewise revised many of the maps you will discover in the following pages, narrowing our focus to cities in some cases and finding unique ways to chart progress and development in others. At the core of our thinking is always the need to provide the most useful information in the most readable format possible.

No book will ever be able to keep pace with the remarkable change brewing is undergoing around the world, but we hope that the snapshot of the moment that this atlas represents will nonetheless fuel curiosity, enliven conversation, and fire the imagination. We suggest that you grab yourself a beer and see if you agree.

Stephen Beaumont
Toronto, Canada

Above: Pale, golden, and brown may be standard, but beer styles cross a multitude of other color divides.

Right: Many craft breweries struggle to simply keep up with the demand for their beers.

Above: Sake, spirits, and "dry" beer might still dominate Japanese beverage sales, but surging craft beer may soon challenge that status quo.

BEER BASICS

Nothing about beer is simple. It is just made to look that way.

As the preferred intoxicant of ordinary people over much—no, over most—of the globe, control of its production or availability empowers the controller. Those who seek to rule us project it as their companion; those who seek to improve us tax it as their enemy; and those who seek to bamboozle us project it as their talent.

Concocted from grain and herbs, tweaked to a thousand local preferences, loved for its association with the best of life, forgiven for its blandness, and fêted for its excellence, how could beer ever be simple?

WHAT IS BEER?

Beer is the world's favorite alcoholic beverage, consumed in one form or another in every country where it is not specifically prohibited, and probably in most where it is. As such, documenting its place in the world is a complex task, made all the harder by its stubbornly evolving and expanding nature. The following pages constitute our attempt to put this changeable picture in order, uncovering beer's past, documenting its present, and doing our best to foretell the future.

The world's biggest beers

In general, little mention has been made of the world's most popular brands. Sadly, within the world of beer, fame is rarely achieved or sustained through maintaining distinctive features but is instead accrued by association with different forms of celebrity or by popular interest, which in turn is bought through sponsorship.

Where global giants such as AB InBev, SABMiller, Heineken, Molson Coors, and Carlsberg are helping to create excellent beers that are relevant to the modern era, we are happy to acknowledge these on the same basis as we would those from a smaller company. Otherwise, we have chosen to pass by the world's largest-selling brands in favor of more interesting ones.

National & regional profiles

With brewing's reach now stretching around the globe, we have had to make difficult decisions about where best to apportion our pages. We apologize in advance to any beer aficionados who feel their country of birth or beer of preference receives short shrift.

Within each entry, further divisions have been made. In relation to many older brewing lands, we have singled out specific styles, while most New World entries have been organized geographically; in some instances, a combination of the two approaches has been used. Beer as a subject matter is amorphous, and no single approach will serve all occasions.

In this edition we have moved away from highlighting particular beers that, in some way, epitomize what is going on in a country. Instead, we have produced short pieces on particular people, firms, or topics that seem to us to have something local to say.

Defining beer

The legal definition of beer varies around the world in both its precise specifications and its purpose. In countries such as Norway and Japan, for example, if a drink is defined as a beer, it will attract a higher rate of tax than other alcoholic beverages of the same strength. In France and Hungary, the opposite applies.

In Ontario, "lager" is not an acceptable label description of the beverage inside a bottle or can, unless the word "beer" is also added. Any brand over 5.6% ABV must include the words "strong beer" or "malt liquor."

In terms of a basic premise, beer is the product of grain, whereas wine is derived from fruit (other than apples and pears, which yield, respectively, cider and perry), and mead is fermented from honey. According to this definition, however, alcoholic beverage pedants will tell you that Japanese sake is therefore a kind of beer. We say it is not, for reasons we cannot define, beyond adding, "obviously."

The categories of beer

Beyond the grain requirement—itself rather broadly interpreted by certain brewing companies—and whatever legal constructs may exist from jurisdiction to jurisdiction, beer is a rather nebulous entity. Unlike wine, which is regulated through appellation controls and convention, restrictions as to what a

Left: Increasingly, today's beer drinkers know what they like and are unimpressed by those who simply like what they know.

Opposite: The battle between uniformity and a beer's terroir is at the heart of defining brewing excellence, seen here at Camden Town, in London.

beer may or may not contain, or how it might be described, are few.

This has created the rather absurd situation whereby the consumer is awarded minimal information as to what he or she is buying. So while no one would expect a Chardonnay wine to boast any flavor profile other than that of a wine made from Chardonnay grapes, an IPA in Britain might be a slender, lightly hopped 3.5% ABV bitter dating from 1915, an attempt to re-create a heavily hopped 5.5% ABV variety from, say, 1850, or one that apes the modern, aggressively bitter Californian type, which is above 7% ABV. Meanwhile, in eastern Canada, an IPA may be similar in appearance, aroma, and taste to a mainstream lager.

As frustrating as this situation may be, especially for the beer novice, this imprecise use of names is the flip side of one of beer's foremost strengths: its diversity of styles, ingredients, and characters. A beer that is thought too strong in one country may be seen as weak in another; some flavors which are considered flaws in one culture might be revered by another; and methods or ingredients that are frowned upon by brewers in one country are actively encouraged by their peers elsewhere.

The bottom line

To attempt a common theme, if you ask for a definition of beer, the short answer is this: It is a moderately alcoholic beverage created by the fermentation of sugars derived in largest part from the boiling of particular specified grains, most prominently malted barley, with seasoning provided primarily by hops (*see* p.20). Catchy, eh?

In a more practical, functional sense, however, beer is anything a brewer can create, beginning with grain, usually with added hops. And it is always fermented by some form of yeast but also potentially incorporates all manner of ingredients not otherwise banned; then it is conditioned or aged in any of a multitude of ways.

Many German brewers may still find solace in the 500-year-old *Reinheitsgebot* or "Purity Order" (*see* p.90), but for much of the rest of the brewing world, and the vast majority of the craft brewing fraternity, such restrictions have never applied.

What has happened in practice is that beer has developed a mechanistic version of terroir. Local laws, the nature of the brewing water, the types of local ingredients available, the skills and preferences of prominent brewers, and the shared tastes of customers have led to beers that are adapted distinctively to their regions.

All definitions of beer within the beer world will tend to confuse and falsify more than they illuminate or clarify, so to dissuade others from wasting their time (and ours) on such work, we have tried consciously not to obsess. To avoid being slaves to any rulebook we have let anarchy reign, wisely or otherwise. Within reason, of course.

ORIGINS

We infer from the pattern of crops planted by the early inhabitants of Mesopotamia and the Fertile Crescent that they were probably brewing a form of beer by 9000 BC, although the earliest direct evidence of a drink derived from fermented grain comes from residues on pottery fragments found in the Hunan province of China dating from 2,000 years later.

By 3000 BC, it seems Egyptian brewers had determined that barley was the best grain for brewing and had developed crude forms of malting. We also know that the Celts were using barley, wheat, and oats by 2000 BC.

Beer making was originally a domestic pursuit, frequently carried out by "ale wives" alongside baking. Even the early "common" or town brewers often employed women to oversee the recipes and the brewing.

The curse of ancient brewers was oxidation. Contact with air rapidly turns the alcohol in sweet, heady fermented grain extracts to nauseating aldehydes and sour organic acids. Beer makers sought for centuries to delay or mask this by adding herbal mixtures called *gruit*, some purveyors of which, such as those in medieval Bruges, became immensely wealthy.

Hops had been used by apothecaries for centuries to add scented bitterness to ancient medicines and may have been used in brewing, too. These bitter weeds contain antioxidants that slow acidification and antiseptics that reduce fungal and other infections. They became the ideal brewers' remedy, spreading slowly across Europe from Bohemia between the eleventh and fifteenth centuries.

Before it was understood to be a living microorganism, yeast, captured in a runny suspension, thick paste, or as dried granules, was revered as a gift from God that made bread dough rise before baking and turned thin oatmeal into intoxicating ale.

Beer has always varied in strength and composition through local circumstances and traditions, but from the seventeenth century brewers gained new options. The new coke ovens allowed lightly cooked malts to be made, from which pale ale could be brewed. The development of brewery-aged porter in eighteenth-century London began the creation of huge oak fermenting vessels. Finally, 1840 saw Alpine ice-storage of beer used for the first time on a commercial scale in Vienna, Munich, and the southern Bohemian town of Pilsen.

The Industrial Revolution made it possible to brew in ever-larger quantities, while the age of steam brought speedier transportation by land and sea, enabling the same beer to be available over vast areas, including overseas.

In 1862, French microbiologist Louis Pasteur and colleagues invented a process that allowed brewers to kill off the tiny creatures that both created and ruined the flavors of beer. By 1870, affordable refrigeration allowed beer makers and drinkers to move away from vinous oak-aged ales to concentrate on crisper, cleaner, and, pivotally, more commercially exploitable ones.

Come 1900, brewery companies the world over had the capability to create and sell a wider range of beers than ever before. Who knows how things would have been by now had 50 years of carnage, economic hurly burly, and prohibitionist politics not descended in 1914?

By the early 1970s only four countries—Great Britain, West Germany, Czechoslovakia, and Belgium—could claim to have a living culture of traditional brewing, and even those were struggling. The game was almost up for handcrafted beer.

Nobody foresaw what happened next.

Above: Modern brewers' control over fermentation owes much to the work of brewing scientists of the nineteenth and early twentieth centuries, such as those pictured here at the Carlsberg laboratories in Copenhagen

Opposite: Egyptian pharoah King Intef II offers milk and beer to the gods Ra and Hathor at Thebes, c.2100 BC.

THE ESSENCE

Policymakers in the European Union make a small, innocent-looking but important distinction between wine and beer. The first, they declare, is "an agricultural product," while the second is "manufactured." This differentiation means that winemakers benefit from an agricultural subsidy denied to brewers—even those who still brew on the farm—that thus far has totaled €13 to €35 billion, depending on how it is measured.

It is not just politicians who see beer as a product of the manufacturing industry. Over the centuries the specialist cooks who were the first brewers evolved into artisans paid to turn grain into a social lubricant. As trading these commodities became big business, some built their reputations on making reliably distinctive and enjoyable beers, whereas others sold ones that were acceptable, affordable, and had greater potential for profit.

The brewing business is in constant flux, its dynamics driven by the age-old tensions between the craftsman brewer intent on making the best-tasting product, and customers often more taken with supplying or seeking intoxication than subtler pleasures.

The turning of barley into beer is at one and the same time a simple technique and an immensely complex balance of science and art. A home brewer might make something acceptably challenging from a store-bought kit using shortcuts, while a modern master brewer might have added a doctorate to his degree before being allowed to design a drink intended for necking unnoticed by those who could not tell a hop from a hobbit.

Such are the complications behind a beverage of multiple personalities: the bringer of warmth and liquid replenishment, of conviviality and menace, the fount of all indolence, and a perfect accompaniment to cheese. Such is the nature of beer.

Yet beer is a deliberate drink. The vagaries of soil or harvest, barrique or cork need rarely be endured by the brewer. Instead, by applying their skills, they get to choose a beer's color, clarity, and intensity; the extent and nature of most of the flavors and aromas held within it; the amount of alcohol it will eventually contain; and even the size, tint, and consistency of its foam.

At every stage, brewers must balance the competing demands of cost and excellence, of individuality and conformity, of consistency and flair. In doing so, they need also do no harm, ensuring that neither rogue microbes nor unwanted oxygen pollute it on its way to your lips, crossing their fingers that their creation will remain well treated throughout its oft-lengthy journey from brewery door to glass. Beer goes wrong through ineptitude, not by an act of God.

The people who design a beer, in theory at least, get to control everything about it. So whether a beer entertains with its perfect balance and imaginative edges, or simply bubbles into the glass with nothing to say beyond its name, it is the result of thoughtful deliberation.

If the beer you are drinking is dull, perhaps its makers are trying to tell you something.

Above: It is a strange truth that for all the disregard by bosses, mistrust by customers, and underrating by authors, most professional brewers love their job.

Opposite top: You can never be too careful. Sampling wort from the lauter tun in one of Bavaria's older breweries.

Opposite bottom: Brewers and beer enthusiasts alike know that aroma is every bit as important as taste in the appreciation of a beer.

MALTED BARLEY & OTHER GRAINS

The heart of any beer is its grain, and malted barley is the grain of choice for the vast majority of the world's brewers. The physical robustness of barley ensures it keeps its integrity throughout the malting process, at the end of which the combination of starch and enzymes in its seedlings creates the best yield of fermentable sugars.

While wheat, oats, rye, and other cereals can also be malted, unlike with barley, the husks around their grains will detach from the kernels during the three stages of production that constitute malting. Thus they tend to disintegrate, making them harder to work with and filter out from the wort at the end of mashing (*see* From Grain to Glass, p.24).

Harvested cereal typically loses a third of its moisture during storage, so the first part of the malting process is to rehydrate the partially dried grain by steeping it in water over a couple of days.

The second stage is germination, as the revived grain, kept warm and damp, springs into life, sprouting a tiny shoot, or "chit." By about five days into this process the action of enzymes in their cell walls turns the starch in the seedling into sugars suitable for fermentation into alcohol and carbon dioxide.

To capture this at its optimum, the maltster kills off the enzymes by a sharp burst of heat delivered by kilning, sometimes followed by further kilning, for color and flavor, or roasting.

During kilning hot air permeates through the grain for around three days, starting at room temperature and building to 212°F (100°C). In contrast, roasting takes place in a huge oven above a furnace, where the temperature of the grain can be set to reach anything between 194°F (90°C) and 446°F (230°C). Only malted grains are kilned, while roasting can be applied to raw barley, kilned malt, or "green" malt that has not been kilned.

Species of barley vary in their resistance to disease, starch content, mix of background flavors, and yield per acre. Some are specifically suited to particular types of beer. British ale brewers often favor Maris Otter, a tasty yet relatively low-yielding variety grown mainly in East Anglia. Their Czech counterparts swear by the Haná varieties from South Moravia, while German colleagues prefer the appropriately named Malz.

Malted barley can be made to a wide variety of specifications, defined broadly by the length of germination and extent to which it is kilned, roasted, or both. Roasted unmalted barley tends to produce more astringent flavors, while roasting green malt creates a slightly caramelized grain called crystal malt, which gives fuller, toffeelike flavors to darker beers.

At the lighter end, pilsner malt is barely toasted and has not browned, allowing its use in the creation of light, blond beers. Pale ale malt introduces an amber tone, Vienna malt brings in ruddy brown, as does the darker Münchener (or Munich). At the roasted end of the spectrum, chocolate malts, which look and taste caramelized, contain little sugar and are used mostly for coloring.

Although barley is the undisputed king of the brewing grains, wheat, rye, and oats have just as long a pedigree. These can be malted or used plain, bringing a heavy sweetness to young beer—particularly so with oats—but greater astringency when their sugars are fully fermented. They bring practical challenges, too, producing a milky protein haze that can be difficult to clear and, if making up much over a third of the mash, clogging up brewing vessels like soggy pasta.

A few brewers have revived the use of older grains such as spelt, buckwheat, emmer, and others, mostly for their different backtastes, while some maltsters are testing the possibilities of quinoa. A wheat-rye hybrid called triticae is appearing too.

Using adjunctive grains like corn (maize), sorghum, and rice, or adding simpler saccharides such as starch, syrup, or crystalline sugar thin out the flavor of beer. While this can make a heavy beer more approachable—a 9% ABV beer will readily withstand substitution of 15 percent of its sugars without suffering—in lighter beers, it is done mostly to keep costs down or flavor subdued.

BREWERS' LIQUOR

The largest component of beer is its least considered—water, also known as liquor in some brewing cultures.

Brewing water needs to avoid contamination that has potential negative effects on health and to contain a deliberate mineral balance for the beer being brewed.

The most important minerals are carbonate and bicarbonate to optimize mashing, sulfate to big out hop character, calcium and magnesium to modify various parts of the brewing process, and finally sodium and chloride levels to optimize mouthfeel. It is complicated.

For our purposes, even the smallest brewers can analyze and doctor the mineral content of their water supply to optimize its suitability, and contamination is a rare event in a production brewery.

Opposite: Traditional floor malting of barley requires that the grain be turned manually so as to ensure even kiln-drying.

HOPS

The common hop (*Humulus lupulus*) is crucial to the smell and taste of a beer. Hops were farmed in central Europe as early as the eighth century and were probably used in brewing long before the king of Bohemia taxed them in 1089. By the fifteenth century, they had become a routine ingredient of most European beers, with Britain a late adopter.

Hop flowers or cones contain a variety of naturally occurring chemicals that reduce fungal and other infections and slow oxidation, while their oils provide floral and herbal aromas and citrus flavors. Bitterness in varying degrees is liberated as alpha acids, which are activated on boiling (*see* p.24) and can be measured in International Bitterness Units (IBU)—though this does not always reflect the consumer experience particularly at the higher end, where estimation may be to blame.

Sour and bitter tastes trigger in-built warning signs in humans that help us spot poisonous foods and liquids. These become more acute in pregnant women and nursing mothers and may account in part for beer's greater popularity with men, although social conditioning probably plays a far stronger role.

Above: "Hop Vine," from *The Young Landsman*, hand-colored lithograph published in Vienna, 1845.

Recent years have seen substantial changes in the acceptability of bitter beers, led by trends in the USA. Hops are little used beyond brewing, so growers must follow the trends of an industry that, until recently, had been moving in the direction of ever less-assertive beers. The consequent fall in acreage saw hop farms disappear altogether from some regions and a loss of over 27,182 acres globally since 2000.

The huge growth in popularity of highly aromatized and bitter styles of pale ale in recent years and the increasingly imaginative use of the flavor properties of some varieties are now impacting so acutely that there are fears of a global shortage lasting the rest of the decade. Is this a driver for the sour and wild beer trend, we ask? Or is this the best opportunity yet for a wee heavy and lower hopped stout boom?

Hop cultivation has never been confined to the European heartlands of brewing, and growers in North America and New Zealand have been exporting for a century and longer. However, China and even Argentina have now joined a reviving international trade.

Over 200 varieties are currently in regular use by commercial brewers, most being fairly recent hybrids. Each has its own profile of antiseptic properties, flavors, aromas, and bitterness. Picking the right hop recipe for a beer is like choosing the herbs, spices, and vegetables to make a stew.

As a rule, single varieties work less well than a carefully concocted mix, but some newer strains are good enough all-round performers to make successful single-hop beers, leading some normally conservative growers to compare these to single-grape wines.

Better-known British varieties include Fuggles, Northern Brewer, Bullion, various Goldings, and the relative newcomer Challenger. German brewers prefer the

BOY HOPS & GIRL HOPS

Hops come in two "sexes"—dubbed male and female. Only female hops are used in brewing, since male hops taste bad.

As hop propagation is vegetative, males are not required to do the deed and are weeded out of hop farms. Even when growing some distance away, they can distract the females, ruining their taste and potency by making them, as one grower put it, "stop work and party." Cultivated males survive only because they are necessary to the creation of new varieties, which is where their true talents lie. Recent years have seen the emergence of hops tasting of oranges (Mandarina Bavaria), mangoes (Mosaic), and even roses (Mapuche).

so-called noble hops like Tettnang, Spalt, the variants of Hallertau, and the Czech staple Saaz.

Although British brewers were importing hops from US growers as far back as the mid-nineteenth century, their boom times have been more recent with winning varieties such as Amarillo, Cascade, Willamette, Columbus (aka Tomahawk), Chinook, Citra, Simcoe, and others. More recently, New Zealand has made its presence felt with oddly fragrant varieties such as Nelson Sauvin, Pacifica, and Motueka, while the new face of Australian brewing is defined in part by the Galaxy hop.

Recent years have seen hop farmers starting to grow nonnative varieties. De Ranke of Belgium for example, famed for their clever use of US, UK, and German varieties in their hop-forward ales, are nowadays supplied all from a Belgian grower.

While the mix of hops is crucial, the form in which they are used is important, too. Whole hops come mostly compressed in bulky and cumbersome sacks, but provided they are fresh they should be considered the gold standard, their exclusive use insisted upon by some brewers. The alternatives are pellets, jamlike extract, and oils.

Brewers can argue long into the night over the relative merits of these various forms but condensing a contentious debate into a few simple points, the use of hop pellets is indistinguishable from that of whole pressed hops, provided they have been crushed when deep-frozen from a fresh state. Some are not, but those that are will actually stay fresh for longer than pressed hops will.

Most extracts and oils struggle to do more than the basics, and where better brewers use them, it tends to be in combination with other forms. That said, we have heard of some well-known brewers experimenting with what we would translate as hop tinctures with results they enthuse about as loudly as the proponents of freshly harvested, whole green hops.

Above: A farm worker loading Saaz hop vines onto a trailer at Lhota, near Žatec in western Bohemia.

Left: The growth of hop-forward beer styles, such as pale ale and IPA, in craft brewing around the world has placed a strain on the world's hop supply.

YEAST

Yeast are the microscopic miracles that shape a beer, creating its alcohol and directing its character. These tiny, single-cell fungi feed on the sugar in wort (*see* p.24), producing alcohol and carbon dioxide as by-products in the process of fermentation.

While there are dozens of grain possibilities and hundreds of hops to choose from, the number of strains of yeast available to a brewer is measured in thousands, each assigning recognizable tastes to a beer regardless of its style.

By convention, yeast are referred to in the plural. Those that ferment ales are known collectively as *Saccharomyces cerevisiae* and when working at room temperature rise initially to the top of the wort—hence ales may be termed "top-fermented." Their lager equivalent *Saccharomyces pastorianus* are better suited to work at lower temperatures, congregating toward the bottom, so "lagers" are sometimes termed "bottom-fermented."

In commercial brewing practice, the distinction between ale and lager has blurred beyond recognition, some brewers pushing lager yeast to ferment beers at room temperature and above in a couple of days, while others ferment lagers with ale yeast made to work in the cold.

It can take a lifetime of beer tasting to appreciate how much the right (or wrong) yeast can maneuver a beer. To take a shortcut, seek out one of the Bavarian wheat beers that use *Hefeweizen* ale yeast to create an intense banana and clove presence (*see* pp.96–7). Then swap to an American "Belgian-style" ale that has attained its spicy character from a specialist yeast strain rather than the addition of spice powders (*see* pp.74–5). Then swap to one of the new breed of earthy saisons that are spreading indiscriminately through the craft beer world, earning their pedigree simply by use of one of a handful of yeast strains recently deemed necessary to make that style.

Brewers of old described their brewery's yeast as its thumbprint, carefully choosing a favorite strain to ferment beers of different styles with a shared backtaste. They used to source yeast by skimming it off the last batch of beer, a technique that also captured some airborne wild yeast, creating a small amount of mixed fermentation.

Nowadays, most use sealed systems that can easily be sterilized between brews, meaning they can choose different yeast for each brew if they so choose, preferring a specialist to a generalist, although yeast sourcing remains critical.

The aim is usually to have a reliable supply of the chosen yeast every time the

Above: Skimming yeast off a top-fermented beer in an open vessel.

same beer is brewed. Larger breweries will manage their own yeast bank on site. Those who cannot afford such a luxury can sometimes rely on an independent yeast bank to maintain supplies of fresh yeast, while others use dried yeast, bought in as needed.

We know a couple of excellent small breweries that produce beers reliably and consistently with dried yeast, but far more who report or display a problem whereby their beers acquire phenolic tastes and aromas ranging from elastoplast via cardboard to stagnant water.

Saccharomyces are not the only yeast, and yeast are not the only microbes that create flavors in beer. The recent expansion in sour and "wild" beers, starting in the USA around 2012 and spreading across the craft beer world faster than the skills required to make them, depends on using slow-acting *Brettanomyces* yeast, pediococci, and other lactic acid generating organisms to create flavors that hover at the edge of acceptability.

These range from regular brews injected artificially with a splash of acid to experimental beers that are oak-aged by people with their eyes, ears, and noses wide open. In our experience thus far they have ranged from exquisite to execrable. Their exploration by brewers and consumers alike is only just beginning.

Right: Stainless steel sealed conical fermenters are now the norm in breweries both large and small.

FROM GRAIN TO GLASS—KEY DECISIONS

All great beers are the products of careful design. Whether the idea for them originated from the creative brilliance of an individual or the methodically collated preferences of the less inspired, all beers are the result of intention. Some of the brewer's design decisions involve having access to particular equipment, although more relate to options of timing, method, and ingredients. Different factors will weigh more or less heavily, depending on the type of beer involved, but whichever it is, the final product is the result of a series of key decisions common to all.

1 PREPARING THE GRAIN

The malted barley and other grains are run into a hopper before crushing and grinding in a mill to produce grist. The resulting mix is sometimes called the grain bill.

Decisions:
Which type of malted barley to use? What proportions? What quantity? Other grains, grain derivatives, or additional sugars, if any?

2 MASHING

Hot, clean brewing water (or liquor) is adjusted to the right alkalinity and mineral content before being delivered into the mash tun, where the grist is mixed in and agitated with a mechanical rake or paddle system. The temperature of the mash in its different phases will determine the type and extent of the sugars extracted. Higher temperatures will tend to yield a greater proportion of complex sugars that sweeten the beer and enhance its body. Typical temperatures are between 140°F and 176°F. Mashing usually takes between one and two hours. Straightforward stewing is called infusion mashing. Where liquid is run off into a separate vessel, warmed, and run back into the mash tun, once, twice, or three times, this is called single-, double-, or triple-decoction mashing.

Decisions:
Any minerals to be added to the water? What ratio of grist to water? Infusion only or with decoction, and if so, how many times? How long to mash? What temperature(s) for the different phases of mashing?

3 SPARGING

At the end of mashing, the sugar-rich liquid, now known as sweet wort, is run off while the residual grain is held back, classically in a separate vessel called a lauter tun, where it is sprayed, or sparged with hot water. This releases more sugar at the cost of dilution. Excessive sparging brings unwanted tastes.

Decisions:
Invest in a lauter tun? Sparge to what final concentration?

4 THE HOP BOIL

The sweet wort is channeled to a brewing kettle, or copper, where hops are added. This hopped wort is brought to a rolling boil, which sterilizes the mix, stops all enzyme action, and releases bittering alpha acids from the hops. A typical boil lasts for between one and three hours and can be sped up by pressure cooking. Further hops may be added at points during a boil for greater freshness and aroma, different effects requiring different temperatures.

Decisions:
Which type(s) of hop? Which forms? Sourced from where? What proportions? Added at what point(s) and in what quantities? How long to boil and at what temperature? Pressurized?

5 PREPARING THE HOPPED WORT

After the boil, the hops are separated out from the mixture by use of a vessel called a whirlpool and/or a sealed unit called a hopback. The suspension is then fed through a heat exchanger to cool it before reaching the fermenting vessel. The aim is to filter out solids while retaining volatile, aromatic taste components.

Decisions:
How much equipment to deploy? What balance of character and clarity is sought?

7 CONDITIONING & PREPARING FOR SALE

Conditioning is what gives a beer its prowess. Most beers are filtered and run into metal conditioning tanks or occasionally into wooden casks for aging. Simpler, mostly industrial beers get a few days rest in a cool vessel before being fine filtered, sometimes pasteurized and sent for sale. The simplest form of longer conditioning, popular in the UK, involves racking (transferring) beer into casks, adding fresh yeast to allow cask-conditioning for up to three weeks. Some beers are filtered before being bottled with fresh yeast and, sometimes, a drop of sugar. Many such bottle-conditioning beers are warm-chambered to spark refermentation. Precise measurement of sugar and yeast content now enables keg-, tank-, and even can-conditioning. The best lagers are cold-conditioned at 39°F or less for 8–12 weeks. Where fresh hops are added during conditioning, this is known as dry hopping.

Decisions:
How long to condition, in how many phases, at what temperature(s), and in which vessels? How much filtration at what point(s)? What, if any, reseeding with yeast? How much warm rooming and/or cold cellaring? When to rack, bottle, or can? Any postproduction doctoring—by blending, dilution, coloring, or sweetening?

6 FERMENTATION

In all types of beer, primary fermentation is vigorous. Open vessels are more vulnerable to infection than sealed ones. Taller fermenters physically stress the yeast. The warmer the temperature, the more volatile the production of esters—organic compounds that contribute "fruity" fragrances and flavors. Lower temperatures lead to greater sulfuring.

Decisions:
Which yeast strain(s) to use in what amount(s)? When and how to prepare, aerate, and pitch the yeast? What size, shape, geometry, and construction of fermenting vessel(s) to use? What starting temperature? Rising to what maximum and controlled how? How to remove the yeast? Whether to recycle it?

THE SELLER'S PART

After all this careful deliberation, the brewer must be resigned to the fact that, ultimately, variables outside his or her control will impact just as much on how the beer presents in the glass.

Transporting a beer from its place of creation to its place of consumption should involve as few stops as possible and "cold chain" logistics that ensure it neither freezes nor rises above 59°F (15°C) at any stage. It should then be stored with care and served with the same consideration one would give to a foodstuff. To do otherwise is to have wasted a lot of time and thought.

THE BREWER'S FIRST COMMANDMENT
Above all other considerations keep everything free of contamination.

THE BREWING WORLD

There may be some question about when the renaissance in modern brewing began—was it in the mid-1960s, with Fritz Maytag's purchase of the Anchor Brewing Company in San Francisco (*see* p.166), Peter Maxwell Stuart's reproduction of Scotland's wee heavy at Traquair House (*see* p.52), and Pierre Celis's revival of Flemish witbier (*see* p. 74); the formation of CAMRA to protect traditional British beer styles in 1971 (*see* p.42); or perhaps the publication of Michael Jackson's first edition of *The World Guide to Beer* in 1977 (*see* p.32)?—but there is no doubt it has now blossomed into a global phenomenon.

The shift in consumer buying patterns in recent years from technically perfect but disappointingly dull industrial beers to better-made, more adventurous ones is no longer measured in millions of dollars, pounds, or euros, but in hundreds of billions.

As each year of this century has seen a relentless rise in its spread across an ever-greater proportion of the world, even beer's most skeptical supporters are feeling good.

INDUSTRIAL BREWING

A 2009 report sponsored by the European Union described the largest brewery company in Europe as "bankers who make beer." It was a concise observation, but was it fair? Perusing the mission statements of the world's six largest brewery companies, one could be forgiven for thinking it was.

Each company focuses on the need to grow, drive costs down, improve business processes, and make higher profits for shareholders. None mentions improving their products, which is odd given that in almost all their traditional markets sales are being lost to smaller competitors who specialize in just that.

In the latter half of the twentieth century, large brewing companies concluded, with some justification, that their customers lacked discrimination beyond knowing a familiar product when they saw one. Several generations of consumer when asked what they wanted in a beer cited less bitterness, less alcohol, lighter color, greater clarity, and fewer calories. We can all condemn what is there—few can imagine what is not there.

As discerning drinkers moved their allegiance to wine, the greater mass continued to follow wherever the beer trend led, smiling at the ads and living the part of a happy, docile flock.

So national and global brand beers lost malted barley to simpler sugars and reduced the hops. High-gravity brewing allowed companies to make more fluid in less space—if a beer produced at 7.5% ABV can be diluted to 5% ABV shortly before canning by adding water, it cuts by one-third the fermentation space required at the brewery.

No beer was too simple. Newer, duller brews were thinned out to become "light" beers, which in turn became "ice" beers, when residual flavor particles were cold-filtered and centrifuged away, leaving a veneer beer consisting mainly of alcohol, sugar, and bubbles. Unpleasant tastes caused by shortcut methods were

Above: High-gravity brewing saves on space during the production process, gaining volume by adding water to the beer at the time of packaging.

dealt with by persuading consumers to imbibe at ever-colder, flavor-obscuring temperatures.

In the history of brewing, the journey from ale wives stirring cauldrons in their kitchens to bankers counting cans off a production line took over a thousand years, although the last part was taken at the gallop.

What sharp-eyed politicians have now spotted is that while the bankers' approach to brewing has been strong on efficiency, tax avoidance, and making cheap alcohol, it is the craft brewers who create employment, pay taxes where their businesses are based, and generate real income and pride for their community and its economy. The global companies are struggling with their vision of the future. They are understandably reluctant to cede western beer markets to the new "craft" class, yet their efforts to make their own craft beers have the faltering feel of elderly relatives grooving to the disco beat at a wedding. Witness AB InBev's Leffe range, Molson Coors' clipping the wings of Sharps in the UK, Heineken's subdued Brand brands, or Guinness's boring efforts with ales of the wrong color.

In reality it is questionable whether their lumbering nature will ever be nimble and fast-paced enough to challenge the craft market or whether drinkers will still want brews with trusted names once they are owned by those who make beers for the more easily pleased.

CRAFT BREWING

The last four decades have seen a global reaction against the simplification of beer. While largely spontaneous, its local champions recognized early the importance of keywords. The UK's Campaign for the Revitalisation of Ale pounced swiftly on "real" as a better "R" by which to define its ales of choice, while Belgium's first consumer champion picked "artisan," refined by Michael Jackson to "craft."

Early enthusiasts believed that small was good and large was bad. Big brewers spent millions on advertising campaigns; small brewers sold their beers in person. Small beer came from down the way; big beer from somewhere anonymous.

Time proved problematic to this idea, however. Some small brewery beers were not at all good. Then brands arose that were made to seem local but came from large breweries trying to capitalize on the growing microbrew trend. The final nail in the coffin came when some of the pioneering breweries grew too large to be described in such diminutive terms. So North America adopted a new term—"craft brewing."

While the romance persists of beer lovingly crafted by hand, rather than forged by sophisticated machinery, the truth is that many craft breweries rely on state-of-the-art equipment and computerization to produce their beers. Indeed, it is exactly this technology that allows them to maintain consistency and character.

So what does separate the craft brewery from the beer factory? The answer, we suspect, is not in terms of equipment, method, or ingredients but rather in ethics and attitude.

An industrial brewer aims to create acceptable beers at an impressive profit; a craft brewer aims to create impressive beers at an acceptable profit.

Hence, in practice craft brewers do not employ high-gravity brewing (*see* p.28) and use of adjuncts such as corn, rice, starch, or liquid sugar is much lower than the full one-third of the fermentable sugars allowed in law and found in many top name industrial brands.

Turning to what they do that makes them "craft," probably the most important aspect is the ability and willingness to revive and innovate. Since the late 1970s, almost every taste innovation in brewing—as opposed to technological—has come from craft breweries. This includes the popularization of American or New Zealand hops; the aging of beers in various sorts of wooden barrel; the use of wild yeast and other microflora during fermentation; sherry-production-inspired, solera-style conditioning; and renewal of many near-extinct or long-forgotten beer styles of the past. The likes of Molson Coors' Blue Moon line, or Guinness's Nitro IPA follow; they do not lead.

Then there is the willingness to add a massive array of flavoring ingredients, including whole oranges and other citrus fruits, wild flowers, spices of almost every conceivable description, and even tobacco leaf. For better or worse.

Whereas the world's largest breweries boast broad brand portfolios consisting of, at best, a handful of flavor profiles, craft

Left: Whereas industrial breweries store their grains in massive silos and leave carefully calibrated computers to do the rest, preparing the grist at a craft brewery is often an exercise in backbreaking manual labor, hauling heavy sacks of grain to the mill and hand measuring the correct combination of malts for each beer recipe.

breweries tend to offer a greater breadth of taste experiences even within a small collection of brands.

Although great in number, craft breweries remain relatively "micro" in terms of the combined volume of their output, rarely accounting for more than 10 percent of market share and in some nations far less. Yet their influence cannot be overstated. Love it or hate it, the US craft breweries' success with hop-forward pale ales may have created the twenty-first century's equivalent of the porter and pilsner booms of centuries past.

Inevitably perhaps, some have grown such fame that they have been bought out or part-purchased, sometimes for eye-watering sums. Such has been the fate or privilege, depending on your viewpoint, of Chicago's Goose Island, California's Lagunitas and Ballast Point, Norway's Nøgne Ø, Ireland's Franciscan Well, Canada's Granville Island and Mill Street, Australia's Little Creatures, the UK's Meantime and Camden Town, Brazil's Wäls and Colorado, and numerous others.

More changes of ownership will follow no doubt, as global brewers in need of a new strategy, and investment companies drawn to any opportunity, see ways to cash in on craft.

But will such "enhanced" companies see the need to give passionate brewers freedom to operate at the heart of the brewery, doing things the expensive way? And will consumers really wish to keep supporting a brand simply because those who first used its name were good people? We shall see.

In the end, what might be more "craft" than size or style innovation, adjunct use, or taste experiences, is the ability of a brewer to connect with consumers on a strongly personal level. And that is something more easily accomplished by a local, regional, or even national business going up against a global corporation than it is for the corporation itself.

Above: One key difference between a craft brewery and an industrial one is the hands-on approach at every stage, including batch testing, as here at Atlas Brew Works in Washington, D.C.

Below: Craft brewing is an attitude of mind. Here, street art meets manufacturing industry in one of the conditioning rooms at Scotland's BrewDog.

Above: Wooden casks with internal linings, such as these in a brewery warehouse in Traunstein, Bavaria, grace many a bar counter in various parts of Germany.

BEER STYLING

A beer style is an informal agreement between a brewer and a drinker, expressed via a label, by which the former tells the latter roughly what sort of beer he or she is about to buy. It is also a way to win prizes.

The first attempt to create a popular catalog of the beers of the world by style came from the late beer-writing pioneer Michael Jackson in his 1977 book, *The World Guide to Beer*. His intent at the time was to clarify and elucidate often obscure and regional beers for an audience that had largely never before encountered them.

Unfortunately, this approach has evolved over time into a morass of confusion, with it seeming at times as if every new thing done to beer should be awarded its own unique style descriptor and prize-winning category.

Much of this style expansionism is rooted in the USA, where a broadly experimental school of brewing has resulted in no fewer than 92 categories being judged at the 2015 Great American Beer Festival and dozens more recognized by the Brewers Association's official guidelines.

The traditional style categories of the kind that Michael Jackson defined still possess some meaning. Readers should be aware, however, that some of the best-known often derive from different traditions connected only by a word. Traditional Dutch *bok*, for example, is clearly the same type of beer as its Norwegian namesake but whether it has much in common with German *Bock* or even modern Dutch *bok* is suspect. Similarly, British pale ale can claim American-style pale ale as its younger, more boisterous offspring, but neither has much in common with Belgian.

Virtually every beer type in the world, from Burton-upon-Trent's pale ales (*see* p.44) to the lambics of Belgium's Payottenland (*see* pp.68–71), is subject to multiple interpretations, revisions, and oft-dramatic variations, leading beer historian Ron Pattinson to observe that they represent, "A shorthand to describe the essential features of a beer and its relative alcoholic strength … neither absolute nor immutable."

The current beer revolution sees not so much style creep as style leap, with some of those who began as imitators now lauding it over the originators. The UK's loss of IPA to the US was understandable given its home country's neglect of its most gifted child, for instance, but recent assumptions regarding the nature, or perhaps denaturing of Belgian *saison* might be a rewrite too far.

It does not help that different nations delineate their beers in different ways. The French, for instance, focus primarily on color as a defining factor, whereas the Italians add strength and cultural

Right: Different beer styles may become distinguished from each other by color, strength, ingredients, method of production, place of origin, or, in some cases, wistful marketing.

inspiration to their system of classification. Americans apply terms like "double," "triple," or "imperial" to high-strength or highly hopped versions of almost anything, even going so far as to "imperialize" some styles that are light refreshers, such as *Berliner Weisse*—in jest, we hope.

Our intention is not to diminish any of the beers that are slotted into these new categories, as some of these can be excellent. Rather, until such time as a much simplified and broadly agreed system of categorization for the fruits of the beer renaissance arises, we recommend readers simply note what might be written on the label and take any style indicator as being similar in

intention to stating the grape variety on a wine label, used without citing its region.

What gets lost in all the enthusiasm is beer's terroir—not in the sense that the local soil shapes the flavor of its ingredients, but for the way local traditions and tastes cause beers to emerge differently around the world. Brewers the world over can source the same hops, grain, yeast, water profile, and machinery, so why add to the already vast sea of American-style pale ales? Better instead to grow or regrow a local tradition that may not even know its name, leaving the prizes for those who value reward over achievement.

Above: Bitter, herbal, earthy, hazy, acrid, sweet, dry, sour, or just beery sir? A bar tender at the Crux brewery in Oregon.

RECENT TRENDS

By the start of 2016 more than 60 nations had become full members of the global beer revival, with a couple of dozen more dipping a toe in the liquor, as it were. Trying to spot patterns amid the resulting chaos is not always easy.

Driven by social media and Internet-based creations such as Ratebeer.com, Untappd, and others, a loose but huge global community of younger and not-so-young beer geeks, aficionados, lovers, snobs, believers, and campaigners routinely feeds off its own enthusiasm for, experience of, and knowledge about beer.

What we see within these wild, swirling currents are three emerging trends.

At its heart is a shared appreciation of what might be termed the classic beers: the longer-established, less immediate styles. Then there are those that push the possibilities of beer making beyond its traditional limits into uncharted territory—the so-called extreme beers. Finally, as the new adherents become familiar with the emblems of modernity they turn their attention to those unique types of beer that have survived in some backwater, archive, or collective local memory—folk beers, if you like.

Classic beers take many forms but share the trait of being more easily identifiable—almost definable—historic types of beer that either were or had recently been produced by many brewers before the recent bonanza began. These might include regional specialties like German *Kölsch* (*see* p.100) or *Altbier* lagers (*see* pp.98–9), national specialties like Irish stout (*see* pp.57–9) or Czech světlý *ležák* (*see* pp.136–7), or the new international beers like hoppy IPAs or strong brown ales.

Extreme beers are usually, though not always, new and experimental, being distinguished by boundary-pushing, bizarre, and not-so-bizarre variations on strong, high-hopped, unhopped, oddly grained, soured, aged, and variously infused brews that come from the minds of the more inventive craft brewing glitterati, and occasionally ingenious dabblers. Brewers get like that sometimes.

We expand on folk beers in our section on Northern Europe (*see* p.112), though there are examples in many beer cultures, through revivals like Dutch *kout* (*see* p.86), German *Leipziger Gose* (*see* p.96), or *Lichtenhainer* (*see* p.114) and some that remained mainstream, such as Belgian lambics (*see* p.68), *Berliner Weisse* (*see* p.96) and arguably British cask-conditioned ales (*see* p.44)—all heritage styles that are or were unique to one brewing culture.

Of course not every legitimate style sits comfortably within one of these categories. Bavarian *Hefeweizen* is both folk and classic; Flemish oak-aged brown ales (*see* p.66) are both extreme and folk; Imperial (Russian) stouts are both classic and extreme; and authentic *gueuze* (*see* p.71) is comfortably all three.

For now, this model is currently unique to ourselves, but for those of us who appreciate bearings by which to make sense of our surroundings, we hope it helps.

Evolving beer styles

Beer's last era of rapid evolution was the 1870s, when brewers reacted to new technologies, growing social concerns, and rapidly changing values.

Pasteurization had for the first time gifted them control over the microbial processes that both created and spoiled their products. Affordable large-scale refrigeration, like that patented by Munich engineer Carl von Linde in 1876, paved the way for year-round large-scale production of lagers. Temperance ideals gained political influence across Protestant Europe and North America, and the urbanization of brewing collided with land availability.

The types of beer produced moved from oak-aged to fast-fermented, light ales became more prominent, and filtration at the brewery and fining in the cask made polished beers more suited to better glassware.

The changes in the first quarter of the twenty-first century are on a comparable scale, as creativity and rediscovery drive diversified beer styling at a giddying pace.

In the table opposite we list 48 of the world's most interesting beer styles and rate them in terms of their relative origins—Folk, Classic and/or Extreme—and how they stack up when it comes to their alcoholic strength, whether they are seen as session beers or beers of serious intent, and the influence the style has had historically in shaping the development of beer globally. The darker the color panel, the bigger the impact.

Above: Some beer festivals are devoted specifically to particular folk beer styles, others to classic beers, and a few, like this one in Boston, Massachusetts, to extreme beers.

EVOLVING BEER STYLES AS THEY SIT TODAY

STYLE NAME	FOLK ORIGINS	CLASSIC STATUS	EXTREME CREDENTIALS	ALCOHOLIC STRENGTH	SERIOUS INTENT	HISTORIC INFLUENCE	COUNTRY ASSOCIATION
CASK BITTER	MEDIUM	MEDIUM	LOW	SESSION	WORKADAY	INTERESTING	UK
CASK MILD	MEDIUM	MEDIUM	LOW	SESSION	WORKADAY	REGIONAL	UK
BRITISH PALE ALE	LOW	HIGH	LOW	SESSION	TROOPER	ROLE MODEL	UK
BRITISH IPA	LOW	MEDIUM	LOW	REGULAR	TROOPER	ROLE MODEL	UK
STRONG BROWN ALE	LOW	MEDIUM	LOW	HEAVIER	IMPRESSIVE	ROLE MODEL	UK
PORTER	LOW	MEDIUM	LOW	REGULAR	TROOPER	ROLE MODEL	UK
MILK STOUT	LOW	MEDIUM	LOW	SESSION	TROOPER	INTERESTING	UK
BARLEY WINE	NONE	MEDIUM	HIGH	ROBUST	STATEMENT	ROLE MODEL	UK
IMPERIAL STOUT	NONE	MEDIUM	MEDIUM	ROBUST	STATEMENT	INTERESTING	UK & USA
SCOTCH ALE (Wee Heavy)	LOW	MEDIUM	LOW	HEAVIER	IMPRESSIVE	INTERESTING	SCOTLAND
DRY STOUT	LOW	MEDIUM	LOW	SESSION	TROOPER	INTERESTING	IRELAND
EXPORT STOUT	LOW	MEDIUM	LOW	HEAVIER	IMPRESSIVE	ROLE MODEL	IRELAND
OAK-AGED ALE	MEDIUM	NONE	HIGH	HEAVIER	STATEMENT	LEADER	BELGIUM
BELGIAN *SAISON*	LOW	MEDIUM	LOW	REGULAR	IMPRESSIVE	INTERESTING	BELGIUM
OUDE LAMBIC	MEDIUM	LOW	MEDIUM	REGULAR	WORKADAY	REGIONAL	BELGIUM
OUDE GUEUZE	MEDIUM	MEDIUM	MEDIUM	HEAVIER	STATEMENT	ROLE MODEL	BELGIUM
OUDE KRIEK	MEDIUM	LOW	MEDIUM	REGULAR	IMPRESSIVE	REGIONAL	BELGIUM
DUBBEL	LOW	MEDIUM	LOW	HEAVIER	TROOPER	INTERESTING	BELGIUM
TRIPEL	NONE	LOW	HIGH	ROBUST	IMPRESSIVE	ROLE MODEL	BELGIUM
WITBIER	MEDIUM	MEDIUM	LOW	REGULAR	WORKADAY	INTERESTING	BELGIUM
BOKBIER	MEDIUM	MEDIUM	LOW	HEAVIER	TROOPER	REGIONAL	NETHERLANDS
BIÈRE DE GARDE	MEDIUM	LOW	LOW	HEAVIER	IMPRESSIVE	INTERESTING	FRANCE
BIÈRE DE BLÉ NOIR	HIGH	LOW	LOW	SESSION	WORKADAY	REGIONAL	FRANCE
HELLES	LOW	HIGH	LOW	REGULAR	TROOPER	ROLE MODEL	GERMANY
MÄRZEN	MEDIUM	MEDIUM	LOW	REGULAR	TROOPER	INTERESTING	GERMANY
KÖLSCH	MEDIUM	MEDIUM	LOW	REGULAR	TROOPER	INTERESTING	GERMANY
ALTBIER	MEDIUM	MEDIUM	LOW	REGULAR	TROOPER	INTERESTING	GERMANY
MÜNCHNER	LOW	MEDIUM	LOW	REGULAR	TROOPER	INTERESTING	GERMANY
DUNKEL WEISS	LOW	MEDIUM	MEDIUM	REGULAR	TROOPER	INTERESTING	GERMANY
SCHWARZBIER	MEDIUM	MEDIUM	LOW	REGULAR	TROOPER	REGIONAL	GERMANY
BERLINER WEISSE	MEDIUM	LOW	LOW	SESSION	WORKADAY	REGIONAL	GERMANY
GOSE	MEDIUM	LOW	LOW	SESSION	WORKADAY	REGIONAL	GERMANY
HEFEWEIZEN	MEDIUM	MEDIUM	LOW	REGULAR	TROOPER	LEADER	GERMANY
WEIZENBOCK	NONE	LOW	HIGH	HEAVIER	STATEMENT	INTERESTING	GERMANY
RAUCHBIER	MEDIUM	MEDIUM	LOW	REGULAR	TROOPER	INTERESTING	GERMANY
BOCK	LOW	MEDIUM	LOW	HEAVIER	IMPRESSIVE	INTERESTING	GERMANY
DOPPELBOCK	MEDIUM	MEDIUM	MEDIUM	ROBUST	STATEMENT	INTERESTING	GERMANY
VIENNA LAGER	LOW	HIGH	LOW	REGULAR	WORKADAY	REGIONAL	AUSTRIA
SVETLÝ LEŽÁK	NONE	HIGH	LOW	REGULAR	TROOPER	ROLE MODEL	CZECHIA
TMAVÉ	LOW	MEDIUM	LOW	REGULAR	WORKADAY	INTERESTING	CZECHIA
SAHTI	HIGH	NONE	LOW	REGULAR	TROOPER	LOCAL	FINLAND
GRODZIŠK	MEDIUM	LOW	LOW	SESSION	WORKADAY	REGIONAL	POLAND
BALTIC PORTER	NONE	MEDIUM	MEDIUM	HEAVIER	IMPRESSIVE	ROLE MODEL	POLAND
AMERICAN PALE ALE	LOW	MEDIUM	MEDIUM	SESSION	TROOPER	LEADER	USA
AMERICAN IPA	NONE	MEDIUM	MEDIUM	REGULAR	TROOPER	ROLE MODEL	USA
DOUBLE IPA	NONE	LOW	HIGH	HEAVIER	IMPRESSIVE	ROLE MODEL	USA
BLACK IPA	LOW	MEDIUM	MEDIUM	REGULAR	TROOPER	INTERESTING	USA
SMOKED PORTER	LOW	MEDIUM	MEDIUM	HEAVIER	IMPRESSIVE	REGIONAL	USA
AMERICAN *SAISON*	LOW	LOW	HIGH	HEAVIER	TROOPER	INTERESTING	USA

THE NEW WORLD OF BEER

It is said that countries divide by their consumption habits into wine drinking, spirits drinking, beer drinking, and abstinence. If that was ever true, it is certainly no longer the case. Beer is universal.

Of the top 40 beer-producing nations, three are in North America, six in South America, seven in Asia, five in Africa, and—with the exception of Australia—the rest in Europe. They include numerous countries traditionally thought of as wine drinking, such as France, Italy, Spain, Portugal, Hungary, Chile, and Argentina.

The global spread of beer brewing owes its origins to European colonial expansion in the eighteenth century and mass emigration to the Americas in the nineteenth. In the twentieth century, beer's growth was driven and shaped by the ambitions of expanding corporations, keen to harmonize and exploit international drinking habits, often associating their brands with the trappings of a desirable, economically independent lifestyle.

By 1975, for reasons outlined elsewhere, while the world was drinking ever more beer, the variety available had shrunk considerably.

Four decades on, there are two distinct ways of mapping beer brewing around the world. One that concentrates on ownership will show an ever-smaller number of large producers holding around 85 percent of world beer production, with the relationships between these companies becoming increasingly blurred. They jockey for position in a few potentially huge but traditionally restrained markets, such as China, Southeast Asia, and India, while sales in their traditional markets are in decline, sometimes alarmingly so.

The other world view, for those more inclined to following the fate of interesting and entertaining beers, shows craft brewing in widely different forms reemerging strongly across every traditional brewing nation, and dozens of others with no such tradition.

It is not far from the truth to say that by 2015 in almost every country where beer is made craft beer sales were rising in both volume and market share. Consumers the world over appear to be giving a clear message that they appreciate interesting beers and want to know more about them, while industrial brands are losing their shine. There is a reshaping of preferences. People are drinking less beer but with greater discernment.

What follows is a snapshot of where quality beer lies in the middle of the second decade of the twenty-first century, beginning with those countries of the Old World whose traditions have most influenced the craft brewing revival to date and proceeding to those in the New World whose efforts are likely to shape future changes.

EUROPE

The battered remains of two millennia of local commercial beer brewing around the world were, by the 1970s, restricted mainly to four parts of Western and Central Europe that were variously the last bastions of cask- and bottle-conditioned ales, cloudy wheat beers, strong ales aged in oak, and those blond and other lagers that were decoction-mashed and cold-stored over months as their originators had intended.

With hindsight, Europe in the 1980s was ripe for a beer revolution. Only Bavaria had a confident beer culture. The UK, Belgium, the Rhineland, and Czechoslovakia nursed wobbly ones, while the inhabitants of other parts of the continent were reduced to mere end-consumers.

Back then, sourcing better brews involved knowing whom to ask about where to look. Nowadays things are a bit different.

WESTERN EUROPE

The story of beer's revival in western Europe mirrored that of other consumer staples such as small batch breads, cheeses, and other local produce, in many places being ahead of the trend. The search for certainty that a one-size-fits-all product represents had lost its appeal.

The flow and content of beer's resurrection has varied from one country to another, but nowhere has it been either static or in decline. In Britain, France, Germany, and the Netherlands, the number of breweries that have opened since 1990 is measured in three figures, with Austria, Switzerland, Belgium, and Ireland each boasting many dozens.

At the same time, there has been a considerable expansion in the number of different styles of beer found. No longer is

Below: Bavaria, Germany's largest and southernmost region, stretching from Franconia to the Alps, home of the *Reinheitsgebot,* and the only place where quality brewing was still thriving in 1975.

pale ale the principal preserve of British brewers, nor stout the specialty of Ireland. Even the Belgians must accept that most of their finest beers have impressive imitators elsewhere.

Germany's obsession with pure, precise, and predictable beers, sometimes cartooned as "five thousand subtle variations on the same six drinks," is giving way to younger brewers and drinkers experimenting with styles their parents and grandparents consider foreign, while, in Britain, the children and grandchildren of the original "real ale generation" are breaking free of their parents' confines.

The growth of such "special beers" has occurred largely at the expense of bigger-brand blond beers and pale lagers more

generally. If Germany's larger producers could concentrate their efforts on quality rather than price, that could change rapidly.

European beer is progressing through the twenty-first century in better shape than it has been for a long while, and nobody is taking bets on it going anywhere else but up.

WESTERN EUROPE ▾
The heartland of Old Europe's brewing belt lies in a corridor to either side of a line drawn roughly from the north of Ireland to Vienna.

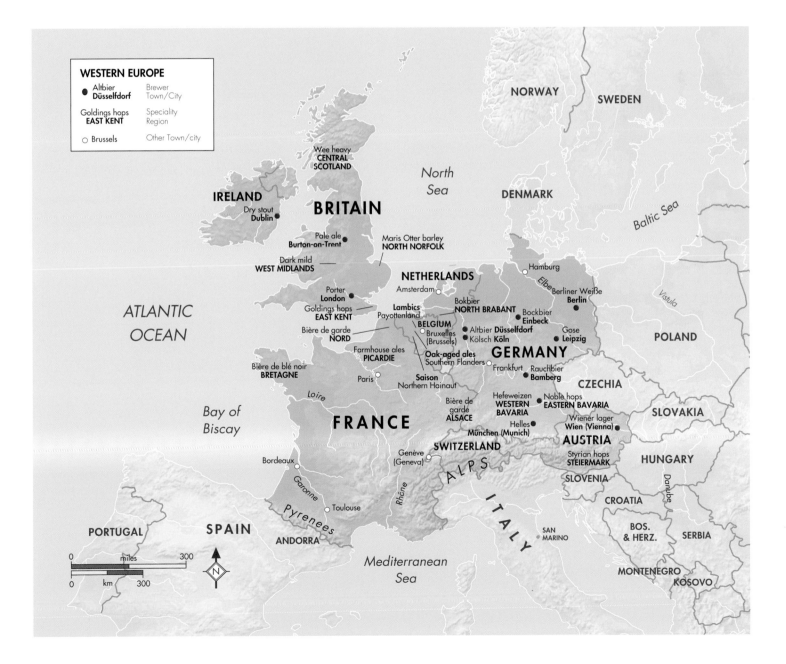

GREAT BRITAIN

Many of the types of beer that feature in craft brewing globally owe their origins to the oddly shaped land masses off the northwest coast of continental Europe known collectively as the British Isles. Pale ale (Indian or otherwise), stout—oatmeal, imperial, or oyster—barley wine, wee heavy, and porter all began life here.

Yet the daily beers of choice in modern Britain are altogether less robust. Industrial lagers dominate markets shared, in the great British pub with low-carbonation light ales and in the take-home, club, restaurant, and hotel trades with lackluster equivalents. Until recently, that is.

The point is that while most of the world is enjoying its first beer revolution in more than a century, Britain is well into its second in 40 years. To follow what we mean by this it is necessary to understand the successes and failures of a quintessentially British institution, the Campaign for Real Ale (CAMRA).

THE NEW LONDON BREWERY SCENE ▶

For the first time in 250 years London is the most influential brewing town in Britain, vying only with Chicago as the most breweried city in the world. The scene changes monthly but is driving extraordinary changes to the beer drinking habits of Londoners and others in the UK.

LONDON

- Brewpub
- Craft mainly
- Cask mainly
- Larger firm
- New commercial
- Pub-based micro
- Pub-chain micro
- Test kit only

Barnet
London Brewing
Finchley
Redemption
Beavertown Brewery
Left Bank
Walthamstow
Wild Card
London Brewing
Brodie's
Hampstead
Solvay Society East London
Signature Brew
Brewhouse & Kitchen
Five Points
Maregade
Camden (AB InBev)
Camden
40-ft
Pressure Drop
Howling Hops
Wembley
Hammerton
Tap East
Crate
Truman's
Stratford
Islington
Plato
Laine's
Moncada
Brewhouse & Kitchen
Hackney
London Fields
Ealing
Portobello
Queen's Head
Fountain
Redchurch
Three Sods
East Ham
Shepherd's Bus
Essex Street
London
One Mile End
Laine's
Dragonfly
Canary Wharf
Thames
Weird Beard
Southwark
Kernel
Anspach & Hobday
Partizan
Hop Stuff
Long Arm
Brew by Numbers
Fullers
Kensington
UBREW
Fourpure
Hammersmith
Thames
Orbit
Monkey Chews
Meantime
Fulham
Mondo
Peckham
Sambrooks
Brixton
Brick
Greenwich
Brixton
Clarkshaws
Zerodegrees
Kew
Florence
Brockley
Richmond upon Thames
Wandsworth
Laine's
Canopy
Late Knights
Rocky Head
Bullfinch
Lewisham
Twickenham
Belleville
Forest Hill
Reunion
By the Horns
Gipsy Hill
London Beer Factory
Wimbledon
Park
Sultan
Wimbledon
Bromley
Kingston upon Thames
Big Smoke Brewery
Volden
Croydon
Cronx

miles 4

km 4

TRADITIONAL BRITISH BEER

In 1971, reacting to what they saw as the demise of traditional British beer, four young English journalists decided to form a protest group to save it. An industry intent on making high-volume convenience brews was about to collide with a crusade promoting less convenient ones. Within two years top-fermented beers that condition in a broached cask had been dubbed "real ale" and in turn became synonymous with "good beer."

CAMRA's early successes made beer lovers who were advancing in other countries take heart, stoking what became a worldwide revival of local brewing. The unintended downside in Britain was to freeze-frame an ideal of what constitutes "proper beer" around 1960, by which time it was already in a pretty bad way.

Only recently, challenged by beers and ideas from foreign revivalists, have British consumers had to work out what they think about the older and grander styles of ale that once upon a time had made their brewers world famous before being allowed virtually to disappear from their lands of origin.

PRE-CAMRA BRITAIN

●	Banks's **Wolverhampton**	Pre-Camra brewery still open in 2015 Town/city
⊗	Vaux **Sunderland**	Pre-Camra brewer closed by 2015 Town/city
●	Samuel Smith **Tadcaster**	Survivors from before CAMRA
○	Cambridge	Other town/city

SCOTLAND

NORTHERN IRELAND

IRELAND

Maclay **Alloa**

Usher (now Heineken) **Edinburgh**

Belhaven (now Greene King) **Dunbar**

Traquair House **Innerleithen**

Northern Clubs Federation **Newcastle-upon-Tyne**

Carlisle **Carlisle**

Vaux, **Sunderland**

Jennings (now Greene King) **Cockermouth**

Camerons **Hartlepool**

Workington **Workington**

Lake District

Tyne

Tees

North York Moors

Flamborough Head

North Sea

Hartley **Ulverston**

Theakston **Masham**

Isle of Man

Okells, **Douglas**

Mitchell, Yates & Jackson **Lancaster**

Yorkshire Clubs **Huntington**

Castletown **Castletown**

Samuel Smith **Tadcaster**

Irish Sea

Timothy Taylor **Keighley**

Selby **Selby**

Matthew Brown Thwaites, **Blackburn**

Leeds

Hull **Hull**

Lees, **Middleton**

Darley **Thorne**

Holt, Hydes, **Manchester**

Oldham, **Oldham**

Greenall Whitley, **St. Helens**

Boddington

Wards **Sheffield**

Higson, **Liverpool**

Burtonwood

Greenall Whitley **Warrington**

Robinsons **Stockport**

Mansfield **Mansfield**

Batemans **Wainfleet**

Border **Wrexham**

Hardy & Hanson **Kimberley**

Home, **Daybrook**

Shipstone, **New Basford**

Greenall Whitley **Wem**

Marston's **Burton-upon-Trent**

Melbourn **Stamford**

Elgood's **Wisbech**

Norwich

Banks's (now Marston) **Wolverhampton**

Hoskin **Leicester**

Ruddles **Oakham**

Snowdonia

All Nations, **Madeley**

Olde Swan

Everards

Cardigan Bay

Aberystwyth

Three Tuns **Bishop's Castle**

Simpkiss **Brierley Hill**

Davenports **Birmingham**

Greene King **Bury St. Edmunds**

Adnams **Southwold**

Batham

Hanson

Holden's **Dudley**

Charles Wells **Bedford**

Cambridge

Tolly Cobbold **Ipswich**

WALES

Hook Norton **Hook Norton**

Greene King **Biggleswade**

Cook, **Halstead**

Donnington **Upper Swell**

Rayment, **Furneaux Pelham**

Ridley, **Hartford End**

Felinfoel Buckleys **Llanelli**

Brecon Beacons

Gloucester

Morrell's **Oxford**

McMullen **Hertford**

Gray **Chelmsford**

South Wales Clubs **Pontyclun**

Brain **Cardiff**

Morland, **Abingdon**

Brakspear **Henley-on-Thames**

LONDON

Arkell's **Swindon**

Bristol

Fuller's **London**

Young's **Wandsworth, London**

Wadworth **Devizes**

Reading

ENGLAND

Shepherd Neame **Faversham**

Gibbs Mew **Salisbury**

King & Barnes **Horsham**

Dover

PRE-CAMRA BRITAIN

By 1973 there were just 92 UK brewing companies operating independently from the six national brewery chains. Between them they ran the 98 breweries shown here Only 34 still remain truly independent. During the same period, a further 53 breweries owned by the national chains were also closed.

Southampton

Gale's **Horndean**

Harveys **Lewes**

Hall & Woodhouse **Blandford Forum**

Portsmouth

Brighton

Beachy Head

Eldridge Pope **Dorchester**

Isle of Wight

Burts **Ventnor**

Exeter

Palmers **Bridport**

Dartmoor

Devenish **Weymouth**

Exe

Tamar

Devenish **Redruth**

St. Austell **St. Austell**

Isles of Scilly

Land's End

Blue Anchor **Helston**

English Channel

FRANCE

Guernsey **Guernsey**

Randalls **St Peter's Port**

Ann Street **Jersey**

Randall's (now Liberation)

St. George's Channel

Twyl

Wye

Severn

Trent

Humber

Ouse

Yare

Strait of Dover

0	miles	50
0	km	50

N

Pale Ale & Bitter Beers

When it comes to packing flavor, variety, and subtlety (or lack of it) into remarkably dilute beer, pale British ales, drawn naturally carbonated from the cask, deserve all the adulation poured upon them. They are also the bedrock of the traditional British pub.

PUNCH'S FANCY PORTRAITS.—No. 89.

SIR ARTHUR M. BASS, M.P.

Above: In the nineteenth century British brewers were so prominent in both the Houses of Parliament that they were known collectively as "the Beerage."

Pale-ale brewing became possible in the seventeenth century when new types of oven allowed maltsters to avoid scorching and smoking their malt for the first time, enabling a paler type to be created by gentler kilning at better controlled temperatures.

A high-hopped variety of pale ale bound for India had appeared in London by 1780, but initially its acrid, unfettered bitterness, which dissipated through perpetual rolling on the long sea journey to Bombay and beyond, made it unpopular at home.

In 1820, Samuel Allsopp's newish brewery at Burton-upon-Trent in the English Midlands decided to ape the style using their local hard water, which is alkaline and packed with gypsum. This they found absorbed the hops' bitterness without harming their floweriness, creating graceful beers that contrasted sharply with the malty sweetness of brown ales and the wall-of-flavor onslaught of porters and stouts.

Burton brewers were well used to exporting beer by this time but had recently lost a large part of their lucrative Russian market in strong brown ale and stout bound for St. Petersburg. The opportunity to ship large quantities of paler brews to the outposts of a growing empire—coupled with the fact that these Burton-brewed beers, bearing the exotic mark of India Pale Ale (IPA), were potentially better suited to immediate consumption in the English market—made the fortunes of Allsopp and of other Burton brewers like Worthington and Bass.

Brewers elsewhere soon learned how to "Burtonize" water by adding sulfates and throughout Britain took to brewing highly hopped pale ales and "bitter beer," which attracted a premium price

Opposite: Traditional oast houses in Kent, where layers of hops are dried in hot air rising from a "kell," or kiln.

WHY IS MOST BRITISH BEER LIGHT?

On August 8, 1914, at the outbreak of World War I, Britain's Liberal government passed the first Defence of the Realm Act. Temperance campaigners had been active in the party for decades. With a single blow the power was created to increase beer duty and impose pub closing times.

Until 1914, British draft beer was generally between 5 and 7% ABV, as elsewhere. By 1917 the maximum allowable strength fell to an eccentric 3% ABV, and remained there till 1921, under teetotal Prime Minister David Lloyd George. The Great Depression that followed the war led to highly taxed stronger beers returning only slowly, and by the time they were nudging back a second cycle of cataclysm and economic recession descended.

Though World War II ended in 1945, food rationing remained in place until 1954, reducing consumer expectations and meaning that beer continued to be a thin drink.

By 1970 an alcohol content of 3.5% ABV was considered normal, and fashionable drinkers preferred the national brands of draft, recarbonated light ale, parroting catchphrases nurtured through television advertising. Those who sought a more challenging drink began migrating to wine, and who could blame them?

Right: Food pairing, UK-style: a light English bitter with pork scratchings—pieces of cold, salt-roasted pork rind.

when it first appeared in the mid-nineteenth century.

Growers in Kent, Sussex, Herefordshire, and Worcestershire sold hop varieties such as Goldings and Fuggles to merchants who

Below: Before the days of statutory paid vacations, working-class families from East London would take a week of paid leave in Kent to help with the hop harvest, pictured here c.1935.

used rail and sea to supply them by the ton to breweries all over the kingdom. Hops were being imported too, though some brewers still preferred to play with pale malt combinations to distinguish their lighter colored ales.

Hoppy pale ale became popular with gentlemen and southerners, coming to enjoy a status somewhere between England's riposte to the blond lagers of

Central Europe and a gauche alternative to darker brews.

The rise of modern British "bitter" and its derivatives is an altogether more recent phenomenon (*see* Why Is Most British Beer Light? p.44). Back in 1910 a light ale like AK would top 5% ABV, with a pale ale or bitter beer around 6% and the drier, stronger, prodigiously hopped Burton Ale around 7%.

Within 60 years these paler beers, once robustly packed with hops, had halved in strength and lost much of their bite. Although the "real" ales CAMRA fought to save seemed to have infinite variety—color ranging from light blond to deep ruddy amber, malt character from wispy to improbably heavy, and hop presence from nuanced to moderately assertive—in truth most were just better-made light ales.

It is largely due to foreigners, re-creating dream versions of Victorian brewing grandeur from historical references, that British brewers are once again being challenged to reconstruct pale ales from the glory days, which are starting to go beyond simply aping Americans.

Below and below right: The changing face of British IPA—Thornbridge Jaipur (5.9% ABV) bottle- and cask-conditioned; Palmers (3.9% ABV) deceased; and BrewDog Punk (5.6% ABV) in grocery stores and bar and pub chains.

Above: As well as exploiting Burton's hard water, the town's brewers used a refermentation method known as the Union System, which is shown here at its National Brewing Centre.

WILL THE REAL IPA PLEASE STAND UP

The original India Pale Ale (IPA) was a hardy warrior. Its job was to survive a journey that took it by train or barge to a British port, there to be loaded onto an ocean-going ship to cross the Bay of Biscay and sail down the coast of Africa to Cape Town before setting out across the Indian Ocean, eventually to off-load in Bombay. The beer inside the tightly sealed wooden casks will likely have risen in temperature as high as 82°F, making the ship's hold an impressive warm chamber, implying that care will have been taken to include as little yeast as possible.

Prodigious hopping offered maximum protection against oxidation, although it was also a feature of many other beers of the day.

Frustratingly, no records have been found that describe what happened to IPA when it arrived in India, but most likely it will have been stored in a cool place to settle for a while before being racked directly into bottles.

Quite what the brewers of Victorian Britain would make of the laundry list of variations that populate today's global canon of IPAs is anyone's guess, though we suspect it would include envy for the kit, perplexity at the choices available for intense hopping, disappointment at the lack of depth and subtlety in many, and surprise at the slow uptake in the UK.

Porters & Stouts

It is hard to believe nowadays that porter was world brewing's first superstyle. Born in London of mixed parentage and spending a lot of time in Ireland in its youth, it had traveled the globe long before IPA strode the world stage or pilsner was even conceived.

Although the image of both porter and stout is closely associated with Ireland, this family of black beers actually originated in early eighteenth-century East London.

Porter evolved in various phases from the brown beers that had fallen in popularity in the early eighteenth century, when hopped pale ales arrived in London. Brewers began to blend a hopped brown ale from different runnings off the same mash, to create a beer dubbed for a time Intire or Entire, though it gained such popularity with stevedores and porters at the docks and in the city that, by 1721, it had become known as porter.

Others later used the Flemish technique of "cutting" young ("mild") and aged ("old" or "stale") ales together to the same end.

When young it was dry and refreshing. However, it was its ability to age beautifully in the barrel, or butt, that secured it a broader fame.

Porter was as revolutionary in its time as Pils would be a century later. It was made in huge quantities for conditioning in massive tuns, its flavor developing on long sea journeys to the British colonies in North America, Australasia, and India, where it outsold IPA three-fold.

The official history goes on to state that stronger—or in the language of the time, stouter—versions became known as "stout porter," later abbreviated to "stout." In truth the word stout was used to describe stronger beers long before the arrival of porter, but either way, it stuck (see below).

Stronger beers were sold successfully in large volumes to Scandinavia and the countries around the Baltic Sea, en route to St. Petersburg, capital of the Russian empire, leaving a legacy to this day of Baltic porters and Imperial (Russian) stouts (see p.52).

As modern brewers are rediscovering, these deep brown ales can take many distinct forms. A much misunderstood

variant on dry Irish stout was oyster stout (see opposite), made by using a layer of nineteenth-century discarded food packaging—crushed oyster shells—to filter the beer before fermentation, thus infusing it with sea salt to bring a drier character and remove solids to brighten its appearance.

WHAT IS THE DIFFERENCE BETWEEN PORTER AND STOUT?

Below: Porter? Or stout?

There are as many theories about the relationship between porter and stout as there are brewers trying to sell two different black-brown ales. No, too cynical. So how about this, then? Nobody really knows whether there was ever any historical difference between porter and stout, but that should not stop us making up a few. No, still too harsh.

In truth, original brewery records reveal a tendency among brewers who made both beers to label the stronger one stout and the lighter one porter. However, where the words "milk," "cream," "invalid," or "sweet" were added, these were usually appended to lower-strength stout, while a Baltic porter was stronger than all but Imperial stout.

There is no consistent evidence for different ingredients or techniques, though the modern tendency is to make porters slightly lighter in color, with a dab more "pale ale" character. This trend may be helpful but it has no clear historical precedent.

That said, the 14 porters that appeared at the 2015 Great British Beer Festival—two bottled and the rest on draft—appeared to have little in common beyond most being dark, matching the stouts for strength, colou, sweetness, bitterness, and rarity.

The coast appears to be clear for a modern convention to be adopted, but whose? And why?

of the WESTMINSTER BREWERY.
SCRIBED.

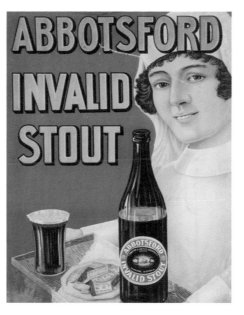

Above: Nurse knows best—the forerunner to oatmeal, sweet, and milk stout was termed invalid stout, as in this Australian example, for its "malty goodness."

Left: Westminster Ale and Porter Brewery, London, c.1840.

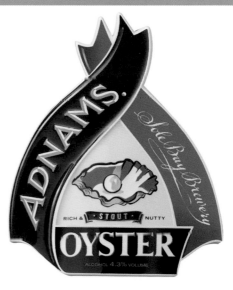

Above: Heavily bearded temperance advocate Sir Wilfred Lawson (1829–1906), pictured in 1890.

A more overtly political beer arrived in the early 1870s, as the previously probeer, antispirits Temperance Society indicated it was about to flay English brewers. "Invalid stout" was a sweetened black beer of 3–4.5% ABV and so rich in malty goodness as to be claimed suitable for the frail and infirm, the elderly, and even nursing mothers.

This sweeter style lived on in forms like milk (sometimes cream) stout, made with the unfermentable milk sugar lactose, and also in the wholesome-sounding oatmeal stout, which takes a more fulsome sweetness from oats added to the mash.

In modern Britain brewers had until recently been shackled by the conservatism of the UK beer market, in particular the belief that a beer of 5% ABV or over is unconscionably strong. Imperial Russian Stout—now a label for Charles Wells of Bedford—dares 10% ABV in its export markets but is near unobtainable in the UK, for example —while newer brewers like London's Beavertown are having greater success with their smoked porter, perhaps the ultimate back to the future beer.

ARE THERE OYSTERS IN OYSTER STOUT?

The straightforward answer is that, sadly, sometimes there are, although this is likely to be a consequence of one of brewing's best hoaxes.

The logic behind using crushed oyster shells to filter beer is that this adds salt and removes proteins. There are other ways to do this, and the economics only make sense if you have a mountain of discarded shells—as was the case in early Victorian England, when pickled oysters were a dietary staple of the urban poor. When consumption plummeted around 1860, however, the economics no longer made sense.

The idea that adding the delicate flavors of oyster meat, in any manageable quantity, to a beer with the pan-palatial character of stout might improve or even impact on the flavor in any way is one of those delicious conceits that naughty smart people sometimes enjoy putting past rich gullible people.

Taking oyster stout to this new level is cited as having first occurred "somewhere in New Zealand" and "in about 1929," but frustratingly —who would be believe it?—no record can be found of this actually having occurred.

Right: Adnams Oyster Stout from Southwold, great with plump local Butley oysters but thankfully not containing any.

Brown Ale & Dark Mild

While the twentieth century may have diminished pale ale in Britain, its effect on those called variously mild, dark, or brown, which reflected a generally sweeter, somewhat softer, and far longer tradition, was withering.

Likely as far back as the time of the ale wives, brown British ales came in three strengths. Regular beer, or "common," was declared around 5–6% ABV. Small beer, made from a thinner wort run off after sparging (*see* p.24), was typically around 3% ABV and provided routine daytime hydration for farm workers and industrial laborers. Then there were stronger ales, as

high as 9% ABV, made for religious festivals, the harvest supper, or, in the case of college breweries at the universities of Oxford and Cambridge, the annual audit.

Until the 1870s regular and stronger ales routinely were conditioned in oak casks at the brewery. As such, they were called "keeping ales." The term "mild" originally indicated a beer that was decanted after a

mere six months, before it had started to turn vinous or acidic, at which point it was called "old ale." Such mild ales could be pale, too.

Prior to 1914 and the Defence of the Realm Act (*see* p.44), many breweries produced a wide range of darker beers seen as neither porter nor stout, ranging from 4–9% ABV, sometimes for blending,

Above: An 1836 caricature from *McCleans Monthly*, entitled "Meeting of the Temperance Society," with Chairman Mr. Drainmedry and his deputy, J. Ditch-Water Esq.

Right and far right: Undistinguished by glass or color, brown British ales need more thought, a commodity found in large measure in The Kernel's modern take on classic varieties.

often for bottling. After the alcohol restrictions of 1915–21, however, they never properly recovered.

The equivalent of "common" lived on in a way through bottled "double brown" ales, mostly in the north of England, but by 1970 Britain's dwindling stock of darker ales consisted mostly of brews in the 3–3.5% ABV small-beer range.

Even the strongest legacy brand, Marston's Merrie Monk, fell short of 4.5% ABV, and when Sarah Hughes's 6% ABV Dark Ruby Mild was re-created at Sedgley in the West Midlands in 1987 it provoked few imitators.

These weaker beers have failed to appeal either to baby boomers or their children, and, while more robust brown ales are now appearing in abundance from better modern brewers like The Kernel in London, these tend to omit the word "mild" from their name.

THE SHILLING TEST

When Scotland came late to the first leg of the British beer revival forty years ago it brought ales named 60, 70, and 80 -/. (shillings), equating in strength if not necessarily character to mild, bitter, and best bitter. The descriptors originated in the early 1800s, when there were twenty shillings to a pound, and represented the wholesale price of a 54-gallon hogshead.

There is something quintessentially Scottish about naming a beer for its price, then continuing to do so long after this has risen immeasurably and the unit of currency disappeared.

By 1975 they represented little more than quirky names for Scottish ales that lacked visibility compared to prevailing lager brands and their English counterparts.

Defining features were sought, based on the erroneous notion that as no hops were grown in Scotland they must always have been low hop brews. In practice, pre-1914 brewing records show a similar range of mostly dark, higher-strength, and highly hopped brews as down south, often coming in at 8% ABV and higher, with shilling counts as high as 160 -/..

Right: The 80 shillings ($6) tax on 54 gallons of beer in the nineteenth century would buy roughly one pint in a pub today.

Far right: An English Queen's shilling.

Wee Heavy, Barley Wine & Stronger British Ales

Britain's ambivalent relationship with stronger beers in the twentieth century explains in large part how it lost touch with its more authentic heritage ales and why the UK has underperformed so badly in the global market for beers in old British styles.

The most poignant illustration of this is the fate of the three strong bottle-conditioned ales that survived the twentieth century—Courage Russian Imperial Stout, Thomas Hardy's Ale, and George Gale's Prize Old Ale—two virtually impossible to source and the third now made in Italy.

Before 1914, many breweries made "keeping ales" of 7–10% ABV—typically designated KK or KKK. Some of these became barley wines, a few finished with wine yeast, while others were termed Burton Ale, in the early eighteenth century a dark sweet ale, though by the late nineteenth century more often massively hopped, paler, and drier.

In Scotland, various stronger, darker, and sweeter beers have become known colloquially as Wee Heavy after the nickname of Fowler's 12-Guinea Ale, an absurdly intense beer that by 1955 had reduced to a 6.7% ABV stripling. These are termed Scotch ale in the export trade, which is where they lingered until Traquair House came along (*see* below).

Quite how "keeping ale" related to English stock ale is less clear. These high-strength beers, often pale ales, were matured in oak and used mainly for

Left: Wee Heavy, a beer of legend diluted to extinction.

Above: Prize Old Ale and Imperial Russian Stout—heritage ales needing attention.

QUAIR FELLOWS

Few breweries will celebrate their fiftieth anniversary in the current decade. The 1960s became the nadir of artisan brewing. In the UK, only one brewery that was created between 1929 and 1974 still survives, yet despite its brilliant absurdity it goes largely unnoticed in its home country.

Peter Maxwell Stuart returned from a career in London to become the 20th laird of Traquair; his family's ancestral home near Innerleithen, in Peeblesshire, is said to be Scotland's oldest inhabited great house. On discovering an intact brewery in one of the outbuildings, he set about renovating it and in 1965, with help from Sandy Hunter of Belhaven Brewery, started to brew a faithful reconstruction of a generic Wee Heavy.

Traquair House Ale is rich and dark, with the typical caramel sweetness that played to changing public tastes in late nineteenth-century Scotland, then the sugar-refining center of the British Empire. It is entirely brewery-conditioned, as such beers usually were, and 60 percent of production goes to export, where it is better appreciated.

Right: Peter Maxwell Stuart, whose small endeavors for the cause of more interesting beer deserve far greater appreciation.

blending into regular beers in the manner of an oak-aged Belgian ale (*see* p.66) to add strength and character. The practice survives in a small way at one mainstream British brewery, Greene King of Bury St. Edmunds, which uses its 5X stock ale to blend into Suffolk Strong.

While other nations struggle hard to find old local beer styles to revive and call their own, Britain sits on a gold mine of mighty historic ones that by recent tradition it leaves to the brewers of other nations to exploit. There is something fundamentally wrong in that.

Below: Traquair, near Innerleithen, Scotland's oldest inhabited great house and home to its oldest new brewery.

New Beginnings

The official story of Britain's first beer revival shows the little guy winning, illustrated by the creation of over 1,400 new breweries to make mostly cask ales. Its second beer revival is more complicated and youthful but driven by exactly the same passion.

The uneasy subplot of UK beer in the last four decades has been a narrow vision imposed on smaller breweries by a conservative beer-drinking audience that mistrusts modern production methods, considers the means of dispensing a beer more important than its flavor, is wary of new tastes, and prefers lower-strength beers of unassertive character.

Meanwhile, as superhighways transport people, goods, and information around the world in previously unthinkable volumes, beer fans from a younger demographic can explore far more easily than their forebears and are more aware of what is going on around the world. A new generation of brewers and drinkers is learning to make or enjoy their own sorts of beer.

The second phase of the UK beer revolution is a work in progress that is now well under way and adopting different rules. Its emerging beers are of mixed pedigree. Some attempt to rekindle old-fashioned styles that may not have been seen inside beer glasses for many decades, while using ingredients and technology that was unavailable to brewers past.

The frustration, in a fast-developing worldwide beer culture where any brewer can create IPAs, porters, and imperial stouts, is that brewers in the lands that invented them have little to say. Why not impose some sort of proprietary authenticity on these old British inventions, rather than imitate the sometimes avant-garde interpretations made elsewhere?

The post-CAMRA redirection of British brewing saw the arrival of innumerable local breweries competing for trade mostly in a shrinking number of pubs in direct competition with longer-established regional or family firms. The leaders of this second phase create beers that push boundaries. They can reach the take-home trade and those drinking places where bulk sale of beer is never going to happen—such as cafés, restaurants, and hotels.

The greatest inroads have been made in urban areas so far. London, which in 1975 had just two independent breweries, now has almost 80, vying with Chicago for the being the most breweried city in the world.

Meanwhile cities like Bristol, Manchester, Edinburgh, Leeds, Cardiff, Cambridge, and

NAMES TO LOOK FOR

Old-school adaptors
National: Adnams, Fullers, St. Austell
Regional: Bathams, Holden's (West Midlands); Harveys, Shepherd Neame (Southeast); Holts, Hydes (Manchester); Donnington, Hook Norton (Cotswolds); Coniston, Hawkshead (Lake District); Harviestoun & Orkney (Scotland)

New-wave creatives
Beavertown, BrewDog, Buxton, Celt Experience, Cloudwater, Cromarty, Fyne Ales, The Kernel, Marble, Moor, Otley, Redchurch, Siren, Tempest, Thornbridge, Tiny Rebel, Wilde

PUNKS ALOUD

Pirouetting at the edge of a trading estate on the outskirts of a nondescript town, a long country bus ride north of Aberdeen, almost as far from the UK's metropolitan and commercial buzz as the mainland allows, is Britain's most successful new brewery in more than a century.

Driven by a heady mix of ego, talent, wit, and opportunist rule-breaking, James Watt and Martin Dickie's 2007 creation BrewDog is the beer-making machine that has helped a new generation of British beer drinkers break away from conservatism and start to define their own tastes.

Impressively oversubscribed crowd-funding helped build a new site capable of almost limitless expansion, which has meant that beers like Punk IPA, 5AM Saint, and Dead Pony Club now reach grocery-store respectability. Yet there is no let up in the experimentation that has led to over 300 different brews thus far, with relatively few dogs and an occasional penguin.

Right: At 32% ABV, Tactical Nuclear Penguin is the lighter of Brewdog's freeze-distilled drinks derived from a much weaker traditionally mashed beer.

Opposite: Britain's larger craft breweries are just like smaller industrial ones, except with stuff going on.

Above: Beerd in Bristol is a younger subsidiary of cask-ale brewery Bath Ales.

Left: After settling, freshly made beer is racked into a cask of real ale at the Dark Star brewery in Horsham, Sussex.

FOR THE TRIP

- In most British pubs, drinks are bought with cash at the bar.
- The otherwise excellent *Good Beer Guide* lists only cask ales.
- Britain's most popular heritage beer comes larger, weaker, costlier, warmer, and flatter than its European equivalents.
- Do not expect to find good beer in many hotels or restaurants yet.
- Must see: The National Brewery Centre in Burton-upon-Trent.
- Must drink: in the Blue Anchor at Helston, one of the world's oldest brewpubs.

elsewhere see burgeoning numbers of specialist beer bars replacing traditional chain pubs. By their second year of operation, the range of styles in these places typically includes better imports, the complete works from experimental local brewers, and even a few better cask ales.

A reversal of the trend away from beers of industrial convenience seems highly unlikely, and a continuing healthy growth in the range and volume of better-made British beers is now inevitable.

Beer in Great Britain has already become more diverse and interesting than it has been for over a hundred years. All that is required now is for the younger generation of craft beer lovers to find common cause with those conservative older drinkers who created the first beer revolution but are now averse to change. If youth knew—if age could.

CAMRA BEER FESTIVALS

If travel is to broaden the mind, the rough must be taken with the smooth, so, for an experience to take home, visit a local CAMRA beer festival.

The first of these modern folk institutions was held at Cambridge in 1974, and the most typical are still run by local volunteers. In the course of a year, around 170 approved ones appear along the length and breadth of Britain (*see* camra.org. uk/events).

Authenticity of sorts is guaranteed, comfort not necessarily. Expect your ale to be poured directly from its cask or pumped to the bar by an enthusiast who does not serve drinks for a living. With luck, you might find a locally sourced pie

or fresh bread and artisan cheese to accompany it. Be pleasantly surprised if the glasses are of sampling size, with somewhere to wash them between pours. Pray there is no music—or that there is somewhere warm and dry to stand while you escape it. If it is under canvas, wear boots.

Welcome to authentic Britain on its day off.

Right: Festivals of real ale are run and attended by enthusiasts. Most serve cider but relatively few offer bottled or international beers.

IRELAND

The fierce independence of spirit that in part defines the Irish character sits uncomfortably alongside the island's wholesale adherence to the corporate brewing culture that controlled its beer scene for half a century, until recently.

The brewing of beer in Ireland may well date back over 3,000 years to the shared cooking area, or *falucht fiadh*, found in the earliest Bronze Age dwellings. Yet Ireland's stamp on world brewing did not arise until the mid-eighteenth century, when England's sweeter, ruby-brown porters were adapted to become drier, darker beers termed *leann dubh*, literally "black beer," nowadays designated Irish stout.

At that time, the London government was aiding English brewers to ship vast quantities of porter across the Irish Sea by imposing a differentially higher malt tax in Ireland. Irish brewers therefore experimented by substituting roasted unmalted barley—though the young and wily Arthur Guinness looked seriously at moving production to North Wales and subsequently reimporting his beers to Dublin.

By the time the tax was withdrawn in 1795, porter and stout already accounted for one-third of the beer drunk in Ireland, most drier than British equivalents by use of unmalted barley and the addition of a little salt to the mash. There were broadly three strengths: "Plain," "Extra," and "Export." The term "porter" tended to be applied to the lighter end, while "stout" referred to the stronger, although the two were interchangeable.

The fate of black beers in twentieth-century Ireland mirrors that of pale ales in Britain. By 1973 the last porter brand had disappeared, and the three domestic brewing companies—Guinness, Murphy's, and Beamish & Crawford—sold only a basic strength stout in their home markets. These covered for heritage, while industrial lager was to be the future, and sweet, light "red" ales of doubtful provenance (*see* p.59) would do for the cusses who liked neither.

The brewing revival that began to engulf the rest of the world in the 1980s

BREWERIES NEAR IRELAND'S ATLANTIC COAST ▲
Ireland's most striking scenery and many of its more interesting breweries are to be found on its western coastline between counties Donegal and Cork on or near the long-distance footpath called the Wild Atlantic Way.

Above: While the imagination might prefer open wooden vessels growing carrageen moss and shamrock, Irish craft brewers use sealed steel like most others.

failed to penetrate an island on which, by then, 99 percent of the brewing capacity was in the hands of multinationals.

The most assertive early revivalist was the Dublin-based Porterhouse brewery and pub chain. Fellow early starters Franciscan Well of Cork were bought out by Molson Coors in 2013, with the O'Hara family's Carlow Brewing Company, the most impressive long-stay case, growing steadily in their third decade, while north of the border pioneer real ale brewer Hilden of Lisburn is in its fourth, under a second generation.

In 2005, tax breaks for smaller brewers were introduced in the Republic, prompting Galway Hooker to start brewing at Oranmore, followed by Trouble Brewing in Kildare and Dungarvan on the Waterford coast. The most adventurous, Galway Bay, has inventive and thorough brewing plus a willingness to invest imaginatively.

The current scene is advancing exponentially, with many small breweries seeking successfully to recapture local sales, while others, such as Eight Degrees of Mitchelstown and Blacks of Kinsale, both in County Cork, have posted wider ambitions.

While 2013 saw an assertive push by US exporters to get Irish craft brewers hooked into making US-style pale ales, more of the

FOR THE TRIP

- The duty on beer in Ireland is the third highest in the EU after Finland and the UK.
- Draft stout is poured in two halves, allowing it to settle between pulls, for no reason known to science.
- Independent restaurants commonly stock a selection of local craft beers by the the bottle.
- *Sláinte*, written by Caroline Hennessey and Kirsten Jensen, captures Irish craft beer brilliantly.
- For more comprehensive information, log onto www.beoir.org.

THE BLACK STUFF

Guinness, part of the Diageo drinks group, is unique in retaining the affection of the world's pickier beer lovers—despite its global reach.

While this gives the company an option to pump the love for all it is worth and accumulate a "world's leading stout maker's take" on the 20 or more styles of stout and porter now found in mainland Europe, this has yet to happen. A good-enough West Indies Porter (6% ABV) has appeared in the UK, along with an underpowered Dublin Porter, but beyond that little imagination has been displayed.

Worse, the company has decided to create, both at home and overseas, a series of "crafty lite"

beers in styles for which it has no reputation and for which it displays no talent.

We sense limits to understanding oft found in the corporate mind, plus possibly an allergy to live yeast.

Right: Dublin Porter, one of Diageo's faltering steps toward reclaiming Arthur Guinness's legacy.

Opposite: Dungarvan Copper Coast, a beer that brought respectability to a dodgy concept.

inspiration for new Irish brewing has come from the busy mind of Cuilán Loughnane, the driver of White Gypsy at Templemore in Tipperary, who experiments with Irish takes on all manner of beer styles and has even sewn hops just to prove they can be grown in Ireland once more.

This sense of locality is echoed by sculptor-turned-brewer Adrienne Heslin of Ballyferriter's West Kerry Brewery, who observed, "A country left sodden by rain three parts of the year and covered by cloud for yet longer, has limited use for tropical hops. A dense porter is a more natural comfort." To which we would add that her Carraig Dubh is a rarely beaten exemplar.

By fall 2015, there were 76 operating breweries in Ireland, a tenfold increase on 1980. Their direction of travel is no more precise than "generally upward," but in the only nation on earth in which stout retained a 35 percent market share even through beer's wilderness years, we suggest that once the younger generation's lust for craft beer has calmed and Ireland finds its place in the global beer trade, there will be a taste for black beers in a whole bunch of styles that begin to challenge the bog-standard one.

Left: Mike Magee, head brewer at Eight Degrees, one of Ireland's cooler new breweries.

Overleaf: Ireland. Dense porters and dark stouts suit the climate of this unique destination.

THE RED STUFF

When is a style not a style? Alternatively, is Irish Red a light French beer?

Industrial brewers faced with a bad-selling beer will look to improve its marketing rather than its taste, so back in the 1980s when two large Irish breweries were struggling with their equally mundane pale ales, they noticed that a French brewery group was pitching its light, sweet *ambrée* as a *bière rousse Irelandaise*—*rousse* meaning "red" in French but only when applied to beer or hair. The solution was but a light switch away.

However, while Irish Red may have begun as a marketing ploy, post hoc respectability has come since some smaller breweries have managed to

make a few fairly decent ones. Dungarven created Copper Coast, named for its local seaboard, and White Gypsy followed with its reddish Emerald Ale, made from all-Irish ingredients.

Latterly, White Hag has produced a suitably up-hopped Red IPA, Dungarven pitched back in with stronger Imperial Red Ale, and Rye River added an inspired one-off called Keeping Red Ale, which would be interesting oak-aged. The only thing missing is a unique selling proposition for the "red" bit. Some rouge up with crystal malt, others with Vienna malt, and a few with subtly roasted barley. If global sales mount, we bet some characteristic will prove to have been present all along.

BELGIUM

Belgium is to beer what France is to wine or the Scottish Highlands to whisky. It is the mother ship of craft brewing. Understand the variations on beer making that emerged from this constantly contested land, and you will be over halfway to appreciating the immense range of tastes and forms that beer can assume.

The organization Belgian Brewers claims that the country produces over 400 discernibly different styles of beer. Some contain virtually no alcohol, while others over 12 percent, their characters ranging from sickly sweet to frankly acidic and accessibility from love at first sip to a lifetime of gradual understanding.

Where other nations' brewers seek perfect presentation, the Belgians have mastered variety. The theory goes that as a legacy of over 30 invasions and occupations by foreign armies in the last millennium, including two in the twentieth century, Belgians developed a parochial mentality that encouraged the retention of local practices in beer making and much else.

This may be so, though Flemish brown ales and the taverns that served them already enjoyed a reputation for excellence among the merchants of the Hanseatic League back in medieval times, when the *gruut* barons of Bruges were among that world's top commodity traders (*see* p.15).

By 1980, the ragbag of small-town Belgian breweries that refused to conform to the global vision of familiar, shiny, white-foamed, easy-drinking lagers stood out above the flood waters, preserving the skills, imagination, and awkwardness that had enabled the world's post-Prohibition and post-1945 generation of brewers to suggest that only industrial beers should be considered "normal."

From barely a mention in economic texts of the 1960s, beer has become one of Belgium's best-known exports, over 60 percent now being sent for sale across Europe and to North America, Australasia, the Far East, and elsewhere.

In most aspects of Belgian life, distinctive threads that look mainly to their locality come together to make the familiar matrix shown to outsiders, though it is predictable that most of Dutch-speaking

Above: *Fin-de-siècle* style meets *oude gueuze* at the café À la Mort Subite in Brussels.

Above: Ghent in East Flanders, one of a dozen top city-break destinations for beer-lovers.

Flanders in the north will follow different patterns from most of those in French-speaking Wallonia to the south.

The country's iconic breweries divide into lambic makers (*see* map, p.69) and ale producers. There are 35 long-established family-owned companies; a small handful of larger ones traded on the stock exchange; some high quality smaller breweries founded since 1975; a new wave of hobby brewers turned professional; and six that are directed to brew by a greater power (*see* Trappist Brewers pp.64–5).

Despite its reputation, by the end of 2015 Belgium had just 180 breweries, consumers being deceived into thinking there are twice that number by the lax nature of consumer law, which in Belgium allows a beer marketing operation to call itself a "brewery," when it clearly is not. Hey ho.

Above: Beers from different vintages aging at a lambic cave somewhere in Payottenland.

Trappist Brewers

The Rule of St. Benedict, the sixth-century text that underpins the traditions of Christian monasticism, allows the daily consumption by those in holy orders of "one hemina of wine"—likely around 10 ounces. It encourages productive labor, too, so here in beer country the creation of "liquid bread" from cereals harvested from the abbey farm plays well to the Benedictine tenets.

Abbey brewing additionally provided an opportunity for excellent public relations; the inns found near the gates of ancient abbeys provided merchants and noblemen—the business travelers and politicians of old—with simple but wholesome food, fine home-brewed ales, and better-informed guests.

When the French abbeys were stripped of wealth and influence by Napoléon in 1793, several moved to the relative safety of the then Southern Netherlands, though it was not until the 1830s, after the creation of the kingdom of Belgium, that a few recommenced brewing on a tiny scale.

Belgium's six brewing abbeys are all run by the Cistercian Order of the Strict Observance, or Trappists. They have been joined by five in other countries (*see* below) with more likely.

Right: Upkeep of the twentieth-century abbey at Villers-devant-Orval is funded largely by the production of its brewery, to the right of the picture.

There is no Trappist beer style as such, though all must be brewed within the walls of an abbey, by or under the supervision of members of the order, and all income must be used to benefit the monastic community or to support charitable work.

In practice, all current Trappist beers are ales. Typically the beers are dark, ranging from 6.5 to 11.2% ABV, although there are also two memorable pale ales and several strong blonds. Many are found only in the bottle though generally less good draft versions have been appearing.

The ancient quality marks of XX and XXX are roughly equivalent to the modern Dutch terms *dubbel* and *tripel*, and are taken wrongly as having monastic

BROTHERS WHO BREW

Growing awareness of its brewing tradition may yet attract more young men into the Trappist Order, but for now most of its involvement is supervisory. The senior overseers are largely self-taught, but the wisdom of some is highly regarded by other brewers.

The recent expansion in the number of approved Trappist breweries means there are now 11 (*see* chart, right).

Only at Westvleteren do members of the order carry out much of the day-to-day activity, made possible in part by its "small country living" dimensions.

Brewery	Since	Abbey or Cloister	Location
Westmalle	1836	Our Lady of the Holy Heart	Belgium (Antwerp)
Westvleteren	1839	St. Sixtus	Belgium (West Flanders)
Chimay	1862	Our Lady of Scourmont	Belgium (Hainaut)
La Trappe	1884	Koningshoeven	Netherlands (North Brabant)
Rochefort	1899	Our Lady of Saint-Rémy	Belgium (Namur)
Orval	1931	Our Lady of Orval	Belgium (Luxembourg)
Achel	1999	St. Benedictus	Belgium (Limburg)
Engelszell	2012	Stift Engelszell	Austria (Upper Austria)
De Kievit	2013	Maria Retreat	Netherlands (North Brabant)
Spencer	2013	St. Joseph	USA (Massachusetts)
Tre Fontane	2015	Sts. Vincent & Anastasius	Italy (Rome)

origins. They originally implied that a beer had double or triple the amount of malt in its mash. The term *quadrupel* was invented for a particular brand in 1990 and had no historical precedent.

In recent years, the output of Chimay and Westmalle has risen to over 3,302,150 gallons a year.

In the twentieth century, a few commercial breweries were licensed by the order, with varying degrees of formality, to produce imitations of Trappist beers on a larger scale to aid fundraising, though all such deals had ceased by 1992.

Other brewers followed suit without invitation, using images and words associated with monks to market beers entirely for commercial gain.

Nowadays, under Belgian law the badge "authentic Trappist product" may appear only on something made at a Trappist abbey, the decision to award it resting with the abbot.

Above: The brewing room at the Abbaye Notre Dame de Saint-Rémy, near Rochefort.

Monks and lay staff at the brewing abbeys are allowed beer but are a sober lot. At Saint-Rémy, the daily ration is 11.6 ounces of Rochefort 8, but consumption is largely confined to the festivals of Christmas and Easter.

Left: The logo that denotes a beer of genuine Trappist origin.

Right: Trappist brewing has now spread to the USA, at St. Joseph's Abbey in Spencer, Massachusetts.

Oak-Aged Ales

There are few more extraordinary sights in the world of beer than the temple rooms at the Rodenbach brewery in Roeselare, where nearly 300 straight-sided oak tuns, most carrying around 4,755 gallons of beer, sit upended on plinths three feet or so above floor level, filled with gently maturing brown ale, intended to reach the same acidity as a typical Sauvignon Blanc.

Oak-aged beers (*foederbier* in Dutch) are a Flemish specialty. Most matured ale is blended or "cut" with its sweeter, younger equivalent to make *versnijsbier*, literally "snipped beer," mirroring the use of stock ale in England (*see* pp.52–3).

Storing beers in oak casks was the norm until the arrival of cheaper metal alloys, a transition sped by World War I, which saw good oak commandeered for other uses and poor casks left to dry out and become useless.

The flavor effects of aging in oak come not from the wood itself but from the microflora that live between its fibers. *Pediococci* produce lactic acid, which sharpens a beer but is otherwise largely tasteless and odorless. Used as a counterpoint to the sweetness of caramelized brown ale, it creates some pretty sophisticated flavor mixes.

Anxious to conform to more conventional tastes and short of oak-aging capacity, mid-twentieth-century producers shied away from releasing these beers in their more intense forms, preferring to use the aged ale as a blending agent, typically adding 20–25 percent of aged beer into a blend dominated by freshly made ale of the same type. However, with the return of interest in craft brewing, it is the more intense products that are attracting attention once more.

In a world grown used to the idea that sour beer is "off," the likes of Rodenbach Grand Cru or Verhaeghe's Vichtenaar can shock at first taste, although those who like aged red wines, particularly a Cabernet Sauvignon, often pick up the drift more swiftly.

Around the market town of Oudenaarde, until the 1980s, some brewers aged the wort of stewed brown ales—brewed overly long to make

Right: Oak-aged Rodenbach Grand Cru—perhaps the most striking brown ale in the world.

BEERS FROM THE WOOD

At Vichte, 12½ miles southeast of Roeselare, the Verhaeghe brothers have enjoyed enough success with Vichtenaar, Duchesse de Bourgogne, and some bespoke brands of aged ales to have been able to swap their higgledy-piggledy, nineteenth-century family-owned deathtrap of a brewery for a brand new one.

Halfway between the two, the commercially successful De Brabandere brewery matures a pale ale on oak in theirs, while newer West Flanders ventures like Alvinne, Struise Brouwers, and Verzet push the envelope in all directions with their experimental varieties, sometimes testing microbes and customers in equal measure.

Across into East Flanders, around the town of Oudenaarde, the residual local variants struggle to re-create authenticity, due to the lack of oak-aging, though both Liefmans Goudenband and Cnudde Oud Bruin make a good fist of taste imitation.

Right: Duchesse de Bourgogne is the fuller, sweeter, more sophisticated aged brown ale from Verhaeghe, preferred by foreigners to the locally favored, sharper, and drier Vichtenaar.

more caramel. Traditionally they aged this in smaller-sized oak casks, though the principle was identical, and the subdivision of these ales into "old brown" in contrast to West Flanders "old red" is hard to justify, especially as none of the East Flanders producers nowadays use traditional aging techniques.

Interest in oak aging is increasing, leading to experimentation with beers that are lighter or stronger, darker or paler, or have fruit added in various forms.

Some brewers are also experimenting with aging beers in brandy, whiskey, port, and wine casks, though the subtle advantages derived from using microflora adapted to surviving the cask's last occupant are, in the case of spirit casks, hard to tease out from the effect of spiking a brew with several residual pints of a fine cognac or single malt!

OAK-AGED ALE MAKERS ►
The heartland of oak-aged ales, which have had so much influence on the recent spate of sour beers from craft brewers everywhere, shows a tiny number of surviving producers and local imitators.

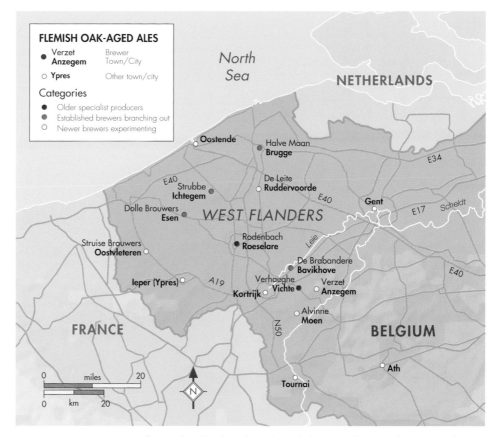

Below: Before blending, the individual character of each and every tun of ripened ale is tested in the laboratory and by experts' palates.

Lambic Beers

Imagine a drink that is brewed as a beer, then fermented like a cider, before being aged in oak like a *grand cru* wine. Such is the progress of a lambic beer. For the beer drinker, the journey from initial revulsion via acceptance and on to adulation often marks their growth from beer supporter to enthusiast and finally aficionado.

Lambics are the only types of beer over which Belgium can still claim sole mastery. Craft brewers in a dozen nations may think they are close to cracking the secret of the ultimate folk beers but we reckon they still have about a century of trial and error to go. Making lambics requires more than technique.

The most refined of the traditional versions of these beers are among the finest and most unusual drinks on the planet, although few ordinary drinkers would consider that they have a primary character anywhere close to beer.

Lambic is the collective name for a clan of beers, distinguished from ales or lagers by their fermentation. The dozen companies that make authentic (or "*oude*") lambic beers are all based within 10 miles of Brussels' southwestern boundary. While all oak-aged ales use the vintner's ways with barreling, lambic makers take a

THE LAMBIC MAKERS OF BRUSSELS AND PAYOTTENLAND ▶
Production of the world's most unusual and sophisticated lighter beers is largely confined to the Payottenland area of Flemish Brabant, south and west of Brussels, where a dozen producers borrow winemakers' methods to coax extraordinary flavors from simple wheat beers.

Left: Lambic ages patiently in the cellars at Brouwerij Boon in Lembeek.

AUTHENTIC LAMBICS: AN INTRODUCTION TO SOME OF THE BEST

3F VINTAGE OUDE GEUZE (7%)
3F SCHAARBEEKSE OUDE KRIEK (5%)
Drie Fonteinen, Beersel (Flemish Brabant)
Armand Debelder blends and steeps lambics from his own and other brewers to sell on draft at his brother's café-restaurant in the village square. Vintage Oude Geuze is his top of the range, made by blending one-, two-, and three-year-old lambics, maximizing the aromas and backtastes of *Brettanomyces* fermentation (*see p.71*), while his Schaarbeekse Oude Kriek uses historically preferred but rare, locally grown Schaarbeek cherries to re-create the quintessential *kriek* taste.
www.3fonteinen.be

BOON OUDE GEUZE MARIAGE PARFAIT (8%)
BOON OUDE KRIEK (6.5%)
Brouwerij Boon, Lembeek (Flemish Brabant)
While others campaigned passionately to preserve lambic, Frank Boon carefully planned to revive it. Now by far the largest producer of traditional lambics, with a tendency to make fuller, stronger *geuzes* and higher fruit *krieks*. Those of his beers designated Oude are where to head, with the rarer Mariage Parfait brands pushing the envelope.
www.boon.be

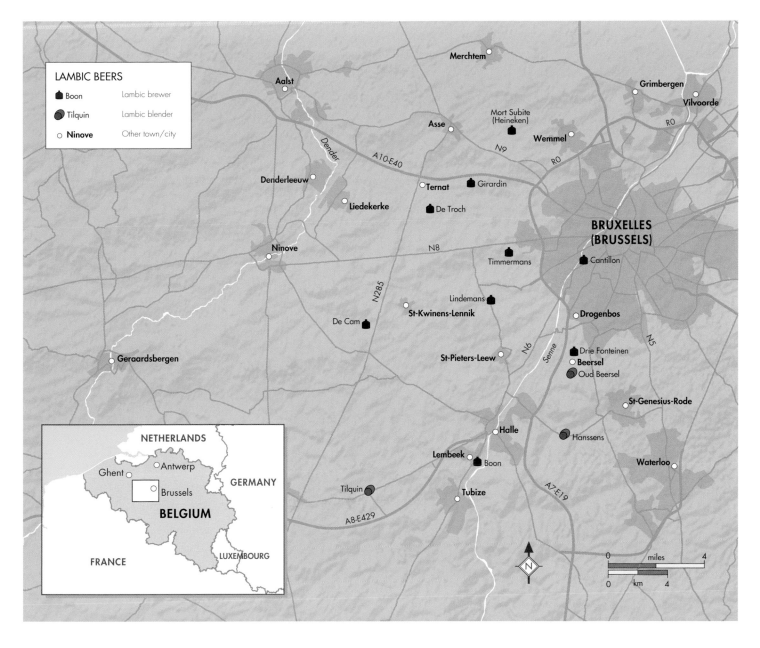

LAMBIC BEERS

■ Boon — Lambic brewer
◗ Tilquin — Lambic blender
○ Ninove — Other town/city

Merchtem
Aalst
Grimbergen
Vilvoorde
Asse
Mort Subite (Heineken)
Wemmel
RO
N9
Denderleeuw
A10-E40
Dender
Ternat ■ Girardin
Liedekerke
■ De Troch
RO
BRUXELLES (BRUSSELS)
N8
Ninove
N285
Timmermans ■
■ Cantillon
Lindemans ■
St-Kwinens-Lennik
Drogenbos
N5
De Cam ■
St-Pieters-Leew
N6
Senne
■ Drie Fonteinen
○ Beersel
◗ Oud Beersel
Geraardsbergen
St-Genesius-Rode
Halle
◗ Hanssens
Lembeek
○
■ Boon
Waterloo
Tubize
A7-E19
◗ Tilquin
A8-E429

Inset map:
NETHERLANDS
Ghent ○   ○ Antwerp
GERMANY
○ Brussels
BELGIUM
FRANCE
LUXEMBOURG

N

0 ——— miles ——— 4
0 ——— km ——— 4

CANTILLON BRUOCSELLA GRAND CRU (5%)
CANTILLON IRIS (6%)
CANTILLON LOU PEPE FRAMBOISE (6%)
Brasserie Cantillon, Brussels
The last lambic maker in Brussels is a center of
brewing excellence and an official museum all in
one. Visitors will find up to a dozen of Jean van
Roy's iconic beers available. Grand Cru is a fully
matured bottled old lambic, so nearly flat. Iris is
deliberately not legally lambic for being produced
from 100 percent malt. The Lou Pepe range is for
his pioneering father and includes a rare, near
perfect, millesimé framboise.
www.cantillon.be

DE CAM FARO (5%)
DE CAM KRIEK LAMBIEK (5.5%)
Geuzestekerij De Cam, Gooik (Flemish Brabant)
Karel Goddeau runs this lambic cave in a folk
museum complex in one of Payottenland's cutest
villages. He steeps and blends several impressive but
rare bottled beers, though try his authentic draft, low
carbonation lambic, cherry lambic and/or faro.
www.lambicland.be

DE TROCH OUDE KRIEK (5.5%)
Brouwerij De Troch, Wambeek (Flemish Brabant)
Pauwel Raes, who took on his family's brewery in
2013, stamped his presence with an *oude kriek*
featuring Schaarbeek cherries on musty lambic.
www.detroch.be

CANTILLON

Grand Cru Bruocsella
1996

Above: Drinking lambic from earthenware crocks. Detail from Pieter Brueghel the Younger's *Fair with a Theatrical Performance* (1562).

MORE AUTHENTIC LAMBICS

GIRARDIN JONGE LAMBIEK (5%)
GIRARDIN OUDE LAMBIEK (5%)
Brouwerij Girardin, St-Ulriks-Kapelle
(Flemish Brabant)
Most of the draft lambic found in Payottenland cafés originates at this publicity-shy farm brewery, hailed by fellow lambic producers as supreme craft producers. Not quite yet of the new world, its officially *oude* products have yet to be so designated, its authentic *gueuze* identified only by its black label.

HANSSENS ARTISANAAL OUDE KRIEK (6%)
HANSSENS ARTISANAAL OUDBEITJE (6%)
Hanssens Artisanaal, Dworp (Flemish Brabant)
The marshaled rows of casks in the old farm buildings where Hanssens' distinctive lambics mature contain a century-old tradition of blending and steeping, distinctive notes of wood smoke, and splintered citrus pervading well-made *oude gueuze*, a smooth *oude kriek*, and the oddball, *Oudbeitje*—the only traditionally made strawberry lambic, retaining its fruit presence long after the color and sweetness have disappeared.

LINDEMANS CUVÉE RENÉ OUDE GUEUZE (5%)
LINDEMANS CUVÉE RENÉ OUDE KRIEK (5%)
Brouwerij Lindemans, Vlezenbeek
(Flemish Brabant)
Renowned brewers of delicate, lemony lambics much prized by blenders, after two decades making mostly sweet fruit beers Dirk and Geert Lindemans' Cuvée René brands mark a return to traditional lambic beers with a lighter touch.
www.lindemans.be

OUD BEERSEL OUDE KRIEK (6%)
OUD BEERSEL GREEN WALNUT (6%)
Oud Beersel BVBA, Beersel (Flemish Brabant)
Gert Christiaens saved the idiosyncratic Vandervelden brewery in 2007, as a place to mature, blend, and steep lambics. Through drive, luck, and local support, he has grown one of the best *oude krieks* and the occasional "out there" experiment, for example by steeping fresh young walnuts.
www.oudbeersel.com

further step toward winemaking by adding no yeast to their beer, relying on nature to spark fermentation.

The common ingredient of all lambic beers is a basic brew, itself also called lambic, the construction of which derives from the wheat beer tradition of central Europe (see pp.74–5). Typically this is mashed with 30–40 percent unmalted wheat. It differs from most other wheat beers in that it is high in hops, though the awkward clash of sour, bitter, and sweet flavors is avoided by ensuring these are old stock, meaning they are low in bitterness and floweriness yet still high in natural preservatives to fight off spoiling.

After brewing, the filtered wort is decanted into a cooling vessel (or koelschip), built like a large paddling pool, where by tradition it cools "under an open roof beneath the night sky" in order to allow airborne or "wild" yeast to land on its surface, as apple or grape skins will.

Where conventional brewers pitch a precise measure of carefully cultured Saccharomyces yeast into their beers to spark fermentation, lambic makers rely on there being enough wild yeast around to provoke "spontaneous fermentation."

In truth the extent to which the fermenting microflora will have come from the atmosphere, night sky, or otherwise is small. At most they feed into the brewery's natural ecosystem, made up of whatever microbes inhabit the walls of the casks into which the contents of the koelschip are racked.

Most of the time, sufficient Saccharomyces arrive to fuel a primary fermentation that is fairly vigorous for two weeks before meandering for another three or four. As with oak-aged ales, pediococci then work to produce lactic fermentation (see p.66), responsible in part for bringing a variety of citrus flavors.

Where lambics enter a world apart is in their third phase of fermentation, apparent in the second and third year in oak. Slow-fermenting yeast strains called Brettanomyces, adapted to live frugally off cellulose in the wood fibers of each cask or tun, develop add-on characteristics conjured up in descriptions such as "old bookshop," "horse blanket," and "hay barn." This is the unique selling point of authentic lambic.

You can still find "raw" draft lambic in some local bars in Brussels and Payottenland, nowadays dispensed from plastic containers as local health inspectors misunderstand and mistrust wood. Served 6–12 months from racking, it is termed jong (young) and tastes of ale laced with lightly pickled mushroom, while after two or three years on oak it becomes oud (old)—in a different sense from the oude of authenticity—and tends to be flat and vinous.

Before 1950, most lambic ended up as faro, a draft form to which sugar had been added to spark lightly fizzy refermentation and soften acidity. This can still be found in a few cafés, such as De Rare Vos at Schepdaal, due west of Brussels.

Nowadays, most traditionally made lambic is used to create bottled beers, such as oude gueuze—geuze in some local dialects—and oude kriek (see below).

Belgian law currently defines the lambic family of beers in a way that includes some with only a passing connection to the authentic version. Thankfully, the European Union has stepped in with some formal designations that mean the term "oude" can be used only to prefix those made in the traditional way.

Oude g(u)euze has a base of young lambic into which is blended a quantity of older lambic before bottling with a drop of liquid sugar. The young provides the body, the old brings the character, and the sugar creates the sparkle. Generally, the greater the proportion of three-year-old lambic, the more characterful the gueuze will be.

Oude kriek is made by steeping cherries (krieken in Old Flemish) in a cask of lambic for six months or so. Though occasionally encountered on draft, most is bottled. It is best to use fruits that are hard, dry, and slightly bitter, always steeped with their pits retained to add a little almond into a mix of fruity, sharp, and musty flavors.

Steeping raspberries creates the equally traditional but rarer framboise. Successful experimentation with steeping grapes, apricots, strawberries, and other fruits has yet to become sufficiently established to earn a title.

TILQUIN GUEUZE À L'ANCIENNE (6.4%)
OUDE QUETSCHE TILQUIN À L'ANCIENNE (6.4%)
Gueuzerie Tilquin, Bierghes (Wallonian Brabant)
Pierre Tilquin's absurd idea to start a business maturing, blending, and steeping lambics from four different brewers produced a first semi-gueuze in summer 2011 and has gone on to see him create a great one. Then he started playing with a damson-plum lambic that tastes like it always existed. Quetsche and gueuzerie are his words.
www.gueuzerietilquin.be

Saison

In Wallonia, the French-speaking south of Belgium, the self-respect of many brewers returned with the renewed interest in a type of beer called *saison*. Dubbed "farmhouse ale" by some proponents, its revival may inadvertently have gone on to cause disappointment, as foreigners use the style name to identify completely different beers.

In centuries past, Walloon farmers brewed in the winter, adding value to some of their grain harvest and keeping farm workers in year-round work. In summer, brewing ceased, as there were other priorities. Additionally, open vessels in overheated fermenting rooms were vulnerable to insect attack and other types of spoiling. So in early spring they brewed and bottled extra beer to tide them over the summer months.

The story goes that such beers were stronger and hoppier than regular beer, as this protected them from oxidation, enabling them to keep better. While this has plausibility—the essential ingredient of a good theory—it lacks a reliable historical record and common sense. For example, why would someone working in the hot sun want to drink a 6.5% ABV beer, and why would an employer needing an efficient, healthy workforce brew them one?

A more likely theory, supported by some surviving production records, suggests that rural Wallonian summer beers, made mainly for farm laborers, were much like *meerts* or *maerts*, lighter forms of lambic still used in blending by some lambic makers.

A different type made year-round for miners and steel-workers in the industrial towns springing up along the major rivers and canals featured mainly water for rehydration and sugar for energy, similar to the lighter mild ales of northern England and the English Midlands.

A third use of the word *saison*, prevalent in the 1980s, described most heavier Wallonian ales, and may originally have been reserved for beers made for the seasonal celebrations around harvest time.

It is known that all these forms were termed *saison* at some point, but whatever the history, the type that rose to fame in Belgium after 1977 and is hailed by some as the inspiration for the American love affair with hoppy pale ales is an aromatically bitter, grainy, pale, medium-strength brew that might be shorthanded as Saison Dupont and beers that want to be Saison Dupont. This beautiful beer, best when conditioned in 26.4-ounce bottles, has little in common with any of the aforementioned types.

All the forms of *saison* survive with varying degrees of success, but in Belgium it is the "Dupont-style" beers that have found their moment, appealing in particular to those who like a prominent aromatic hop-yeast presence without stinging bitterness.

Meanwhile, across the rest of the world, a fifth type of *saison*, emanating from the USA, has arrived as a sort of catch-all for beers that are neither sweet or sour, bitter or necessarily pleasant, largely defined by use of particular patented yeast strains.

It remains to be seen how Belgian brewers will react to hearing that several successful—and delicious—Belgian *saisons* were prevented from entering the second round of a prestigious US beer competition for not being "true to the *saison* style."

A SELECTION OF DIFFERENT BELGIAN SAISONS

IV SAISON (6.5%)
Brasserie de Jandrain-Jandrenouille, Jandrain (Wallonian Brabant)
Delicate yet vibrant, cleverly hopped, pale *blonde* new-style *saison* from a recently constructed brewery, housed on an old farm.
www.brasseriedejandrainjandrenouille.com

SAISON CAZEAU (5%)
Brasserie de Cazeau, Templeuve (Hainaut)
Light *blonde* ale that looks the part despite liberties having been taken with the style, thanks to elderflowers being added, showing off its hops and bringing a distinctive summery twist.
www.brasseriedecazeau.be

SAISON D'EPEAUTRE (6%)
Brasserie de Blaugies, Blaugies (Hainaut)
Overtly *rustique* with the aroma of a hay barn. Spelt substitutes for some barley malt, but the hoppy character is partly yeast driven.
www.brasseriedeblaugies.com

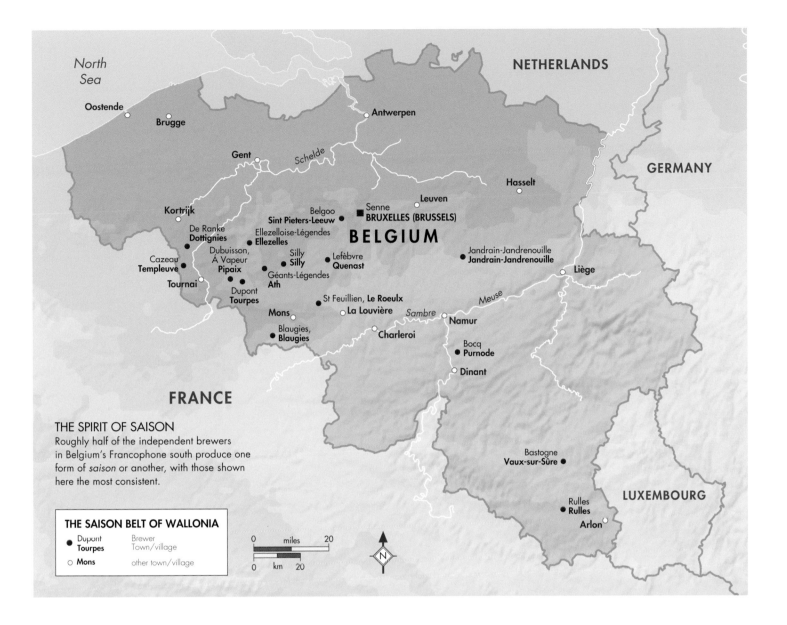

North Sea

NETHERLANDS

GERMANY

Oostende

Brugge

Antwerpen

Gent

Schelde

Hasselt

Kortrijk

Belgoo

Senne

Leuven

Sint Pieters-Leeuw

BRUXELLES (BRUSSELS)

De Ranke

Dottignies

Ellezelloise-Légendes

Ellezelles

BELGIUM

Cazeau

Templeuve

Dubuisson,

À Vapeur

Pipaix

Silly

Silly

Lefèbvre

Quenast

Jandrain-Jandrenouille

Jandrain-Jandrenouille

Liège

Tournai

Géants-Légendes

Ath

Dupont

Tourpes

St Feuillien, **Le Roeulx**

Meuse

Mons

La Louvière

Sambre

Namur

Blaugies,

Blaugies

Charleroi

Bocq

Purnode

Dinant

FRANCE

THE SPIRIT OF SAISON
Roughly half of the independent brewers in Belgium's Francophone south produce one form of *saison* or another, with those shown here the most consistent.

Bastogne

Vaux-sur-Sûre

LUXEMBOURG

Rulles

Rulles

Arlon

THE SAISON BELT OF WALLONIA

● **Dupont**
  Tourpes   Brewer Town/village

○ **Mons**   other town/village

0   miles   20

0   km   20

N

SAISON DE PIPAIX (6%)

Brasserie à Vapeur, Pipaix-Leuze (Hainaut)
Jean-Louis Dits assures all that this distinctive, dry spiced beer is from an ancient brewer's recipe found at the unique steam-powered village brewery he saved from closure in 1985.
www.vapeur.com

SAISON DUPONT (6.5%)

Brasserie Dupont, Tourpes (Hainaut)
The leading light of the new genre makes its beers in a modern plant sited within Wallonia's cutest-looking ancient farm complex. Wafts of herb and haystack augment a hop bitterness best appreciated when in 26.4-ounce bottles.
www.brasserie-dupont.com

SAISON VOISIN (5%)

Brasserie des Géants, Ath (Hainaut)
The best of the sweeter, lighter *saison* beers originated at the Voisin brewery in Flobecq and, after its closure, was re-created in 2002 with the former brewer's assent.
www.brasseriedesgeants.com

Château-Brasserie   Castle-Brewery
Kasteel-Brouwerij

Saison Voisin

℮ 33 cl   alc. 5% vol.

Belgisch Bier - Bière Belge - Belgian Beer

Regional Belgian Ales

The great joy of drinking beer in Belgium is exploring the fabulous diversity of styles and one-off creations found among the local brewers, known collectively in Dutch as *streekbieren* or in French as *bières regionaux*. Forming these into neat, obedient columns for easier assimilation might seem sensible but takes no account of the Belgian character.

Spiced wheat beers

From as early as the ninth century AD, records survive of brewing with wheat across much of the north of Charlemagne's Holy Roman Empire, suggesting at some level a shared history.

A tradition of lacing Flemish beers with spices may have survived from the times when *gruut* mixes acted as preservatives and flavorings (*see* p.15) and was recalled as occurring by the legendary Pierre Celis (*see* below) when he revived the style. Whether it was routinely spiced

before 1966 is a moot point. Up the way in Leuven, the now-defunct *peeterman* style was definitely unspiced, but Celis's imitators, who came in droves, mostly included dried peel and coriander because this made their cloudy beers full of the taste of fresh bread, subtly perfumed, and enjoyably drinkable.

Such so-called "white" beers have since diversified to include spelt, buckwheat, rye, and other grains. Some have gone spicier or plainer, weaker or stronger, clearer or murkier, and occasionally dark.

The British influence

Created at the 1830 London Conference, Belgium, according to France's president Charles de Gaulle, was invented by the British to annoy the French. Its first king was Queen Victoria's brother-in-law, and before the end of the century the person holding most influence over its brewers was another Briton, George Maw Johnson.

This Canterbury brewer became involved in advising colleagues in the town of Hal (now Halle), south of Brussels, and from this he earned the editorship of *Le*

| Coriander | Cumin | Wheat | Oats | Dried orange peel |

THE HERO OF HOEGAARDEN

In 1966, dairy manager Pierre Celis decided to revive a type of beer he recalled from the Tomsin brewery, near his childhood home. He added coriander, a little cumin, and the dried peel of Curaçao oranges to flavor a mash with 30 percent unmalted wheat and a few oats. He named it Oud Hoegaards, after his home town of Hoegaarden, and sold it in stoneware bottles inscribed in a shaky hand with blue lettering.

Celis did not set out to become either a hero or a millionaire. He was a small businessman, a bit of a dreamer, and a likable old-fashioned grafter who recognized a good opportunity. His beer had the advantage that it both looked

and tasted completely different from regular beers at a time when conformity was going out of fashion.

Oud Hoegaards eventually mutated into Hoegaarden, the first craft beer of recent origin to become a worldwide hit for a global brewer, although by the time that happened it had left behind its suitably enriched creator and most of its panache.

Right: Few brewers write an autobiography, but Pierre Celis of Hoegaarden, here shown mashing his beer in the early days, wrote his in three languages.

Petit Journal du Brasseur in 1899. Johnson it was who persuaded Belgian brewers to greet the new century by creating a light style of pale ale called *spéciale*. Sweet black beers based on British milk stout followed, as did strong, dark, malt-packed Scotch ales and robust export stout.

To this day, a variety of old British brewing names—brands as well as styles—appear on Belgian beer menus, alongside the Worcestershire sauce and hot steaming Oxo.

Local specialties

As one would expect in a country as perversely uncoordinated as Belgium, provinces retain local beer traditions with variable degrees of exclusivity.

In Limburg, they make light blond ales with the aroma of summer grass that ape the polished style of their Dutch neighbors.

Brewers in Brabant and elsewhere blend lambic into some of their ales to make a *versnijsbier* (*see* p.66) that crosses the

Below: Brewers' wheat at a farm in Flanders.

fermentation divide, causing them to end not far from the character of an oak-aged ale.

Antwerp brewers claim originality for pale ales they had made for decades before the *spéciale* fad of the early twentieth century, while Mechelen and Diest were each famed for their robust brown ales.

Many southern brewers vaguely follow the *blonde*, *brune*, and *ambrée* principles found in neighboring France and elsewhere, also absorbing the traditions of *bière de garde* (*see* pp.108–9).

More widespread, especially among the established family brewers is the one-brand range consisting broadly of a lighter blond and brown, heavier *dubbel* and *tripel*, plus a strong ale, tagged with a distinctly religious name, the badge of honor being a formal fundraising deal with a functioning abbey (*see* below).

For the last two decades, Belgian regional brewers have seen everything they own turn to gold, as their beers are exported to all corners of the globe. It remains to be seen whether they retain the inventiveness to create and follow new types, as opposed to brands of beer or, failing that, display the confidence to let their brewers play and spot when those games create new classic beers.

Above: The brewery at Silly in northern Hainaut continues to produce a classic Scotch ale long after Scottish brewers had forgotten how.

ABBEYS OF THE BEER ORDER

After the Trappist order licensed a couple of breweries to imitate and commercialize their beers, other brewers sensed an opportunity—as did some abbeys.

Arrangements became more confused when various abbots signed up to deals licensing the use of their abbey's name or location as a brand name. Sadly, the link between image and authenticity was often an early casualty.

Some of these so-called "abbey beers" are undoubtedly accomplished brews, a few more so than the Trappist originals. Others, however, are dull and sweet, with little to recommend them beyond an allusion to godliness.

Attempts to confine use of the term to brands supported by a monastic order are difficult to justify from a consumer viewpoint as the best ranges over time often have no such link, while some of the licensed but less interesting brands can be highly lucrative.

If consumer support continues to be sought, keeping simple blond or brown beers out of any range of abbey beers would be a smart gesture.

Right: St. Bernardus of Watou make better beers than some of their Trappist godparents.

The Belgian New Wave

Trying to improve Belgian brewing from a position at the head of the field is not easy. Many better-established brewers adore their export sales, which, in recent decades, have seemed to expand effortlessly. However, a new breed sees complacency and an opportunity to shape the future differently.

Not all new Belgian beers are products of imagination. Nor is everything of high quality. A recent vogue for making "fruit beers" to mimic the tradition of *oude kriek* (*see* p.71) saw few brewers create beers with any a degree of authenticity, most preferring to use syrups or juice concentrate to create banal drinks that insult a great cultural tradition. The use of spices and other flavorings can be suspect, too, especially in the hands of hobby brewers.

However, there are newer brewers—we would say "younger," but many have passed 40 and a couple are nearer 60—who see an altogether different trajectory for Belgian beer.

Down south, few can match Gregory Verhelst of La Rulles brewery either for his dedicated localism or the buzz he gets from seeing his near-perfect beers on sale in Manhattan. Rising stars Brasserie

Right: Taras Boulba from Brasserie de la Senne—small but perfect.

BELGIAN-STYLE ALE

Belgian brewers recognize no "Belgian style" in their ales. Indeed, many object to the implication that their country's beers might be characterized by a simple theme—the opposite being the reason for their renown.

Belgian-style ale is the invention of North American home brewers, who noticed back in the 1980s that some beers from Belgium tasted spicy. This was mostly down to brewers adding herbs and spices in subtle amounts to enhance the flavor of some beers and in industrial quantities to drown that of others.

When specific yeast strains that could create similar flavors during fermentation were isolated

and patented, commercial yeast banks had new products, brewing competitions found new categories, and US consumers got to experience the drift without having to pay import prices.

Such yeast strains are, of course, perfectly legitimate and allow brewers to do useful new things to their beers. However, a more appropriate style name might be "American Spicy."

Right: Homage or derivative? The equally excellent Long Strange Tripel from Belgian-owned Boulevard Brewing in Missouri and Bam Bière from Jolly Pumpkin in Michigan.

FOR THE TRIP

- Most cafés prefer table service with a running tab.
- Few restaurants or hotels stock special beers yet.
- Specialist beer warehouses in most towns sell direct to the public.
- *Good Beer Guide Belgium* is the indispensible beer visitor's bible.
- Must visit: Brasserie-Brouwerij Cantillon in Brussels to see the lambic process.
- Must drink: slowly but adventurously.
- Visiting beer aficionados often know more about Belgian beer than waiters, customers, and many bar owners.

Left: Belgium is also blessed with more than its fair share of elegant cafés.

Opposite: Some Belgian ales have become big business, as seen in the high-tech brewhouse of Duvel Moortgat, at Breendonk near Antwerp.

THE WORLD'S LOCAL CRAFT BREWER

One of the world's most remarkable breweries sits in an industrial estate at the edge of an unassuming East Flanders town, looking like a components factory that supplies some great industrial enterprise—which, in many ways, it is.

The Proefbrouwerij in Lochristi, East Flanders, has links to one of Ghent's brewing schools, and was set up to help professional, semiprofessional, and amateur brewers experiment with creating new beers. It casts hundreds of new beers a year, saving many from ever seeing the light of day but creating others that go on to become modern classics.

While it may sound like a production line, in practice some of the world's most imaginative brewers come here to have their concepts turned into liquid reality—Danish beer designer Mikkeller,

for example, is said to be its biggest customer. The secret is a brewing team possessed of strong professional acumen, great kit, and a tolerance for being permanently inventive.

Over 3,000 definably different beers have been made so far, and tours are impossible, even for eminent international beer writers—we assume because some of the tags on the fermenters might break confidences.

Right: Dirk Naudts, brewmaster at Proef in Lochristi, East Flanders, has produced over 3,000 different beers for clients from Belgium and beyond.

de Bastogne, Belgoo, and Cazeau get the same excitement from seeing theirs in the bars of Brussels, which is also the local hunting ground for Yvan de Baets and Bernard Leboucq at Brasserie de la Senne, whose combined eye for both beer and label design makes them perhaps the best of breed.

Up north, the supreme hop work of Nino Bacelle and Guido Devos at Flemish-Wallonian Brouwerij De Ranke and the impressive catalog of Dutch-Belgian Ronald Mengerink's Brouwerij De Dochter van de Korenaar put them among the world's best. Urbain Coutteau and Carlo Grootaert at De Struise Brouwers have also drawn

international fans to their inventive and sometimes challenging beers.

All of which, we hope, brings comfort to Kris Herteleer and his team at De Dolle Brouwers in West Flanders and the Caulier family at La Brasserie de Blaugies in Hainaut, whose efforts over three decades have inspired these protégés.

Left: Danish "gypsy brewer" Mikkel Borg Bjergsø relies on the breweries of colleagues to make his distinctive beers.

NETHERLANDS

Most Europeans have seen their beer scene improve in the past decade but none more than the Dutch. Where once a tiny cabal of mighty breweries thrived by the clever application of advertising, a swarm of characterful imports and new local brews in a wide range of styles now claims one-sixth of the pie.

The Netherlands is a nation of traders. Its wealth, like much of its land mass, comes from the Dutch ability to conquer the seas.

In the Protestant north, drink was eschewed as a sign of human weakness, while in the Catholic south, it was celebrated as God's way of helping mankind survive a trying world. The western provinces of North and South Holland, and their respective port cities of Amsterdam and Rotterdam, took the sailor's view.

Meticulous excise records mean we know more about beer sales here in past centuries than in most other countries. For example, we know that beers made in Louvain (Leuven) and Bremen were shifted in vast quantities through the ports of Holland in the fifteenth century.

Historically, the Dutch drank regular brown ales, with traditions of special brews made for the fall, New Year, and possibly the coming of spring. This transformed around 1870 when refrigeration and improvements in brewing technology saw new breweries appear, especially in the south, following a pattern that had swept through Germany.

The Netherlands' better-known contribution to world brewing was its role in forming a global vision of simple, shiny beer for all, embodied in the world of beer's first and arguably greatest marketing man, Freddie Heineken (*see* p.82), whose lowly family brewery he transformed into a global giant.

By 1970, most small-scale commercial brewing had disappeared from the Netherlands and those regional independent brewers that survived aped the giants. Even the brewery at the Trappist abbey of Koningshoeven near Tilburg produced mainly a blond lager called Abdij Pilsener.

The Dutch beer revival began in 1968, when Piet de Jongh of the Beyerd café in Breda and two other bar owners began to import bottled ales from Belgium. By 1975 they had joined others in a string of independent cafés called ABT, which started to sell unusual bottled beers, mainly imported from Belgium and elsewhere. The consumer group PINT (rhymes with "mint") followed in 1980.

Interest built in a traditional seasonal beer style, the dark fall lager called *bok*, which to this day has its own national beer festival, held each October (*see* Beer Festivals, p.256).

Yet to most Dutch people, beer remained a ritually poured, blond, foam-topped drink made by one of two global corporations with a national connection. The older regional brewers that survived—Budels, Gulpener, Alfa, and Lindeboom, dotted along the Belgian border—failed to trade on their independence, and new small breweries brought imaginative recipes and technical flaws in equal measure.

What new Dutch brewing needed was a brewer of pioneering spirit, with a talent for invention, an understanding of sound methods, and strong self-belief. What it got was Menno Olivier and De Molen of Bodegraven near Gouda, south of Amsterdam (*see* New Dutch Brewing, p.84).

In our first edition, we said Dutch craft brewing had a long way to go to catch up with the rest of northern Europe but that at least its ship had left the harbor. We forgot that this nation of sailors had all the skills to sail fast.

The old Belgian joke—that, if it is Dutch and does not play soccer, it is probably rubbish—is wearing thin.

Above: The shadow of brewing giant Heineken looms large over the Netherlands, but smaller Dutch breweries are making progress.

Above: In contrast to much of its landscape, the Dutch beer scene is anything but flat.

THE BREWERIES OF THE DUTCH BEER REVOLUTION

In little over a decade the Netherlands' beer culture has advanced more rapidly than anywhere else in Europe. Its head count of breweries passed 200 in 2015, and for a while was growing at the rate of one a week. Those captured here have either made the greatest impact or have the most potential to do so.

West Frisian Islands

Texel

North Sea

NETHERLANDS

Leeuwarden
Bax of Groningen
Groningen

Us Heit
Bolsward

Maallust
Veenhuizen

Assen

Texels
Oudeschild

Den Helder

Mommeriete
Gramsbergen

Alkmaar

Praght
Dronten

Berghoeve
Den Ham

IJ (Duvel Moortgat)
7 Deugden, Butchers Tears, Oedipus, Prael,

Jopen Uiltje
Haarlem Pampus **AMSTERDAM**

Sallandse
Raalte

Apeldoorn

De Eem
Amersfoort

Leckere
Maximus
Utrecht
De Molen Oudaen
Kompaan **Bodegraven**
DEN HAAG (THE HAGUE)

Rodenburg
Rha

Arnhem

Duits & Laurel
Everdingen

Pelgrim
Rotterdam Kaapse, Noordt

Hemel
Oersoep
Nijmegen

Dordrecht

Muifel
Berghem

Ramses
Wagenberg

Emelisse
Kamperland

Beyerd, **Breda**

Tilburg
La Trappe
Koningshoeven

Hertog Jan (AB InBev)
Arcen

Kees
Middelburg

Kievit
Klein Zundert

Pimpelmeesch
Chaam

Stadsbrouwerij Eindhoven,
Van Moll
Eindhoven

Budels
Budel

Lindeboom
Neer

GERMANY

BELGIUM

Fontein
Stein

Alfa
Schinnen

Brand (Heineken)
Wijlre

Gulpener
Gulpen

Maastricht

North Sea

IJssel

Waal

Rhine

Meuse

NETHERLANDS

- **Muifel**
  Berghem — Brewery Town/City
- ○ **Eindhoven** — Other Town/city

- Long-established smaller breweries
- Trappist breweries
- Influential brewpubs
- First wave new independents
- Second wave new independents

0 — miles — 20
0 — km — 20

N

Bokbier

The Dutch *bokbier* tradition is held to be an extension of German *Bock* (*see* pp.92–3). However, the custom of using up the previous year's residual malt shortly after the new harvest to brew an extra-strong beer for consumption in the fall is common across Europe.

From the mid-twentieth century, the first week of October saw virtually every Dutch brewer launch a seasonal dark brew that was typically available only for a couple of weeks. By 1980 every one of these was a dark lager of exactly 6.5% ABV, within a narrow range of caramel sweetness, backed by low to medium hopping.

The last three decades have seen major style creep. Most are now ales, color runs from amber to jet black, and the alcohol content has been nudged upward. Some contain wheat and other grains, and several are smoked. Many have adopted the name *herfst* (harvest) *bok*. If ever the *bokbier* family was related to German *Bock*, they are now but distant cousins.

Mei- ("May") or *lente-* ("spring") *bok* is a more recent development, the honeyed sweetness of these generally light amber ales and lagers being more obviously related to German *Maibock*

(*see* p.93). These appear in the first week of April, exactly six months apart from their fall equivalents.

The tradition of *nieuwjaarsbier* ("New Year beer") has been succeeded by "winter beers," typically first appearing in late November, thus ending the opportunity to launch a summer style in the first week of July to complete an agreeably neat marketing cycle.

Left: Budels Lentebock, the paler *bokbier* from springtime, from the smallest Dutch legacy brewer.

Opposite: The Dutch beer consumers group PINT presents several beer festivals, including the Meibokfestival (pictured) in spring and Bokbierfestival in the fall.

THE HEINEKEN LEGACY

More than in any other country, the rise and fall of brewing in the Netherlands is the legacy of one person, Alfred "Freddie" Heineken (1923–2002), the man who said, "In the end, life is all about advertising."

The Heineken family brewery, though small, had been good enough to win international awards in the late nineteenth century, but it hit bad times in the interwar period and it fell out of family control —a fact that irked Freddie badly.

After spending time in the USA in the late 1940s, he came to understand the power of product imaging and determined that he would use this to create for Heineken a "brand."

Even after the company's empire had grown beyond his wildest expectations, he continued to take a keen interest in the minutiae of its advertising campaigns and logos, as important to him as the architecture of its financial success.

A huge character, he survived three weeks as a kidnap victim in 1983, but eventually succumbed, as he had predicted, to the effects of "too much smoking."

Right: Freddie Heineken, the architect of an empire and the world champion of brand awareness.

New Dutch Brewing

In contrast to the conformity and orderliness of the large-scale Dutch brewers, there are far fewer patterns of production among the newer, smaller ones, now numbering over 200 and set to rise further.

In the 1980s, new microbreweries emerged that rejected the mainstream styles of the larger corporations but also, sadly, ignored their technical standards. Yeast infections and other forms of spoiling became a routine hazard as naive owners tried to save money by skimping on key production safeguards.

The small collection of established Dutch family brewers has only recently begun nudging toward the bravery demanded by new beer followers. Meanwhile, from the first wave of microbrewers, four have emerged to become the new regionals—Texel, Jopen, Us Heit, and 't IJ, the last of these recently acquired by Belgium's Duvel Moortgat.

The country's long-established lone Trappist brewery has recently been joined by a second (*see* pp.64–5). Legendary La Trappe is now operated by Bavaria, an independent family-owned brewer that otherwise concentrates on making canned beers for grocery store contracts. In its abbey brewery, however, it makes smooth, rounded versions of *dubbel*, *tripel*, and its own invention, *quadrupel*, plus some increasingly experimental fine strong ales. Meanwhile, a small brewhouse called De Kievit (The Lapwing), based in a retreat south of Breda, makes Zundert, a beer that epitomizes the best of new and old Dutch ale brewing—polished, sweetish, strong, and well-hopped all in one.

Trying to characterize the new wave of Dutch brewers so simply is less easy.

Some look to be set on spending a decade to perfect a range of maybe four beers, but others find making fewer than a dozen varieties each month an unacceptable constraint.

A few brew solely for one café, but far more are taking advantage of national distribution afforded by block national deals with drinks specialists Mitra and one or two of the grocery store chains.

The sticking point for many remains quality, though those at the top of the tree now make reliable production quality their top priority, recognizing

Above: The Netherlands' second Trappist brewery, De Kievit, opened at Zundert, south of Breda, in 2013.

HOW TO KNIT SUCCESS

The extraordinary progress of Dutch brewing in the past decade is a helpful case study in how to improve a country's beer culture.

The key has been the bringing together of minds. Importers, distributors, retailers, publicists, and brewers now recognize that taking sales from industrial brands, grocery store wines, and sugary sodas means accepting the difficult premise that, by helping to sell your beers, I will sell more of my own because between us we will attract more people to better-designed beers.

The approach appears to be working impressively. Regular visitors to the Netherlands comment on how the perception of beer is visibly shifting from the ritually poured and skimmed *pintje* (Dutch for "little pint" of pils) to the enjoyment of diversity and interest.

In hushed tones, some even speak of Dutch brewing becoming as good as Belgian. There is a way to go before that is generally true, but it is fair to say that newer Dutch brewers tend to be better than their Belgian counterparts at creating tasty, well-made beers and that they have a far higher conversion rate from beer draftsman to brewery owner.

The superiority of a broadly collaborative approach over competitive animosity is mirrored in Denmark and, on a much larger scale, in the USA. It is a lesson others might do well to learn.

Above: At the Arendsnest in Amsterdam, only Dutch beers feature on a list of nearly 200 brews.

Above: The bar may be makeshift and the color scheme random, but there is no doubting the attitude at the Oedipus brewery tap in Amsterdam.

Left: Fresh green hops bound for another experiment at De Molen brewery in Bodegraven.

Below: The heavyweight Imperial Russian Stout (11% ABV) from Emelisse and playful Thai Thai (8% ABV) spiced *tripel* from Oedipus—two of the 800-plus new ales that are stretching the Dutch scene.

that the "folksy" and "alternative" nature of their products is no longer enough to impress.

The best were unquestionably inspired after following the gradual development of De Molen, where international beer styles old and new are re-created and sometimes even invented with great aplomb.

A majority of newer brewers are mimicking British, Belgian, American, German, and other styles but are starting to add their own spin.

The Dutch beer scene is one of adolescent brilliance within which any teacher might spot the naturally gifted, the determined plodders, the hare-brained enthusiasts, the easily led, and the challenged. Whether by businesslike devotion or sheer weight of numbers, we are certain the class of 2015 contains within it some of the stars of the future, their lights shining ever brighter.

FOR THE TRIP

- In cafés every fresh glass is rinsed to cool it and control the foam.
- Bars with peanuts expect the shells to be thrown on the floor to keep it oiled.
- Tim Skelton's excellent book *Beer in the Netherlands* tells it all.
- For up-to-date tips, try www.cambrinus.nl.
- Must see: a traditional smoke-stained brown café or *kroeg* while stocks last.
- Must drink: beers from most Dutch breweries at the Arendsnest in Amsterdam.
- If your hotel has no good beer, locate your nearest Mitra store.

OLD BEERS FOR NEW

Some farseeing beer purveyors have predicted (correctly, in our view) that for a nation's brewers to gain authority in export markets, they will need to have a few national beer specialties to call their own. The Netherlands has *bokbier*, but this is seasonal, so what else has potential?

For now the front runner is an earthy folk style called *kout* (also *kuit*, *kuyt*, or *koyt*). Referred to by some as the Dutch *saison*, it already mimics the trait of inventing its authenticity on the hoof. This is easily defensible, as original brewing records from centuries past are scant, and what does survive tells different truths. A folk beer is, after all, the beer of ordinary folk, not an exclusive treasure. We do know, however, that oats were often a major ingredient.

We predict the crunch will come when someone has to decide what role today's "folk" should have in what it should become. We pray that this will not be determined by the discovery and incidental patenting of a narrow range of modified yeast strains deemed essential to its fermentation— all the property of a single, highly organized yeast lab. But who knows?

Right: The residue from *kout*, thick with oats, was used to make rough cookies and for animal feed.

Left: De Molen present—top quality kit for top quality beers.

Below: De Molen past—makeshift machinery sat below a beautifully preserved windmill in Bodegraven.

GERMANY

Germany is the world's fifth-largest beer producer, brewing almost 3 billion gallons annually, yet it is alone in the top 40 for the fact that less than half its output—38 percent—comes from breweries owned by global companies.

Not that Germany is immune to the fancies of the brewing behemoths. Four of the Big Six companies that show at Munich's Oktoberfest each year, plus many instantly recognizable German beer brands such as Beck's and Paulaner, are owned directly or in effect by them.

However, their influence is subdued, and in general the larger producers—such as the Radeberger and Oettinger groups, Bitburger, and Krombacher—are broadly German-owned.

The remainder of the market is split among roughly 1,500 breweries, almost half based in Bavaria. While some are little more than commercialized hobbies and many others are single-pub concerns, a high proportion are diminutive, local companies happily mired in approaches to brewing that are centuries old.

The natural conservatism of the market owes a great deal to the strictures of the legally defunct 500-year-old "Purity Order" (*see* p.90), which ensured that German beer was always among the best, albeit within narrow parameters.

Historically, German brewers seek to produce beers of high quality, with a tight ceiling on price, thus quietly mitigating against the success of smaller breweries and arguably seeing off the interest of global groups. It is rarely their purpose to create something spectacularly different or, until recently at least, to ape other countries' brewing preferences. However, the emergence of new consumer tastes from abroad and the enormous blunder by some larger brewing groups of producing cheap beer at all costs, is forcing smaller established brewers to think how they position themselves.

Northern Germany has innumerable *Hausbrauereien* (brewpubs), most created within the last 25 years and offering a predictable portfolio of a pale lager, a dark one, and a wheat beer—plus, from time to time, a seasonal brew.

In the south, older, small-town, and typically family-run breweries dominate, ranging from single beer producers to those that offer a broad array of brands, some following the light-dark-wheat triptych while others happily do their own thing.

The established contrasts across the country are compelling. A Munich *Biergarten* will offer beer in 34-ounce *Maß*, or stein, but venture north to Cologne and the glass shrinks to a 7-ounce *Stange*.

Märzen in Bamberg may arrive smelling like a smoked ham, whereas in Augsberg—at the other side of Bavaria—it will be clean, malty, and warming. The traditional wheat beer of Berlin should be light and tart, while one from Bavaria should yield a fruity, spicy brew.

The nomadic drinker will enjoy the greatest selection of beers and make the most enjoyable discoveries. Germany's greatest brewers are local heroes, little known beyond their parish. You will need to find them because they are unlikely to find you.

German-style craft brewing is arriving, most prominently around Berlin, with outposts in Bavaria and the Rhineland. Dutifully creating interpretations of US styles but on occasion dabbling in revivals of more traditional German styles like *Leipziger Gose* or *Berliner Weisse*, with many others out there to rediscover.

In the bigger picture the question remains whether German-owned brewing groups will stop their obsessive chase for the cheaper gallon and, as even the most undemanding of drinkers begins to tire of industrial beers, cash in on their mastery of quality large-scale brewing and claim the biggest prize in brewing today—supplying the world with better international lagers.

Left: As the third-largest city in Bavaria and home to a major German university, it is perhaps not surprising that Augsburg boasts five breweries.

Above: The new face of German beer. At the Vagabund brewery tap in Berlin the emphasis is on good beer, not just our beer.

Left: More typical of recent German brewing history is the city's Lemke Brauhaus, under the railroad arches on Hackescher Markt.

Helles & Other German Pale Lagers

The word used in southern Germany to describe a pale-gold, lightly to moderately hopped, crisp and refreshing, bottom-fermented beer is *Helles*, meaning "light" or "bright," whereas "lager," derived from the German *lagern*, meaning "to store," is reserved for a few slightly aged beers.

Helles is the everyday drinking beer of Munich—the one that fills the imposing steins featured in countless images of jubilant Bavarians. At its best, it is a refined and elegant thirst-quencher, a sublime expression of subtlety and finesse in the brewing arts, while even at its most awkward it should be a pleasing if mundane quaffer.

Possibly as early as the fourteenth century, brewers in southern Bavaria came to realize that whatever it was that ruined beer brewed in the summer months could be prevented from doing so by refrigerating it in cold caves under the foothills of the Alps. By storing their late-spring brews there, lowering the temperature of conditioning, they unwittingly encouraged the propagation of what we now know to be cool-activated lager yeasts that had evolved naturally centuries earlier.

The technique to produce pale malts is thought not to have arrived in southern Germany until the early nineteenth century,

not long before light blond lagered beers appeared in Bohemia. These German brews have a drier, leaner, and paler malt profile than *světlý ležák* (*see* p.136), attributed in some cases to using infusion rather than decoction mashing, leading also to a greater degree of perceived, if not necessarily measurable, bitterness.

Common German use of the term Pils began in the 1960s. Travel north toward the Teutonic pilsner heartland of Lower Saxony and the Upper Rhine, and pale German lagers grow by stages more aggressively hoppy and less elegant, increasingly distant from the Pilsen original.

Left: The one-liter (33-ounce) *Maß* is the preferred drinking vessel for *Helles* throughout Bavaria.

THE SURROGATE PROHIBITION OR REINHEITSGEBOT

In 1516, Duke Wilhelm IV of Bavaria issued with his coruler, Duke Ludwig X, a masterpiece of legislation, accepted by historians as the world's longest-lasting consumer protection law.

A price war had developed between brewers and bakers over the purchase of wheat. Coming on top of longstanding concerns that brewers were putting all sorts into local beers, including herbs, root vegetables, fungi, and animal products, this latest annoyance brought a response known until the late nineteenth century as the Surrogate Prohibition and more recently the Purity Order (or *Reinheitsgebot*). This diktat stipulated that beer must be made only with barley, hops, and water. Yeast escaped mention, as it had yet to be

discovered. Within a decade, an exemption was made, ironically, for malted wheat.

As the German states came together under Bismarck, many adopted the standard, outlawing numerous historic local beer styles in so doing. It only became universal in 1919, when Bavaria made it a condition for accepting its amalgamation into the new Germany.

The *Reinheitsgebot* was formally withdrawn in 1988 after the European Union declared it a restraint of free trade, although many German breweries to this day refuse to use the sugar, substitute grains, and additives allowed by the law that has replaced it.

Above: Like all classic pieces of legislation, the original *Reinheitsgebot* was mercifully short.

Above: The interiors of many a Bavarian beer hall are dwarfed by the great expanses of an outdoor *biergarten*, the largest of which can seat more than 10,000 people and sometimes does.

Above: Enjoying a beer and the last of the daylight
at a café in Lower Saxony.

Dark Beers & Bock

The new kilning techniques allowing the production of pale malt did not arrive in the toy box of German brewers until the early nineteenth century, and it was not till the 1860s that brewers and drinkers alike took to blond beers with gusto, consigning to the margins many darker local varieties.

With the revival of interest in "anything but Pils" that began to jog the German beer market in the 1980s, southern varieties of darker lager began to cluster together under the name *Dunkles*, or sometimes *Münchner*, though the latter should strictly be made in the city of Munich from Munich malt.

The same period saw the reemergence from the former East Germany of yet darker beers known as *Schwarzbier* (literally "black beer").

However, unquestionably the most significant of the holdouts is *Bock*, said to date from fourteenth-century Einbeck, a city in Lower Saxony once also recorded as Eimbock. This being the case, it was probably first a stored ale, and records indicate it might also have been a wheat beer before it ultimately became an all-barley, cool-fermented lager.

Bock was also strong perhaps because Einbeck brewers, dependent as they were on creating beers for exports, believed —rightly—that high potency would help

protect the beer during its journeys to Munich, France, England, and beyond.

Today's *Bock* is usually sweetly malty and dark, although a few light-hued ones exist, sometimes known as *Maibock* ("May *Bock*"). Typically they measure between 6 and 7 % ABV, although there is a more formidable variant known as *Doppelbock* ("double *Bock*"), brands of which are usually designated by the suffix -ator.

Incredibly, these beers were used as a form of "liquid bread" to sustain fasting monks. Indeed Martin Luther was thus sustained throughout his most challenging debates at the Diet of Worms in 1521, supping from a donated barrel of Einbeck beer. This may explain why he lost.

Left: Because of their higher strength, *Bock* beers are sometimes served in smaller, more stylized glasses than other German lagers.

GERMAN BEER CLASSIFICATION

In Germany, beer categorization is based more on format than character. For example, there are yeast-containing varieties, essentially bottle- or even barrel-conditioned in the manner of British cask ales, known variously as *Zwickel*, *Ungespundet*, *Kräusen*, and *Kellerbier*, some of which are at best amber and a few plainly dark, with some being low in carbonation. For *Landbier*, literally "country beer," read rustic branding for a filtered, carbonated Helles.

A few beers are named "Lager," but more generally *Märzen* is the name given to those beers traditionally sent to cold storage for consuming over the summer before brewing recommenced in September, the remainder being seen off at

late summer festivals, where they are now termed *Oktoberfestbiers* (see right). Classically of light amber hue, they tend to be stronger, maltier, and richer.

The newer names Export and *Spezial* may indicate varieties that are not necessarily aged but lie on a spectrum of strength that stretches out toward the paler forms of *Bock*. Franconia (see pp.94–5) has some additional rules.

Right: Munich Hofbräuhaus's famed Oktoberfestbier is really an end-of season *Märzen*.

The Beers of Franconia

The Germans consume a lot of beer annually—29 gallons per head in 2014. This figure is said to double in Bavaria and is even higher in its northern area, Upper Franconia (Oberfranken), home to close to 300 established breweries, more per head than anywhere else on Earth.

Most are small, local operations producing no more than 264,172 gallons per year in a wide variety of local styles that use subtly different terminology from other parts of Germany. Here, visitors will encounter *Vollbier* (used to identify the brewery's main beer), *Landbier* (denoting a local brew but little else), and the modestly carbonated, fresh-from-the-barrel *Ungespundet* or "unstoppered" beer.

The region is best known for its *Rauchbier* (smoke beer, *see* below), a specialty gloried in Bamberg, a wonderful city supporting ten breweries, a gorgeous UNESCO-designated cityscape, innumerable artfully preserved buildings, and cultural events through the year, making it the obvious base for touring Oberfranken, an area that belongs on the itinerary of any traveler visiting Germany and every beer lover's bucket list.

Left: The brewing town of Bamberg is also an architectural wonderland, recognized by UNESCO as a World Heritage Site.

FOR THE TRIP

- Most German breweries sell beer directly to the public during working hours.
- Over half also have their own taphouse at or near the brewery.
- Sharing tables in a pub is normal, but always request permission first.
- The exception is the *Stammtisch*, reserved for regulars and accessible by invitation only.
- For updates, follow www.german-breweries.com or, for Franconia, www.bier.by.
- Local beer festivals, common in Bavaria, are usually part of larger celebrations.
- Must visit: Bamberg, Munich, Düsseldorf, Cologne, and Berlin.

BAMBERG'S RAUCHBIER

Before the arrival of better ovens allowed for more controlled kilning of barley, all malt had a degree of color and smokiness to it, from the wood fire used to dry the germinated grains. While most of the world's breweries moved away from this flavor profile, in Bamberg it persisted, eventually becoming an acclaimed local specialty.

Known collectively as *Rauchbier*, the smokiness of these brews varies considerably depending on the percentage of smoked malt that appears on the grain bill and on where it was smoked.

At the Heller-Trum brewery they kiln their own malt over a beechwood fire to create the best-known and perhaps most heavily smoked example of the style, Aecht Schlenkerla, a frequent find at specialist beer stores around the world, while across town at Spezial more gently smoky beers delight with their subtlety, again using grain smoked at their own maltings.

An estimated 70 other brewers in the region now brew this way, most only on an occasional basis, while brewers in other nations play with the style, often sourcing smoked malt from Bamberg's own Michael Weyermann Malzfabrik.

Right: The Aecht Schlenkerla brands—here the classic *Märzen* and less well-known wheat beer— are generally the smokiest and most practiced in Franconia.

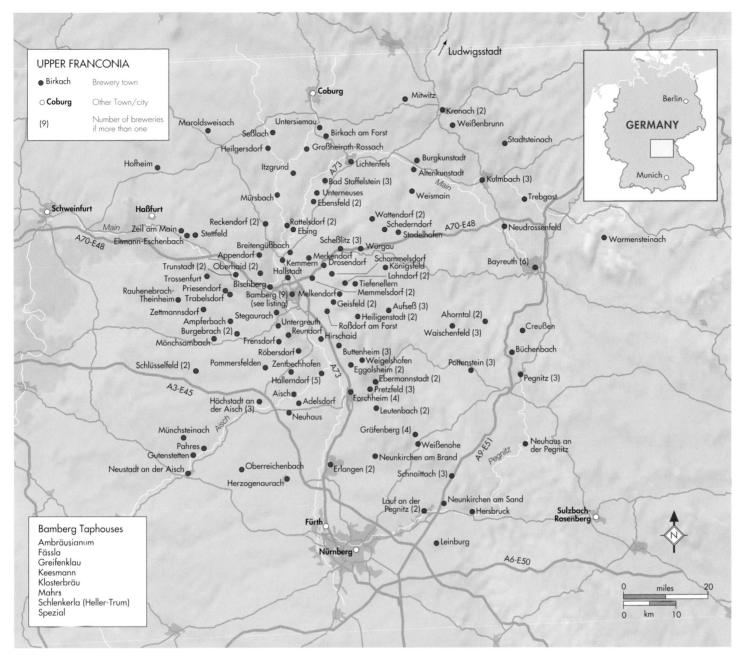

UPPER FRANCONIA

- Birkach — Brewery town
- ○ Coburg — Other Town/city
- (9) — Number of breweries if more than one

↑ Ludwigsstadt

Coburg

Mitwitz

Kronach (2)

Weißenbrunn

Stadtsteinach

Maroldsweisach

Seßlach

Untersiemau

Birkach am Forst

Burgkunstadt

Heilgersdorf

Großheirath-Rossach

Lichtenfels

Altenkunstadt

Kulmbach (3)

Hofheim

Itzgrund

Bad Staffelstein (3)

Weismain

Trebgast

Mürsbach

Unterneuses

Ebensfeld (2)

Wattendorf (2)

Schederndorf

Schweinfurt

Haßfurt

Reckendorf (2)

Rattelsdorf (2)

Stadelhofen

A70-E48

Neudrossenfeld

Main

Zeil am Main

Stettfeld

Ebing

Scheßlitz (3)

Würgau

Warmensteinach

Eltmann-Eschenbach

Breitengüßbach

Merkendorf

Schammelsdorf

Bayreuth (6)

Appendorf

Kemmern

Drosendorf

Königsfeld

Trunstadt (2)

Oberhaid (2)

Hallstadt

Lohndorf (2)

Trossenfurt

Bischberg

Tiefenellern

Rauhenebrach-Theinheim

Priesendorf

Trabelsdorf

Bamberg (9) (see listing)

Melkendorf

Memmelsdorf (2)

Ahorntal (2)

Creußen

Zettmannsdorf

Stegaurach

Geisfeld (2)

Aufseß (3)

Ampferbach

Untergreuth

Heiligenstadt (2)

Waischenfeld (3)

Büchenbach

Burgebrach (2)

Reundorf

Roßdorf am Forst

Mönchsambach

Frensdorf

Hirschaid

Röbersdorf

Buttenheim (3)

Schlüsselfeld (2)

Pommersfelden

Zentbechhofen

Weigelshofen

Pottenstein (3)

Pegnitz (3)

Hallerndorf (5)

Eggolsheim (2)

Ebermannstadt (2)

Aisch

Höchstadt an der Aisch (3)

Adelsdorf

Pretzfeld (3)

Forchheim (4)

Neuhaus

Leutenbach (2)

Münchsteinach

Gräfenberg (4)

Pahres

Weißenohe

Neuhaus an der Pegnitz

Gutenstetten

Neunkirchen am Brand

Neustadt an der Aisch

Oberreichenbach

Erlangen (2)

Schnaittach (3)

Herzogenaurach

Lauf an der Pegnitz (2)

Neunkirchen am Sand

Hersbruck

Sulzbach-Rosenberg

Fürth

Leinburg

Nürnberg

A6-E50

GERMANY

Berlin ○

Munich ○

Bamberg Taphouses

Ambräusianum
Fässla
Greifenklau
Keesmann
Klosterbräu
Mahrs
Schlenkerla (Heller-Trum)
Spezial

0 — miles — 20

0 — km — 10

OTHER SMOKED BEER VARIETIES

With experimentation an obsession among craft brewers, it is possible to find almost any type of beer in a smoked format, if only fleetingly. Of the Old-World styles only Polish Grodzisz (see p 144) is known to have survived the centuries. The one most likely to reach similar permanence is that pioneered by the Alaskan Brewery Company as Alaskan Smoked Porter (6.5% ABV), which first saw the light of day in 1988 and now also comes in single vintages. Like its *Märzen* cousin from Bamberg, thankfully it travels well to all parts of the globe.

Left: The wood-fired kilns are still loaded by hand at Heller-Trum's on-site maltings in Bamberg.

THE BREWERIES OF UPPER FRANCONIA ▲

The geographical boundaries of the Bavarian district of Upper Franconia are defined more by spirit than local government. It is an area of intense natural beauty peppered with striking old towns and more densely populated with heritage breweries than anywhere else in the world. This map shows the location of the traditional breweries, most of which run taphouses.

Bavarian & Other Wheat Beers

Before the invention of modern lagers in the 1840s, there were broadly two types of beer in Bavaria
—smoky, strong, lagered brown ales and light, fresh-tasting white or wheat beers. The latter live on
in a variety of forms, most prominently in western Bavaria and parts of Baden-Württemberg.

Ironically, although the original purpose of the *Reinheitsgebot* (*see* p.90) was to curtail the use of wheat in brewing, this was rapidly reinstated, with volumes being held down by the application of heavy taxation over and above regular beer duty.

In 1602, the elector of Bavaria, Maximilian I, removed this tax differential and instead licensed its production. With the fall in production price, wheat beers enjoyed a massive increase in popularity, which played well for the elector's family, the Wittelsbachs, who had bought all the licenses!

This family monopoly ended in 1798, by which time the popularity of wheat beer had faded, and it was not until Munich brewer Georg Schneider (*see* p.97) bought his license in 1872 that efforts were made to revive types of beer that by then were badly on the wane.

Bavarian wheat beers, particularly when they appear with the prefix *Hefe* (roughly "with yeast") are notable for more than just their grain content. Properly, such beers are fermented with one of a distinctive

family of yeast that imbue the beers with bananalike esters (*see* p.25) and/or clove-accented spiciness. Citrus notes may also come from the wheat, along with some peppery character.

Filtered and clarified, they are often termed *Kristall*, while with darker malts they become *Dunkel Weiss* ("dark white")

WHEAT BEER BREWERS IN BADEN-WÜRTTEMBERG AND BAVARIA ▶
While wheat beers are found in brewpubs across Germany their heartland is the southwest, where specialists in all types abound.

Below: Skimming yeast from a traditional open fermenter at a wheat-beer brewery.

THE WHEAT BEER BELT OF MEDIEVAL EUROPE

Beers brewed from wheat were once found widely across Europe, and other parts of Germany have wheat beer traditions that are quite different from those of the south. *Gose*, said to originate from the town of Goslar, near Hannover but adopted in the nineteenth century as a Leipzig specialty, is a tart style made, as with Irish stout, by the addition of salt to the mash. It died out in the 1960s but was revived after the fall of both the *Reinheitsgebot* and the Berlin Wall, to be made by a handful of breweries using recipes that include coriander.

Another renowned local variant, *Berliner Weisse*, was typically of low strength (2.5–3.5% ABV), with a trademark tangy lactic acidity. It became the case that the best of these were brewed in the

USA, though recent experiments by craft brewers like Brewbaker of Berlin and Braumanufaktur of Potsdam have prompted improvements to the Oetker Group's widely available market leader. The beer's engaging tartness is muted, indeed vanquished, by the faddy and unnecessary addition of sweetened syrup flavored with raspberry or the herb woodruff.

Expect to see more revivals as brewers experiment with re-creating beers from archived brewing records that identify local traditions of adding smoked malt, fruits, herbs, older grains, and much else besides, many outlawed when the all-powerful *Reinheitsgebot* obliterated diversity in non-Bavarian Germany in 1919.

Above: *Berliner Weisse* is currently enjoying a tentative revival in its home city.

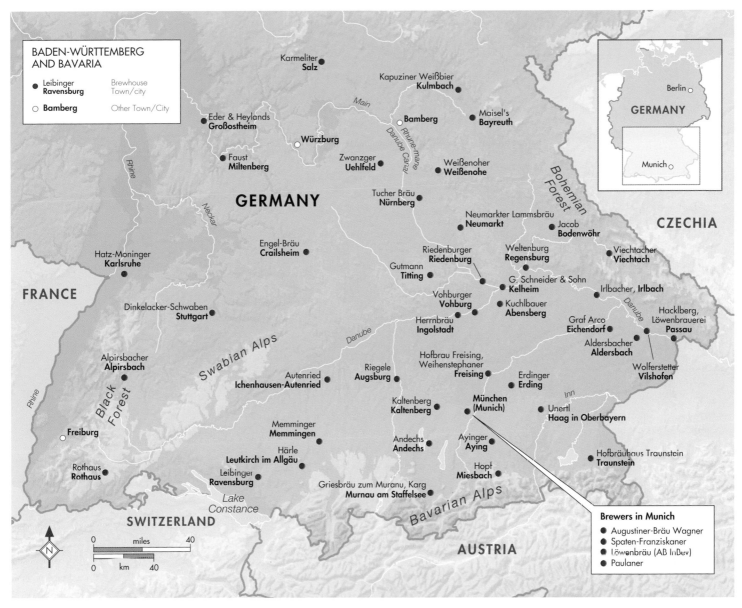

BADEN-WÜRTTEMBERG
AND BAVARIA

● Leibinger
Ravensburg   Brewhouse
Town/city

○ **Bamberg**   Other Town/City

GERMANY

Berlin ○

Munich ○

CZECHIA

FRANCE

SWITZERLAND

AUSTRIA

Karmeliter
Salz

Kapuziner Weißbier
Kulmbach

Maisel's
Bayreuth

Eder & Heylands
Großostheim

Main

○ **Bamberg**

Faust
Miltenberg

Würzburg

Zwanzger
Uehlfeld

Weißenoher
Weißenohe

Danube Canal

Rhine-maine

Tucher Bräu
Nürnberg

GERMANY

Neumarkter Lammsbräu
Neumarkt

Jacob
Bodenwöhr

Bohemian Forest

Viechtacher
Viechtach

Rhine

Neckar

Engel-Bräu
Crailsheim

Riedenburger
Riedenburg

Gutmann
Titting

Weltenburg
Regensburg

G. Schneider & Sohn
Kelheim

Irlbacher, **Irlbach**

Danube

Hacklberg,
Löwenbrauerei
Passau

Hatz-Moninger
Karlsruhe

Dinkelacker-Schwaben
Stuttgart

Vohburger
Vohburg

Kuchlbauer
Abensberg

Graf Arco
Eichendorf

Aldersbacher
Aldersbach

Wolferstetter
Vilshofen

Herrnbräu
Ingolstadt

Danube

Alpirsbacher
Alpirsbach

Black Forest

Swabian Alps

Autenried
Ichenhausen-Autenried

Riegele
Augsburg

Hofbrau Freising,
Weihenstephaner
Freising

Erdinger
Erding

Inn

Freiburg

Memminger
Memmingen

Kaltenberg
Kaltenberg

Andechs
Andechs

**München
(Munich)**

Ayinger
Aying

Unertl
Haag in Oberbayern

Härle
Leutkirch im Allgäu

Hopf
Miesbach

Hofbräuhaus Traunstein
Traunstein

Rothaus
Rothaus

Leibinger
Ravensburg

Griesbräu zum Murnau, Karg
Murnau am Staffelsee

*Lake
Constance*

Bavarian Alps

Brewers in Munich
● Augustiner-Bräu Wagner
● Spaten-Franziskaner
● Löwenbräu (AB InBev)
● Paulaner

N

0   miles   40
0   km   40

or occasionally even *Schwarzer Weiss* ("black white"). Stronger *Weizenbock* and *Eisbock* beers have gained popularity in recent years, too, although whether the latter revives an older style or creates a new one is debatable.

The extent to which the modern wheat beer diaspora is beginning to stretch its wings is nowhere better demonstrated than in the range of the original German revivalist, Georg Schneiider & Sohn of Kelheim—this generation's head being Georg VI—which still sets the standard for German wheat beer old and new.

Right: The Wasserschloss in Titting, home of Gutmann brewery.

The Two Beers of North Rhine Westphalia

There are beer styles that can be understood almost at first sip. Dry stout, American-style pale ale, and many types of wheat beer show themselves quickly and may be reasonably defined in a word or three. Then there are those that take their time in revealing themselves, best tracked to their source in order to be properly appreciated. Such are *Alt*, or *Altbier*, from Düsseldorf, and *Kölsch* from neighboring Cologne (Köln).

Altbier

Literally, *Altbier* means "old beer," and its heartland is Düsseldorf's Altstadt, or "old town," although there are variants throughout the region.

As cool-temperature fermentation and cold-conditioning spread across Germany and other parts of Europe in the late nineteenth century, pockets of resistance formed, particularly in Germany's northwest. In Düsseldorf, concession was made to lager's long and cool conditioning period (*see* p.25), but top-fermenting ale yeasts were retained, creating a hybrid between the two families of beer.

Yet there is more to the enigma of *Alt* than this. Although often deep brown, it typically displays more earthy than roasty character, and its significant hoppiness speaks more to dryness than bitterness. Additionally, its cool conditioning means

THE CITY WITH NO STYLE

The firmly malty style of the pale lager called *Dortmunder*, for its association by foreigners with the northern city of Dortmund, is not recognized in Germany. As with Pilsener and Budweiser in Czechia, all that a German will understand from the term *Dortmunder* is that the beer will probably have come from the single large brewery that remains in the old capital of Westphalia, more famed nowadays for its high-performing soccer club, Borussia Dortmund.

In practice, the city's beers are largely indistinguishable from those produced by others in the country's major brewing groups, and few, if any, are either stronger or fuller-bodied.

The myth evolved after World War II, when an intense local spirit to rebuild the city after the devastation caused by bombing of the industrial Ruhr region coincided with the presence of thousands of UK and US military personnel and some snappy advertising by two local breweries.

This does not stop Dutch and American brewers producing stronger blond lagers bearing the name or competition organizers giving prizes for the best beers of a nonexistent style.

Right and opposite left: Dutch Alfa Super Dort and Dog Days from Two Brothers, Illinois—disciples without a prophet.

THE ALTBIER AND KÖLSCH BREWERS OF NORTH RHINE WESTPHALIA ▶

Visitors are advised that the relationships between those brewers and imbibers who prefer either *Altbier* or *Kölsch* resemble those between major league soccer teams from the same city. Asked which you prefer, express a preference for the home team or else avoid passing any opinion.

that the round, alelike qualities, although apparent, are restrained.

Further, just when you think you might have grasped the style, the Düsseldorf breweries complicate matters with the occasional production of special *Sticke* or "secret" *Altbier*: stronger, often darker, but no less beguiling.

Düsseldorf's convenient location, the seductive appeal of its riverside Altstadt, and the short, manageable walks between its taphouses make a compelling case for pilgrimage. Additionally, a few easy trips out on a DB train will bring you to small towns where they do *Alt* in their own way.

Opposite: The brewery at Zum Schlüssel in Düsseldorf often goes overlooked amid the bustle of the beer hall.

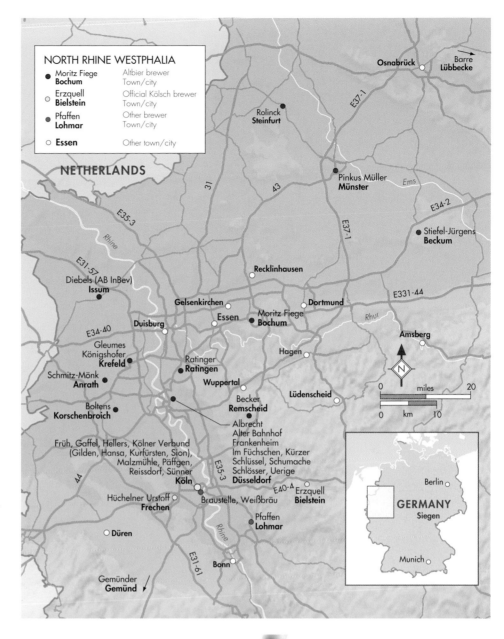

NORTH RHINE WESTPHALIA

- ● Moritz Fiege **Bochum** — Altbier brewer Town/city
- ○ Erzquell **Bielstein** — Official Kölsch brewer Town/city
- ● Pfaffen **Lohmar** — Other brewer Town/city
- ○ **Essen** — Other town/city

NETHERLANDS

Osnabrück · Barre **Lübbecke**
Rolinck **Steinfurt**
Pinkus Müller **Münster** · *Ems*
Stiefel-Jürgens **Beckum**
Recklinghausen
Diebels (AB InBev) **Issum**
Gelsenkirchen · Moritz Fiege **Bochum** · Dortmund
Essen
Duisburg
Gleumes Königshofer **Krefeld**
Schmitz-Mönk **Anrath**
Ratinger **Ratingen** · Hagen · Amsberg
Wuppertal
Boltens **Korschenbroich** · Becker **Remscheid** · Lüdenscheid
Albrecht Alter Bahnhof Frankenheim Im Füchschen, Kürzer Schlüssel, Schumache Schlösser, Uerige **Düsseldorf**
Früh, Gaffel, Hellers, Kölner Verbund (Gilden, Hansa, Kurfürsten, Sion), Malzmühle, Päffgen, Reissdorf, Sünner **Köln**
Hüchelner Urstoff **Frechen** · Braustelle, Weißbräu · Erzquell **Bielstein**
Pfaffen **Lohmar**
○ **Düren** · Bonn
Gemünder **Gemünd**

N — 0 miles 20 / 0 km 10

GERMANY — Berlin, Siegen, Munich

Left: Schlüssel (pictured here), along with Schumacher, Füchschen, and Uerige are Düsseldorf Altstadt's four heritage brewers, while Kürzer Alt has the new kit on the block.

Kölsch

Pale of hue and delicately fragrant, with neither high strength nor aggressive hopping to trumpet its presence, *Kölsch* is often dismissed unfairly as trivial. Rather it is a teaser.

Its dozen or so makers have achieved the tightest style protection afforded to any beer in the European Union and may yet attain a full *appellation contrôlée*. Within the EU, all claimants to the name must be brewed within an area of the city and its environs outlined in a 1985 Convention, plus a few specified older producers from nearby.

The emphasizing effects of adjectives such as "premium" are banned from labels and advertising, and even the shape and size of its glass, the 7-ounce *Stange* are proscribed.

All of this might seem a lot of fuss for a pale beer that is, like *Altbier*, fermented at ale temperatures and conditioned like a lager. To understand why *Kölsch* should not be dismissed as just another "lawnmower beer," you need to sample it at its best, which means visiting Cologne and finding it served straight from an unpressurized barrel that has been tapped within the hour.

Between an initial soft fruitiness and a dry, appetizing finish, *Kölsch* should segue through a range of subtle palate tweaks, some hoppier, others almost pillowy on the tongue, still others portraying a more assertive maltiness.

Many of the city's brewery taps (*Ausschänke*) sit on twisting laneways in the shadow of the brooding cathedral, offering beers and environs that vary, though the rituals are the same: the blue-clad waiters (*Köbesse*) wandering the aisles with trays of freshly poured beer, replacing glasses the moment they empty and marking the sale on a coaster beneath.

The cycle stops when the customer places the coaster atop their glass, at which time the pencil marks are counted, the bill is tallied, and the party moves on.

To optimize the experience, locate those brewers that have retained their independence from the larger groups, such as Päffgen, Malzmühle, and Sünner, and target their taps.

Above: The Päffgen beer hall is filled every evening with a mixture of locals and scattered tourists.

Below: Cologne's Cathedral is a good starting point for a tour of the city's *Kölsch* breweries.

New German Beers

That even large German breweries have traditionally produced uniformly "good enough" beers probably accounts for Germany's lack of noisy groups protesting about the parlous state of beer making. However, national detachment is being challenged by demands for beers that reflect best modern practice elsewhere, even if this turns away from purity.

The nascent German new wave has thus far concentrated on making "me too" brews, mainly of US origin, ahead of the recent arrival of US craft brewers. Additionally some producers, including longer established ones, have sought to grow new styles out of existing ones.

Among longer established breweries, Bavaria's Brauerei Hummel Merkendorf of Memmelsdorf stands out among the out-of-Bamberg Franconian brewers. In addition to wheat beer originator Schneider & Sohn, whose high-profile innovations include Weisse Tap X Mein Nelson Sauvin, look for the evolution of the Weihenstephaner range, or go smaller with Brauerei Gutmann, based in Titting, south of Nürnberg.

Brauerei Schönram, from Petting, near the Austrian border, is one of the first established brewers to create its own range of Anglo-American ales, rather than creating them to order for copious crafty beer firms on one-off contracts.

New brewers to watch include Camba Bavaria in Truchtlaching; Störtebeker Braumanufaktur from Stralsund in northern Mecklenburg-Vorpommern; Häffner Bräu, at Bad Rappenau in Baden-Wurttemburg; and Gänstaller Bräu of Schnaid, north of Nürnberg, which smoked its recipe to create Affumicator (9.6% ABV), the most credible rival for best *Rauchbier* ("smoke beer") beyond the gently evolving range of Aecht Schlenkerla beers from Brauerei Heller-Trum.

Better brewery hirers include Crew Republic in Bavaria and Freigeist from the Rhineland.

The "craft" component of the German beer market may be small at present, but do not doubt its serious intent. With Germany's larger brewers seemingly set on serving a tight walleted gray mass and the smaller established brewers afraid to challenge the stranglehold of price restrictions, these newer players see limitless opportunities to entice the world's greatest beer drinkers toward new horizons.

Above and top: CREW Republic is one of the firms daring conservative Bavarian drinkers to wake up and smell the hops that don't come from Hallertau.

AUSTRIA

It is never easy running a smart shop next to a popular discount store, especially when there is a well-respected boutique on the opposite corner. Austria's brewers may be forgiven for feeling unsure about how they should stand out from their neighbors in Germany and Czechia.

Austrian brewer Anton Dreher has the strongest claim to have first commercialized lager brewing at Schwechat near Vienna in 1841 (*see*

Above: Austrians are the third-largest consumers of beer in Europe.

below), where he used Vienna malt to create ruddy, amber-hued *Wiener* (Viennese) lagers. Although Brau Union at Schwechat and Viennese independent Ottakringer recently re-created such a beer, in general neither brewers nor bar owners in Austria today fête this style as a local specialty, preferring to mimic German *Helles*, *Märzen*, *Dunkles*, and *Schwarzbier*.

Austria never had to accept the restrictions of the *Reinheitsgebot* (*see* p.90), leading some Germans to be sniffy about beers made here at the southeastern end of the German-speaking world. Meanwhile, had the end of the Austro-Hungarian Empire in 1918 been different, who knows what similarities Austrian beer would now share with those of Bohemia?

Austria has around 220 operating breweries, of which 60 percent are

brewpubs. Over half of Austrian beer comes from Brau Union AG, part of Heineken, which runs nine separate breweries, eschewing the one-size-fits-all model and likely explaining its continued success locally. Numerous family-owned companies trace their origins back an implausible number of centuries, of which nine have formed a collaborative group, Brau Cultur.

The hop-growing area that stretches from Steiermark into Slovenia gave the world Styrian hops, many of which are now grown organically, adding to the growing desire by Austrian brewers to source local ingredients to produce fully organic beers, termed Bio.

If they come to need another national specialty they might consider *Steinbier* (stone beer), emerging as Austrian by

WHERE DID LAGER ORIGINATE?

The question of who can be credited with making the first lager depends very much on what you consider a lager to be.

For centuries, much of central Europe had a brewing season that reflected the difficulties which prevented beer from spoiling during fermentation in the warmer months. In Munich, this stretched from St. Michael's Day (September 29) to St. George's Day (April 23).

Various parts of Europe developed their own supply solutions, which involved storage in oak casks, as represented by the traditions of lambic, *bière de garde*, *saison*, and *Märzen*. In parts of Bavaria, Bohemia, and Austria, it was known that Alpine caves and underground vaults that remained cold throughout the summer were excellent for keeping beer sound—the colder they remained, the better.

The first definite commercialization of natural cold storage, or lagering, was Dreher's Vienna lager in 1841 (*see* above), followed in 1842 by Josef Groll at the Burgher brewery in Pilsen, credited with creating the first blond beer to be cold-conditioned. Claims are made for earlier dates—Austria in 1835 and Munich in 1837—but clear evidence is hard to pin down.

Initially such beers gained renown only as a local specialty, occasionally exported. It was advances in commercial refrigeration techniques in the 1870s that led to their global spread.

Right: Austrian brewers do not lack imagination. Kiesbye's Waldbier (or forest beer) is fermented for three days below fir trees to attract wild yeast before being aged in oak—indoors—for 6–12 months.

Right: Roast pork knuckle and voluminous beer are the specialties of the Schweizerhaus in Vienna.

dint of disappearing elsewhere. In this tradition the wort is brought to a boil by dropping in red-hot stones, causing it to caramelize and go slightly smoky—a pleasing combination.

Austrian takes on German styles can excel. The Pils from both Trumer and Zipfer are among the best in the world, and the range of wheat beers impresses. A typical Austrian *Märzen* is leaner and often more immediately appealing than its German cousins.

The country's emerging craft brewers number around 20 currently, creating ales in a ragbag of global styles, varying hugely in both design and technical quality between producers, brands, and brew

runs. As yet there is no national equivalent of BrewDog, De Molen, or Nøgne Ø, though Austria has been gifted a Trappist brewery in the shape of Stift Engelszell on the banks of the Danube in Upper Austria—with no café sadly.

AUSTRIAN BREWERIES THAT WELCOME VISITORS ▾

With 60 percent of Austria's 220 or so breweries making beer only for the pub, hotel, or guesthouse where they are based and many of the rest having ornate, folksy, or grand taphouses, there is no better way to examine the country's reviving beer culture than to absorb its sometimes spectacular beauty on a brewery tour.

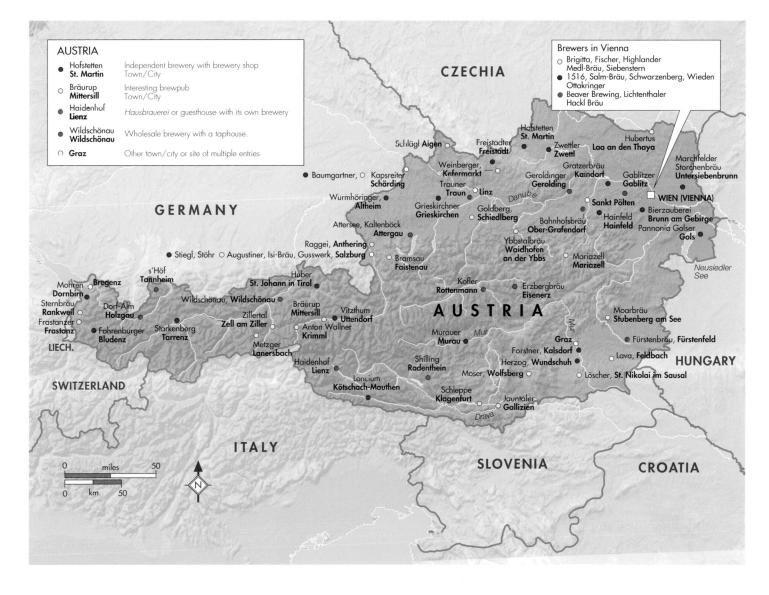

SWITZERLAND

Until the mid-nineteenth century, beer consumption in Switzerland was tiny, but now, on paper at least, the Swiss have more breweries per head than any other nation. Where once brewing was held back by poor transport links, nowadays complex trade restraints are the worry.

The number of breweries is made artificially high due to home brewers being allowed cheap licenses in order to sell a little beer to their friends. However, there is no denying an impressive underlying trend.

We noted in our first edition that the nation that might feel most aggrieved at not being granted its own space was Switzerland, which, depending on who was asked, had between 130 and 190 breweries at that time.

The headline figure is now nearing 600, or one to every 13,500 people. However, up to half of these are those home brewers selling tiny amounts of beer rather than true commercial enterprises.

There is also a yawning gap in size between the smallest of the 14 long-established independent breweries and the largest of the new wave, which despite their number can claim only 3 percent of the market between them.

There is no uniquely Swiss style of beer and the country's three language regions reflect the respective brewing habits of their linguistic homelands, the German-speaking east being mostly lager country, while the Francophone west is Belgian-influenced and pro ale. It has been a slow journey, but Swiss beer is getting there.

Right: Massive, high-speed bottling lines, such as this one at the Carlsberg-owned Feldschlösschen brewery in Switzerland, package more beer in a few minutes than most craft breweries do in a day, and with far fewer employees.

Opposite: Even in summer, Switzerland's Alpine landscape is spectacular, though for centuries the terrain held back indigenous brewing.

NAMES TO LOOK OUT FOR

In Deutschschweiz, Switzerland's large German-speaking region, the best of the established brewers is Locher of Appenzell, with Felsenau of Bern not far behind. There is regular craft stuff from Storm & Anchor in Zurich; Bier Factory of Rapperswil-Jona, St. Gallen, shows occasional excellence; and Doppelleu Brauwerkstatt of Winterthur is a traditional German brewer gone to ale.

The French-speaking region, La Romandie, has extreme beers from Brasserie des Franches-Montagnes (BFM) in the Jura. There are consistently beautiful ones from Brasserie Trois Dames, on the other side of the Jura in the Vaud canton, while La Nébuleuse of Lausanne impresses, too. Sadly the leading craft brewery in the Italian-speaking canton, Ticino, recently went under.

Left and above: With the more interesting Swiss beers appearing in the take-home trade brewers like Locher of Appenzell, pay close attention to their bottled beers.

FRANCE

We refuse to arbitrate on the question of whether it was a Belgian or a French brewer who first coined the term *bière artisanale*—literally craft beer—beyond noting that we have seen the term used on a French beer label said to date from 1969.

The word *bière* did not enter its modern usage in the French language as the term for a fermented grain drink until the fourteenth century, although there is evidence of communal brewing in monasteries in the Alsace region as early as the seventh century.

Alsace has remained one of the traditional centers of brewing, and from the sixteenth to the nineteenth centuries the city of Strasbourg, like some other parts of France, had the same brewing season as Munich—from St. Michael's Day to St. George's Day.

The French Revolution in 1789 was a spur to independent brewing, and within a century France had over 4,000 breweries. In 1890, the first French brewery group, Brasseries de la Meuse, formed as a confederation.

While the 1914–18 war inflicted significant damage on breweries and maltings in northern France, it was the Second World War (1939–45) that undid French brewing structurally and economically.

When Charles de Gaulle became president of France in 1959, it remained home to an economically battered but recognizable network of small regional breweries, but by the time his successor, Georges Pompidou, died in office 15 years later, all but a handful of local artisan breweries had been absorbed into six corporations, none of which proved solid enough to remain French owned.

The first new brewery to open in a generation was Deux Rivières at Morlaix in Brittany, in 1985, ahead of a small outbreak of regional brewing. By the turn of the millennium, there were a few signs of a revival of French brewing culture in other regions where wine production is absent or low key, such as in the far north along the Belgian border.

Fifteen years on, the whole of France is seeing a massive increase in the number of small breweries, from the Alps to the Pyrenees and La Manche to Le Med, such that only three of the country's 95 mainland *départements* have none, and the national total now tops 750.

While many French people remain delightfully chauvinistic about food and drink, turning rapidly scornful of poor quality, lack of familiarity with higher-quality beer has made the public forgiving of unimaginative brewing. The 1992 decree that defines minimum standards for beer requires only 50 percent of the fermenting sugars to come from malt.

As recently as 2011, it was fair to say that few of the beers from these new *artisanale* ventures would make the brew masters of Belgium or Bavaria begin quaking in their boots; it is now the case that there are modern French exemplars in many of the ale styles that emanate from both western Europe and North America, plus several styles that the French are beginning to call their own.

Many newer producers brew less beer in a week than some people keep in their cellar, while others are no more than brewpub franchises making rather dull beers not far off the mainstream. However, as we predicted last time around, impressive and consistent performers are emerging, and, in a country famed not just for its wines but also for its brandies, pastis, and *eaux de vie*, it would be naive to assume that among these pioneers there are not dozens of Europe's cult brewers of tomorrow.

Above: Northern France's bars, like the Java in St. Malo, shown here, have more in common with the pub traditions of northern Europe than the café culture of Paris and the south of the country.

BREWERY DENSITY IN FRANCE ▶

At the start of 2016, there were 760 licensed breweries known to be operating in France, a 20-fold increase on the position in 1975. Only one mainland *département* was without a local brewery —with Nord boasting 40. The number had doubled in five years, and no region witnessed a reduction. To appreciate the changes graphically, compare this map to its equivalent in our first edition.

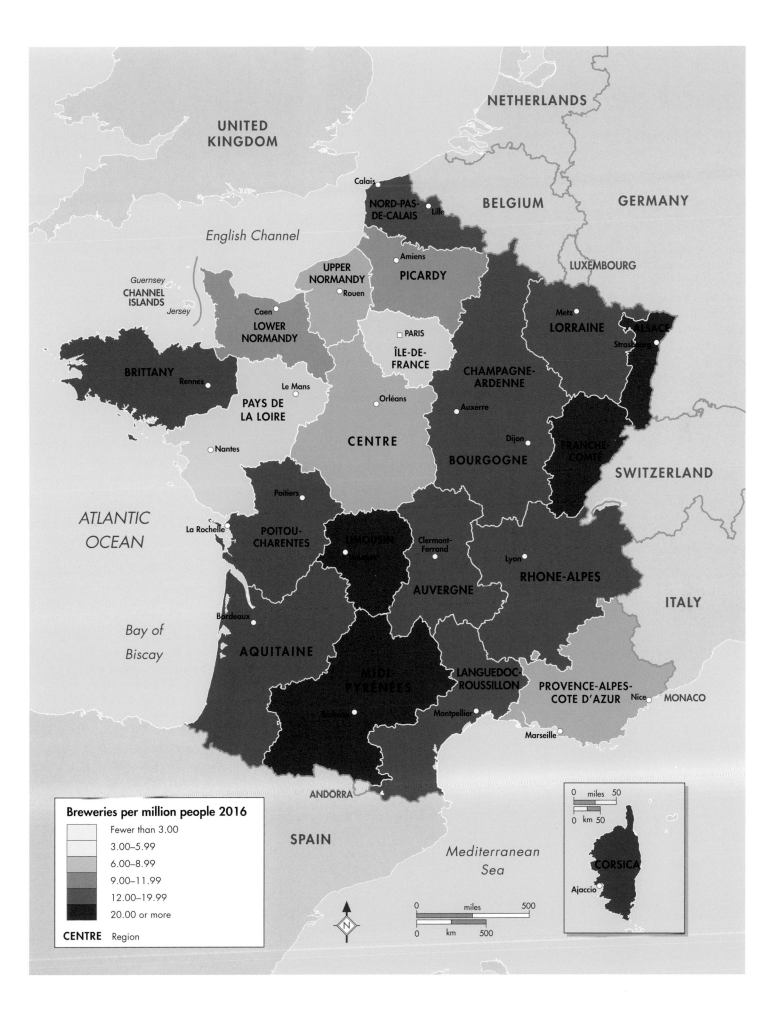

NETHERLANDS

UNITED
KINGDOM

BELGIUM

GERMANY

English Channel

Calais

NORD-PAS-
DE-CALAIS

Lille

LUXEMBOURG

Guernsey
CHANNEL
ISLANDS

Jersey

Amiens

UPPER
NORMANDY

PICARDY

Caen

LOWER
NORMANDY

Rouen

PARIS

ÎLE-DE-
FRANCE

Metz

LORRAINE

ALSACE

Strasbourg

BRITTANY

Rennes

Le Mans

PAYS DE
LA LOIRE

Orléans

CENTRE

CHAMPAGNE-
ARDENNE

Auxerre

Dijon

BOURGOGNE

FRANCHE-
COMTÉ

SWITZERLAND

Nantes

ATLANTIC
OCEAN

Poitiers

La Rochelle

POITOU-
CHARENTES

LIMOUSIN

Clermont-
Ferrand

Lyon

RHONE-ALPES

ITALY

AUVERGNE

Bordeaux

*Bay of
Biscay*

AQUITAINE

MIDI-
PYRÉNÉES

LANGUEDOC-
ROUSSILLON

PROVENCE-ALPES-
COTE D'AZUR

Nice

MONACO

Montpellier

Marseille

ANDORRA

Breweries per million people 2016

Fewer than 3.00

3.00–5.99

6.00–8.99

9.00–11.99

12.00–19.99

20.00 or more

CENTRE Region

SPAIN

*Mediterranean
Sea*

0 miles 500
0 km 500

N

0 miles 50
0 km 50

CORSICA

Ajaccio

Bière de Garde & Farmhouse Ales

France's leading beer writer, Elisabeth Pierre, makes two key distinctions between *saison* (*see* p.72), farmhouse ales, and *bière de garde*. These are that the concepts overlap but are not interchangeable and that the latter two are fundamentally French.

The term *bière de garde* means "stored beer." Although its origins predate the development of ice-cold lagering by some centuries, its principles are similar (*see* p.25), referring to the practice of letting a beer mature at the brewery for a time before dispatch, lying in oak tuns like a fine wine.

Although these French beers likely share some common heritage with the *saison* beers made in the five former French *départements* that became the southern provinces of Belgium, and with the oak-aged ales of Flanders (*see* p.66), they share no tradition of aging to earthiness or acidity. Rather they are known to have been brewed, in whole or in part, to a traditional cycle.

Before the 1870s revolutionized brewing—French microbiologist Louis Pasteur showing the biological nature of fermentation, affordable large-scale refrigeration arriving, and brewery kit being upscaled—September marked the beginning of a well-worn brewing routine.

September was the month in which the new season's hops arrived at their freshest and last year's barley started to be replaced by the new harvest, so October 1 marked the traditional time for brewing those beers made for storing 80 days before release prior to Christmas—*bière de Noël*.

December 23 or thereabouts then saw the second cycle of beers being brewed again for release after 80 days of storage, on or around March 13—termed *bière de Mars*. These were therefore available ahead of Easter and before the end of the brewing season, allowing a third and final big brew before brewing ceased on April 23.

Bière de garde's home territory runs from that part of northeast France between Calais and Lille sometimes referred to as French Flanders, down through Picardy, the French Ardennes, and on into Lorraine and Alsace, a wide strip of country that borders Belgium and the German Rhineland.

This is also one of the heartlands of the *ferme-brasserie*, literally "farm brewery," though the hyphen implies a single inseparable business running in cycles, rather than a brewery that happens to be based on a farm. While some will undoubtedly have joined in the production of *bière de garde* like a town brewer might, they will also have concentrated on adding value to whatever was the grain crop for that year by making beer from it. This was a normal part of French agricultural practice, which happened to survive in the Belgian *saison*-making area.

Left: The landscape of French Flanders is, like its beers, in many ways similar to neighboring Belgium.

Left: In the northeastern *départements* of France, beer making is as much a part of the fabric of life as is wine-growing in the valleys of the country's south and west.

Bière de Blé Noir & New French Brewing

Urban French brewers have tended to define their beers on the tricolor principle of one *blonde*, one *ambrée*, one *brune*, still found commonly across much of the Francophone beer world and beyond. What is beginning to emerge from the brewing revival is a thirst for experimentation and a new identity.

Even in self-styled French Flanders, the northern brewing heartland where several breweries can trace their roots back to the nineteenth century, the entrepreneurial Duyck, whose Jenlain beers are widely exported, St. Sylvestre's well-regarded 3 Monts brand, and Pays Flamand of Blaringhem use color as their beers' principle designator. Among the new breed, Thiriez of Esquelbecq, whose locally hopped Étoile du Nord (northern star) is in our view modestly named, promotes hue above style.

Driven by mistrust of anything that goes on in the capital and annoyance at being excluded historically from the national tourism map, the region is growing its distinct local culture, along with its own dialect, in which increasingly distinctive ales and some fabulous authentic estaminets play no small part.

Distance from Paris matters in Brittany too—a region that shares many characteristics with Cornwall, on Britain's southwestern peninsula. As with the Cornish, remoteness from the capital and familiarity with the skills of surviving winter on a gale-blown granite-cragged shipping hazard peninsula jutting out into the North Atlantic have bred a strong regional spirit among the Bretons. This is seen in their music, plain cooking, and, in recent decades, the creation of their own underrated beer style.

Bière de blé noir is as Breton as the pipes and pancakes, although whether local brewers of old used to mash with the blackened buckwheat for which it is named is anyone's guess. Regardless, their descendants adopted it as their own and in so doing have created a distinctive type of session ale that lies somewhere between Bavarian *Weizenbier* and Irish plain porter, without being either.

At the latest count, 20 producers had joined in making versions of this smooth, caramelized, mellow but jagged-edged ale, though you may well have to travel to the region to sample it, none having yet appeared in England's Western Peninsula, or Southern Ireland as far as we know.

In a nation of chefs serving a people who delight in discovering and celebrating flavors cultivated over centuries, French craft brewing is in its infancy. Most modern French beers and their styles are derivative for the present, though a trend is emerging for novel spice combinations and other additives that nudge toward Belgian and Italian in equal measure, with a healthy blast of North American, including Québécois, German, and, heaven forbid, British.

Most French craft breweries are tiny and thus far at least tend only to sell their beers locally, or at best within their own region, though Paris now has half a dozen top rate beer bars and even more specialist beer stores that take French *bières artisanales* seriously.

For more reliable regional brands, in the northeast, between Calais and Strasbourg, visit the lovely estaminet, shop at Brasserie Thiriez in Esquelbecq, and also look out for Brasserie du Pays Flamand, Vivat, Le Paradis, St. Rieul of Picardy, La Sedane, St. Alphonse, and Alsace's La Perle.

In the northwest, between Caen and La Rochelle, bag *blé noir* and others in Brittany at Philomenn, Tri Martolod, and Sainte Colombe and all sorts from La Piautre of Anjou.

In the center, within a 62-mile radius of Paris, try to find La Sancerroise, Vallée Chevreuse, La Bière du Vexin, Brasserie Rabourdin, La Mandubienne, and the creations of Scottish expatriate Craig Allan.

In the southeast, between Geneva, Lyons, and Marseilles, Brasserie des Garrigues is spreading its wings, as are L'Agrivoise and Mont-Salève, while Brasserie d'Ancelle, Brasserie de la Loire, Pleine Lune, Ninkasi, and Galibier are found mostly in their region for now.

Even the least beery region historically, in the southwest, south of Bordeaux and west of Toulouse, brewers like La Caussenarde, La Lutine, and Aliénor are receiving nods of the head from those normally taken only with wine.

FOR THE TRIP

- On entering a café nod, make eye contact, and wish customers "Bonjour!"
- Expect to pay eyewatering prices for craft beers in Paris.
- Must read: Elisabeth Pierre's *Le Guide Hachette des Bières*—the French beer bible.
- To keep abreast of developments, browse www.brasseries-france.info.
- The hilltop town of Cassel, 12½ miles from the Channel ferries, is a great base for touring the far north, with numerous beer stores and restaurants, the hilltop Kasteelhof café-shop, and gorgeous Kerelshof beer café (*see* opposite).

Opposite top: The continuity of the Celtic fringe drinking culture is seen in bars like Ty Elise in Plouye, Brittany, where French real ales are served in a public bar littered with bric-a-brac.

Opposite bottom: In the heart of French Flanders, Kerelshof is an atmospheric, relaxed, and thoroughly beery tavern on Cassel's main street.

NORTHERN EUROPE

If any part of the world embodies the unexpected nature of the beer revival, it is Scandinavia and the Baltic States. The nations that in winter make up Europe's icy north have taken to craft beer as a cultural obsession, despite the obstacles put in their way by well-meaning governments.

The destruction inflicted on Scandinavian brewing in the twentieth century did not come from Europe's 1914–18 war but mostly from self-inflicted wounds.

Born out of an odd mix of religious conviction and concern for public health, an almost fetishistic belief in the evil of alcohol has pervaded the politics of northern Europe for over a century. People here, it seems, prefer to elect politicians who take the potential harm of alcohol far more seriously than its life-enhancing properties.

While only Norway, Finland, and Iceland ever voted to criminalize the beer trade, all bar the Danes have at times introduced tight controls on its production, importation, and sale, giving governments an overrated sense of control over alcohol problems and generating considerable cash for their treasuries.

Alcohol in beer was often taxed more punitively than that in wine, as beer drinkers were considered in greater need of protection from their own proclivities.

Ironically, it was high taxation that eventually fueled the return to making bigger, stronger beers. Emerging craft brewers reasoned that, if beer drinkers were condemned to pay an exorbitant price for the ordinary, they may as well be invited to part with even more for something excellent.

The earliest stirrings of the Scandinavian beer revival were in the last years of the old millennium. Denmark has enjoyed the most success, although Sweden, Norway, Finland, and most recently Iceland have all made remarkable progress against steeper odds.

The most interesting player is the Copenhagen-based Carlsberg group of companies. While it would be exaggerating to see them as instigating the craft-beer revolution in the region, they put up little resistance to its emergence and in some cases provided training, practical assistance, and moral support to aspiring newcomers.

Their reasons were not entirely altruistic. Other global brewers lined up to take chunks out of their home market, backed by massive resources. The products from these incomers had little to recommend them beyond being new, so Carlsberg reasoned that a rash of genuinely innovative small-scale producers might usefully queer their rivals' pitch.

They followed through with some interesting beers of their own, creating a microbrewery (Jacobsen) on their Copenhagen site and more recently another in the Latvian capital, Riga.

What held back other brewery developments in the Baltic States was red tape and the absence of investment, though recent years have seen a swathe of new breweries bent on reviving and evolving both New World beer styles and old-fashioned local ones.

Porters and stouts have been around this part of the world for 250 years (*see* The Origins of Baltic Porter, p.144), but this is just a blink of an eye compared with the beers of folk origins.

Below: Culturally conservative and environmentally aware, Denmark is not a place known for its revolutions, but beer is different.

The Folk Beers of Northern Europe

It may have something to do with the long, cold winters and the fact that fewer things can be grown and eaten in icier climes. Either way, northern Europe is awash with unique food traditions, not least among its beers. As respect for beer grows, a host of older beer traditions is reemerging (*see also* Evolving Beer Styles, p.34).

Usually the domain of the farmstead brewer, Finnish *sahti* (a word of two distinct syllables) may be as old as Nordic civilization itself. Traditionally, it was mashed in a hollowed-out tree trunk, heat and caramel coming from the addition of red-hot stones.

Found mostly on farms in the central southern part of Finland, to the northwest and southeast of Tampere, its main ingredient is malted barley, sweetened by rye or wheat. The first commercialization in the early 1980s saw stainless steel *kuurnas* replace wooden ones, the wort being infused with and filtered through juniper branches before being top-fermented by baker's yeast, to add ripe banana to the mélange of flavors (*see* p.22).

High on spicy esters but free of hops, its short shelf life renders it virtually unexportable, although you will still find it in some Helsinki beer cafés such as Villi Wäinö (4 Kalevankatu).

Head westward to find the smokier, honeyed, often juniper-infused *Gotlandsdricka*, brewed by farmers on the Swedish island of Gotland and Norwegian revivals of *Gulating* beers, such as the tangy, smoky Norwegian Wood, from Haandbryggeriet in Drammen. The latter tries to re-create the beer likely to have been made by Norway's farmers under a legal obligation to brew.

Heading south from Helsinki across the Baltic to Estonia finds an even more rustic tradition in the *koduõlu*, literally "home brew," of Estonia's westernmost island, Saaremaa. These all-wheat ales shock with their milky-yellow appearance but also feature juniper instead of hops, suggesting a link to *sahti*.

Further south, the *kaimiskas* beers of northeastern Lithuania also contain wheat but compromise with "normal" beer by containing hops. However, these are stewed separately then added to the mash in the form of a tea; the filtered result is then fermented rapidly at room temperature. The yeast mixtures used come from skimming yeast off previous brews and have not been refreshed for generations, defying laboratory identification.

The substyle *kleptinis* employs a crumbly bread, made from the spent grain of a prior brew, as happens with some types of *kvass* (*see* p.148).

Continue down the Baltic to Poland and into Germany, and the folk beers meet and meld with the pre-*Reinheitsgebot* survivors from the European wheat beer belt (*see* p.96) such as the Polish smoked wheat beer *grodzišk*, Berlin's light, sharp *Weisse*, salted wheat beer *Gose* and the nearly mainstream *Lichtenhainer*.

Strong allegiances formed between local communities and some of these beers to the extent that they are sometimes excluded from legislators' bright ideas. For example, the right to continue brewing *sahti* (and making fruit wines) on the farm continued throughout the Finnish Prohibition.

Home production also means they are not easy to control. Some old *kaimiskas* breweries on Lithuanian farms still brew their hop tea in an underground cellar, while mashing in an outbuilding. The enticing explanation for this is that mashing smells much like baking, while the aroma of boiling hops identifies a brewery. Preparing the hops in a sealed space made it easier to hide it from Soviet apparatchiks intent on eliminating private enterprise, not to mention EU officialdom trying to impose excise duties and health and safety regulations.

It is a great story, but we cannot imagine honest brewers being so devious.

Left: Haandbryggeriet's Norwegian Wood re-creates the type of beer farmers made in centuries past.

Far left: Pivo Grodziskie has enjoyed a comeback in Poland and elsewhere.

Opposite: Making *kaimiskas* in Lithuania, commercially and on the farm.

DENMARK

The foundation of a brewers' guild in Copenhagen around 1525 marked the point at which beer making in Denmark tipped from being a traditional role for women in farm kitchens to one for men in trade. Another three centuries were to pass before the next big transition.

Until the 1840s, the dominant Danish brews were variants of *hvidtøl*, or wheat beer. Then a young, self-taught brewer called Jacob Jacobsen became aware of the potential of a new style of beer from Bohemia that was clearer, lighter, and had a longer shelf life. Within a decade he purified a strain of yeast suited to fermenting this new "lagered" beer and in so doing enabled his Carlsberg brewery to change the face of Scandinavian brewing.

Fast forward to 1995 and a well-researched trip to Copenhagen yielded two basic ales from a newly established brewpub in the city center, plus a couple of half-interesting porters from larger producers. Nothing else unusual crossed the radar. Venturing outside the capital would have added little.

Yet two decades on, Denmark has over 120 operating breweries and several other famous craft beer makers without one to call their own. Brewers pull on the finest habits of the American new wave, classical German, older British, and ingenious Belgian brewing spectrum to create countless beers that range from local takes on simpler styles to experimental ones designed to shock even the most world-weary beer hunter.

There is no such thing as a typical Danish craft brewery. Some originated as brewpubs, others were created by enthusiastic home brewers, and a few arrived with business plans written by graduate brewers with a second business degree. A handful result from little more than artistry and imagination. Across the board, green credentials are prominent.

The country's most acclaimed new-wave brewery company, Mikkeller, does not even own a commercial-sized brewery, its principal product being owner-brewer Mikkel Borg Bjergsø himself. His inventive and sometimes striking beers are made mostly at Proef in Belgium (*see* p.78). His reputation is such that several other Danes, not least his not-so-identical twin brother Jeppe, have set up companies on a similar model.

As everywhere, the most successful of brewers combine rigorous technical quality with an eye for a winning style, a desire to add recognizably homespun originality, and a sound understanding of business, though cultural conservatism means few have ventured into export thus far.

The many fine specialist beer cafés that have sprung up are just as likely to serve Belgian and American beers as homegrown creations, yet despite this

THE SEARCH FOR A DANISH BEER

Many Danish beer lovers fear their country lacks a style of beer that is identifiably Danish.

One new development that is exciting techies and beer glitterati in equal measure is *Ny Nordisk Øl*, or new Nordic ale. While nodding to the tradition of beers flavored with botanicals, proponents of these sometimes bittersweet, more often mellow, hop-free alternative ales are clear that they are inventing a new concept for modern times, not reviving an old one. Still a work in progress, many contain ancient ingredients like sweet gale but at the same time deploy new yeast strains not previously used by brewers.

Meanwhile, to the casual visitor it is obvious that the massive range of different types of porter and stout brewed in Denmark can match that of the USA, which is 40 times its size. Full-flavored

brands include recognizably light Irish; lactose-sweet, heavy-lagered Baltic, or thick, Imperial Russian, some with additional coffee grounds, cocoa powder, coconut, vanilla extract, or the historic favorite, licorice.

A classic case, perhaps, of tourists seeing what the locals pass by.

Right: Ny Nordisk Øl is encapsulated in Thagaard, Faddersbøl, and Klithede, three herbal brews from Agrotech.

Opposite: Herslev Bryghus, one of 120 new Danish breweries, has since 2004 made about a hundred beers for itself and half as many again for beer designers.

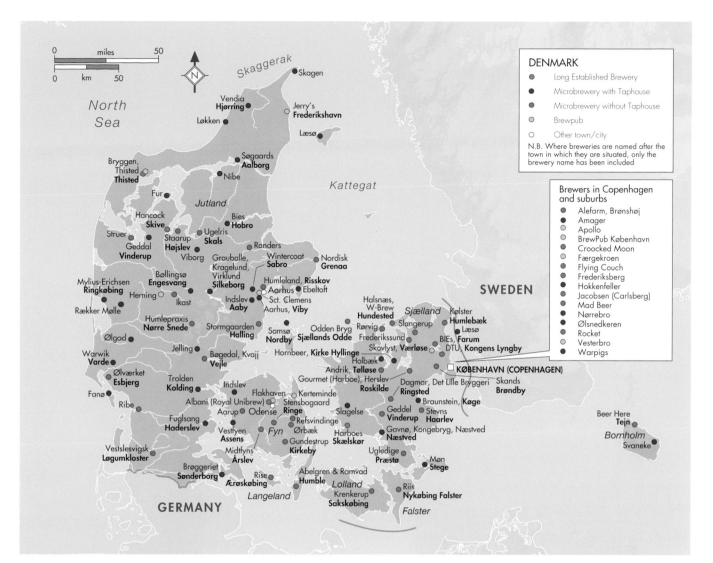

DENMARK
- ● Long Established Brewery
- ● Microbrewery with Taphouse
- ● Microbrewery without Taphouse
- ○ Brewpub
- ○ Other town/city

N.B. Where breweries are named after the town in which they are situated, only the brewery name has been included

Brewers in Copenhagen and suburbs
- ● Alefarm, Brønshøj
- ● Amager
- ○ Apollo
- ● BrewPub København
- ● Croocked Moon
- ○ Færgekroen
- ○ Flying Couch
- ● Frederiksberg
- ● Hokkenfeller
- ● Jacobsen (Carlsberg)
- ● Mad Beer
- ● Nørrebro
- ● Ølsnedkeren
- ○ Rocket
- ○ Vesterbro
- ● Warpigs

Skaggerak
North Sea
Kattegat
SWEDEN

Skagen
Vendia **Hjørring**
Løkken
Jerry's **Frederikshavn**
Læsø
Søgaards **Aalborg**
Nibe
Bryggen, Thisted **Thisted**
Fur
Jutland
Hancock **Skive**
Bies **Hobro**
Struer
Staarup Ugelris **Skals**
Geddal **Vinderup** **Højslev**
Viborg Randers
Graualle, Kragelund, Virklund Wintercoat **Sabro**
Bøllingsø **Engesvang** **Silkeborg** Nordisk **Grenaa**
Mylius-Erichsen **Ringkøbing** Herning Humleland, **Risskov**
Ikast Aarhus ● Ebeltoft
Indslev **Aaby** Sct. Clemens
Rækker Mølle Aarhus, **Viby**
Humlepraxis **Nørre Snede** Stormgaarden **Halling** Samsø **Nordby** Odden Bryg Sjællands Odde
Ølgod Jelling Bøgedal, Kvajj Hornbeer, **Kirke Hyllinge**
Warwik **Varde** **Vejle**
Ølværket **Esbjerg** Trolden **Kolding** Indslev
Fanø Flakhaven Kerteminde
Ribe Albani (Royal Unibrew) Stensbogaard
Aarup ○ Odense **Ringe**
Fuglsang **Haderslev** Vestfyen **Assens** Refsvindinge Slagelse
Vestslesvigsk **Løgumkloster** Midtfyns **Årslev** Ørbæk Harbøes **Skælskør**
Bøgedal, Kvajj Gundestrup **Kirkeby**
Brøggeriet **Sønderborg** Rise
Ærøskøbing Abelgren & Ramvad **Humble**
Langeland *Lolland* Krenkerup **Nykøbing Falster**
GERMANY Sakskøbing *Falster*

Halsnæs, W-Brew **Hundested** Rørvig Slangerup
Frederikssund Kølster
Skovlyst, **Værløse** **Humlebæk** Læsø
Holbæk BIEs, **Farum**
Andrik, **Tølløse** DTU, **Kongens Lyngby**
Gourmet (Harboe), Herslev Dagmar, Det Lille Bryggeri
Roskilde **Ringsted** **KØBENHAVN (COPENHAGEN)**
Skands Braunstein, **Køge** **Brøndby**
Geddel **Vinderup** Stevns **Haarlev**
Gavnø, Kongebryg, **Næstved**
Ugledige **Præstø** Møn **Stege**
Riis
Sjælland
Beer Here **Tejn**
Bornholm Svaneke

THE CRAFT BREWERIES OF DENMARK ▲

As Europe's most mature new beer culture, Denmark's craft breweries are spread evenly across the kingdom, often named for their towns. This map features the most reliable.

Right: Jacobsen microbrewery, under master brewer Morten Ibsen, allows the world's fourth-largest brewery to play.

the small brewery sector has taken 6 percent of the Danish beer market in just over a decade.

The reputation of new-wave producers for audaciously challenging convention led some old hands to fear that too great a gap would grow between the regular beer drinker and those seeking ever more radical brews. However, in practice, the better brewers are taking different paths to immortality, some specializing in extreme beers, while others stick to brightening up the mainstream.

Today's brewing scene seems both disparate and confident. If you know where to go, you will find beers that stretch from soft and toffee-sweet to hard, acrid, and desert-dry, in strengths as low as 2 percent and as high as 15 percent, encompassing flavors that range from delicate to glaring.

Ask craft beer nuts to name great Danish brewers, and they will likely single out Mikkeller, perhaps also drawing down To Øl and Evil Twin from their memory. While these are all excellent beer makers, each pushing the boundaries of brewing culture, the beers of the first two are mostly made at Proef in Belgium (*see* p.78), and the last, while Danish owned, is US-based.

Beyond these rock star creatives lie the hard slog brewers, whose beers have consolidated the Danish beer revival.

The most frequently found outside its borders come from Amager, though numerous others are at a point where they should be—such as Hornbeer, Det Lille, Indslev, and Midtfyns, as well as craftier Croocked Moon and WinterCoat. Thisted is the best of the legacy brewers.

FOR THE TRIP

- The strength of a beer typically bears little relation to its relative price.
- For draft beers, "small" is 6.3–10.6 ounces and "large" is 11.6–17.6 ounces.
- If the beer is both dark and Danish, try it.
- Copenhagen's separate Beer Celebration and Øl Festival bookend a week in late May, offering contrasting but complementary experiences.

Copenhagen also has two extraordinary brewpubs in Nørrebro, a sophisticated operation that seems to knock out classic versions of limitless varieties of beer in older and newer styles, and Warpigs, a sort of shabby chic industrial setup in the old meat market, said to be bringing Mikkeller horribly close to a real estate commitment. Svaneke, on the distant island of Bornholm, impresses too.

However, our favorites are Bøgedal, a brewhouse in wood and iron, where ales are made by old-style methods and designated by numbers rather than brands to avoid the need for accurate reproduction, and the Ebeltoft farm brewery, where experimentation is held in higher regard than reliability, a trait forgiven by their occasional excellence.

Danish brewers still have no idea where they are heading, but we believe they will know when they get there. With the madness of adolescence behind it, the best days of craft brewing in Denmark are only just beginning.

Above: Once a city awash with golden lager, Copenhagen is now one of northern Europe's great beer destinations, with breweries, brewpubs, beer bars, and a company of global reach.

SMALL WORLDS APART

The windswept Faroe Islands (population 49,000), blessed by fabulous scenery and the world's best-looking sheep, form an archipelago in the North Atlantic roughly halfway between Iceland and the Shetlands. Largely self-governing, they remain part of the kingdom of Denmark but have separate "national" teams in soccer, swimming, and handball, print their own banknotes, and have an alcohol regulatory system more akin to those of Norway, Sweden, Finland, and Iceland.

Take-home sale of beer above 2.8% ABV is restricted to the state-owned chain of nine Rúsdrekkasøla Landsins (or Rúsan) stores, which is remarkably loyal to the Faroes' two independent breweries, Föroya Bjór of Klaksvík and Okkara of Velbastaður, whose most memorable beers are their stronger porters.

The most remarkable Faroese beer is Okkara's Rinkusteinur, a 5.8% ABV amber ale made in the manner of a Steinbier (*see* pp.102–3) but

using lava rock heated to 1,472°F for heating and caramelizing the wort. Whether for the sulfurous nature of the stone or the power of imagination, it seems more mineralized than its Austrian counterparts.

While American, Belgian, and other foreign beers have been starting to appear, thus far the representation of Danish mainland craft brewing has remained limited to beers from Amager, Hornbeer, and Ørbæk.

Above: The remote Faroe Islands, between Iceland and the Shetlands, with two local breweries and remarkably little outside influence.

SWEDEN

Sweden is one of the most expensive countries on Earth in which to buy a beer, but this does not stop it being one of the most exciting. The state-owned Systembolaget chain of liquor stores, which holds the take-home monopoly for regular and stronger beers, now has a theoretical range of nearly 1,200 different local and imported brands.

The system of alcohol control is tough but logical and generally even-handed, the only exception being that direct advertising of beers above 3.5% ABV is not allowed, while for wines and spirits it is. The drinking age is 20 and photo ID is checked for any customer who looks under 25.

While Systembolaget clearly sees its primary social role as the control of alcohol provision, it makes its full product range available across the whole country via its 430 stores and 500 order points serving smaller communities. Sweden's expanding swathe of new breweries, of which there are now over 180, get to serve one branch immediately and three if their beers sell well enough. Access to the whole chain—the holy grail of commercial success—then depends on popularity and the price-to-quality ratio being right.

Exporting beer to Sweden can, however, carry risks, as one monastic brewery

FOR THE TRIP

- Do not hand beer to your children for tasting as you can be prosecuted.
- Food is normally available in Swedish pubs.
- The word "slut" on a beer tap means it is not available.
- Some better Swedish beers appear in lighter grocery store versions.
- Follow Swedish breweries and beer bars on www.svenskaolframjandet.se.

Left: Sweden's Systembolaget liquor stores sometimes carry a phenomenal range of craft beers from around the world—but at a price.

Opposite: In a country with fewer than 10 million people, nearly 600 inhabited islands, and high tax on alcohol, Swedish craft brewers like to think small and stay top quality.

STRENGTH IN WEAKNESS

There have always been low-alcohol beers in Sweden, possibly related originally to the *kvass* tradition (*see* p.148). Long predating the beer revolution, the ultralight beer *svagöl*, later *svadricka*, contained so little alcohol that from 1919 they dropped under the radar of the alcohol monitors and could be sold in general stores with little difficulty.

They became so popular by the mid-twentieth century that whole breweries were dedicated to their manufacture, although we think the last has closed.

For Sweden's new local breweries, creating low-alcohol beers that taste of something is technically

challenging but worth the effort, as it enables the brand to appear in grocery stores before the bigger, bolder beers start to appear in local Systembolaget stores.

Hantverksbryggeriet's Kusken is such a beer, banging out maximum malt intensity without cloying sweetness, with a hop-yeast combo that makes it absurdly tasty for its strength.

Right: Hantverksbryggerie Kusken, a tiny beer using some neat tricks to get a big taste.

discovered to its embarrassment a few years back. The Swedish authorities not only regularly check that the alcohol content declared on the label is correct, they also inform their counterparts in the country of origin if they discover any anomalies.

The number of breweries in the country peaked around the end of the nineteenth century and hit an all-time low of 13 in 1990, the bulk of the expansion happening since 2011. Two-thirds of the market is held by Carlsberg's Pripps and Falcon brands, followed by those from local established independents Spendrups and Åbro, the brewing arm of a cider maker. The most successful of the newer breweries are Nils Oscar from Nyköping and Oppigårds of Hedemora, with

Jämtlands of Pilgrimstad and Nynäshamns of Nynäshamn not far behind.

The recent explosion in the number of breweries has its fair share of start-ups who need more brewing classes but perhaps two-thirds lie somewhere on a spectrum between useful and worthy of global respect. Among the latter are longstanding superstar Närke of Örebro, creator of immense beers in both retro and proto styles. Names like Mohawk, Dugges, and Malmö are worth noting. Omnipollo tries to riff like a Swedish Mikkeller, though we felt its mango lassi *gose* was perhaps a note too far, and Brekeriet is up for anything sour.

One interesting recent initiative is Carnegie's, a brewing enterprise backed by

Carlsberg, New York's Brooklyn Brewery, and others, which thus far has avoided the modish appeal of being an American brewer abroad to play instead with elderflower wheat beer, *Kellerbier*, and the like.

The average Swedish beer drinker still takes light lager to be the norm, but this is gradually changing as newer breweries adopt a largely uncoordinated two-pronged approach of creating a few memorably fabulous beers at the top end of the spectrum and an increasingly impressive array of well-made beers in simpler styles at the other. The idea of having a local brewery is still a novelty.

Quite where things will be in five years time is anyone's guess.

NORWAY & SWEDEN
- Player
- Role model
- Interesting brewpub
- Long-established
- Other town/city

miles 0 — 200
km 0 — 200

Svalbard, Longyearbyen

N

Brewers in Oslo and suburbs
- Amundsen
- Crowbar
- Dronebrygg
- Grünerløkka
- Little Brother
- Oslo
- Schouskjelleren

Hammerfest

Mack **Tromsø**

Skavli **Evenskjær**

Lofotpils **Svolvær**

Norwegian Sea

Bådin **Bodø**

Nausta **Slagnäs**

SWEDEN

South Side **Skellefteå**

Beer Studio **Umeå**

Gulf of Bothnia

Inderøy **Inderøy**

Klostergården, **Frosta**

○ **Trondheim**

Austmann
To Tårn
Trondhjem ○

NORWAY

Jämtlands **Pilgrimstad**

FINLAND

Kinn **Florø**

Hubertus **Dovre**

Atna Øl **Atna**

Helsinge **Söderhamn**

Balder, **Leikanger**

Espedalen **Espedalen**

Lillehammer **Lillehammer**

Baran
Hansa
Waldemars

Ægir, **Flåm**

Voss, **Voss**

Ryentorps **Falun**

Bergen

Lysefjorden, **Fana**

Aass
Haandbryggeriet
Aja

Oppigårds **Hedemora**

Gavle

Skebo Bruks **Skebobruk**

7 Fjell, **Bønes**

Eiker, **Mjøndalen**

Sundbytunet
Jessheim

Coppersmith's,
Hantverksbryggeriet

Bålsta **Bålsta**

Jackdaw, Slottskällans, **Uppsala**

Veholt, **Skien**

○ **OSLO**
Drammen

St Eriks, Sigtuna, **Arlandastad**

Fjellbryggeriet, **Åmotsdal**

Færder

Borg (Hansa Borg)

Ølkultur, **Eskilstuna**

Västerås

Apotekergaarden
Nøgne Ø (Hansa Borg)

Tønsberg

Lindheim

Sarpsborg

STOCKHOLM

Lervig, **Stavanger**

Gvarv
Sandar

Ego,
Nøisom

Närke **Örebro**

Adelsö **Adelsö**

Pang Pang Hökarängen, **Farsta**

Berentsens
Egersund

Sandefjord

Arendals
Fredrikstad

Vänern

Nils Oscar, **Nyköping**

Ångbryggeri
Nynäshamn

Nynäshamn Køltur, **Hölö**

Lindesnes, **Lindesnes**

Arendal
Grimstad

Qvänum **Kvänum**

Vättern

Central **Linköping**

Provianten, **Mandal**

Kristiansand

Poppels, Rådanäs
Mölnlycke

Nääs **Ydre**

CB (Hansa Borg)
Christianssand ○

Beerbliotek, Ocean

Stigbergets, Vega, West Coast
Göteborg

Dugges, **Landvetter**

Gotlands (Spendrups)
Visby *Gotland*

Qvart

Sahtipaja, **Sätila**

Byaregårdens
Veddige

Folkared 15
Varberg

Ängö **Kalmar**

Kattegat

DENMARK

Höganäs **Höganäs**

Oland

Brygghus 19, **Karlshamn**

Brewski, **Helsingborg**

Klackabackens, **Kristianstad**

North Sea

Remmarlöv, **Eslöv**

Baltic Sea

Lilla
Malmö
Malmö

Brekeriet
Staffanstorp

Hyllie, **Vintrie**

Brewers in Stockholm and suburbs
- CAP
- Fjäderholmarnas, Lidingö
- Köksbryggeri, **Sundbyberg**
- Mohawk, **Täby**
- Monks Café
- Nya Carnegie (Carlsberg/Brooklyn)
- Stockholm Brewing Co, **Stockholm**

ESTONIA

Gulf of Finland

Gulf of Riga

LATVIA

Klaraven

THE BEST OF NEW NORWEGIAN AND SWEDISH BREWERS ▲

The antisocial tax rate levied on alcohol in Norway and Sweden has prompted
a new wave of brewers who figure that if people are charged a lot for plain lagers
they will pay yet more for fine ales. The best exponents of this idea include a few
longer-standing companies, a large number of independent producers that can be
seen as leading players, and a few top breweries that can be seen as role models
for the rest. Only brewpubs are allowed to sell beer direct to the public.

NORWAY

Although there is no recorded instance of this happening, the ancient Gulating code stipulated that any Norwegian farmer who did not brew ale (øl) would be fined. By 1919 attitudes had changed so much that the production of beer and all other forms of alcohol had been criminalized.

Prohibition lasted until 1926, when the French government, lobbied by the major wine houses, reacted to the loss of this wine market by excluding Norwegian fish from France. The political compromise that followed created a state-controlled network of alcohol producers, importers, and retailers called the Vinmonopolet (or "wine monopoly").

Ninety years on, the monopoly part is confined to take-home sales of wines, spirits, and beers over 4.5% ABV—leaving it a modern chain of over 300 well-stocked retailers selling supertaxed goods, including a range of domestic and imported beers that tops 800.

The beer market remains dominated by Ringnes (part of Carlsberg) and the large independent Hansa Borg, with only two other established independent breweries, Aass and Mack, having survived the twentieth century.

Old-style production was mostly blond lager and lower-tax light beers (lettøl), with some darker lagers, such as deep amber *bayer* based broadly on *Münchner*, *bo(c)k* that is dark, autumnal and leans more Dutch than German, and spicy brown Christmas *juleøl*. The Aass Bock is a classic of its kind.

Then, in 2002, came Nøgne Ø ("Naked Island") and its strapline,

Below: The old harborside at Oslo, which welcomed brave explorers like Amundsen, Nansen, Heyerdahl, and Norwegian craft brewing.

Det Kompromissløse Bryggeri (The Uncompromising Brewery), a firm that did what it said in the bottle. Its name refers to Norwegian playwright Henrik Ibsen's description of a storm-battered rocky outcrop off Norway's southern coast, resilient against all that nature can throw at it.

At a time when sky-high taxation and a strong krone were conspiring to mean Norwegian bars had to charge three times as much as in Western Europe for adequate but uninspiring lagers, Nøgne Ø risked asking twice that price for the brewery's bold experiments in massively framed beers, proving in the process that there is always a market for excellence. They soon attracted importers from abroad, founding a trade into which others have followed. It was a daring journey that their Viking forebears would appreciate.

Fifteen years on, Nøgne Ø is now controlled by Hansa Borg but is as yet none the worse for that, and Norway has around 70 breweries, the best of them emulating the original's heroic efforts. Those with the most entertaining lists include Haandbryggeriet of Drammen, north of Oslo, 7 Fjell of Bønes near Bergen, Kinn of Florø, between Bergen and Ålesund, and Ægir of Flåm, with Lervig of Stavanger popping up all over Scandinavia and beyond.

Above: Nøgne Ø's first Grimstad brewery was located within a converted hydroelectric plant.

Left: Adding hops at Nøgne Ø. The southern Norwegian brewery is the vanguard in the country's youthful but growing craft brewing movement.

THE MOST NORTHERLY BREWERY IN THE WORLD

For many years, the Mack brewery in the city of Tromsø, northern Norway, claimed to be the most northerly in the world, fending off rumors of small plants in northern Siberia and a possible tiny commercial rival just outside Tromsø itself.

But in 2015 a newcomer trumped it by a full nine degrees of latitude, by setting up on the Norwegian dependency of Svalbard (Spitsbergen), a mere 78 degrees north of the equator, 764 miles from the North Pole, serving a small mining and Arctic research community year round and a particularly intrepid type of visitor in summer.

The Svalbard Bryggeri began planning in 2011 and produced its first batch in the summer of 2015. The eventual plan is to try to make four beers, brewing in summer, with export to the mainland via Tromsø.

What we love about them most of all is that they have added a visitors' center and tasting facility. Beer heroes or what?

Above: Beers from Longyearbyen, on Svalbard, the world's northernmost brewery.

ICELAND

When President Ronald Reagan and General Secretary Mikhail Gorbachev met to discuss nuclear disarmament in Reykjavik in 1986, they could not share a *bjór* (beer), as to do so would have been illegal. Their talks ended without agreement.

All alcohol was banned in Iceland by a referendum that took effect in 1915. Wine reappeared in 1921, after a Spanish boycott of Icelandic fish, and in 1935 a further referendum reinstated spirits. Beer of more than 2.25% ABV remained illegal until March 1989.

Having to create a brewing industry on a large, remote, sparsely populated, volcanic island close to the Arctic Circle was always going to be interesting. In practice the multinationals shied away from direct investment, leaving existing drinks producers and entrepreneurs to try their luck.

Thus far almost a dozen new enterprises have entered the market, and, despite that all the ingredients must be imported, some pretty impressive brews have been created, particularly by Borg in Reykjavik, Ölvisholt, near Selfoss, and Gæðingur,

in remote Skagafiröi. More widely seen abroad are the beers commissioned by Einstök, from the Viking brewery in the north coast fishing fleet port of Akureyri, one of the most remote breweries in Europe.

While drinking beer in Iceland remains an expensive hobby, the state-owned Vínbúðin chain of liquor stores, which enjoys the take-home monopoly, seems to allow all local producers theoretical access to their stores.

Beer liberation is still celebrated each year on March 1, the anniversary of its legalization, with pubs staying open until 4 a.m., causing the sort of predictable problems that made prohibition look like a good idea in the first place. At other times, start exploring from the Micro Bar in Reykjavik's Center Hotel.

Above: Iceland's Ölvisholt brewery, whose Lava (9.4% ABV) smoked imperial stout is considered among the best beers in the world.

FINLAND

Modern Finland is not sure whether it is Scandinavian. Its language is unique, and it only ceded from Russia in 1917. It prefers to see itself as Nordic, though a quarter of its population lives in or around the capital, Helsinki, on the Baltic coast. Most of the rest live in the country's southern third, which is why its 60 or so breweries huddle there.

It is remarkable that any new breweries emerge in this nation, given the Finnish politicians' obsession with taxing and otherwise restricting locally made beers beyond people-friendly limits. Containing the consumption of alcohol has been a live issue since the mid-nineteenth century, leading the newly established Finnish state to "celebrate" independence from Russia by enforcing prohibition in 1919 that lasted until 1932.

A paternalistic attitude to alcohol has shaped Finnish brewing since that time. The country's nationwide chain of state-owned liquor stores, Alko, remains the only source of take-home beer above 4.7% ABV—a strength chosen for being just below the standard strength of German beers at 4.8% ABV. However, as in Norway and Sweden, the range carried is now impressive, and smaller Finnish brewers have gained the right to supply locally.

Prohibition ended because the smuggling it fostered fueled rampant criminality that was in turn linked to increased solitary drinking at home. Sadly, the flawed belief that applying the highest alcohol taxes in the EU will reduce problem drinking remains politically popular, despite this experience.

Pub sales have halved since 2000 as the population once more takes to drinking at home to minimize the cost. In another rerun of history, the easiest source of cheap alcohol now comes through massive importation by ordinary Finns via the Estonian ferry, equivalent each year to more than the total amount sold by Alko.

It is hard to imagine worse conditions in which to be a craft brewer, let alone to try to preserve one of the world's longest-surviving traditions of folk brewing —the heavy, pungent beers known as *sahti* (*see* The Folk Beers of Northern Europe, p.114).

Yet Finland is seeing the same upsurge in beer interest as everywhere else in northern Europe. Depending on how one classifies Olvi, the country's largest independent brewer, special beers now take between 4 and 8 percent of the market and rising, before including the better porters from Carlsberg subsidiary Sinebrychoff, which still wins plaudits two centuries after it became the region's first dedicated producer of the style.

For the best of the new breed, look out for Malmgård, Plevnan, Stadin, Huvila, Beer Hunter's, and Maku and splash out on something north of 4.7% ABV.

Below left: Pekka Kääriäinen of Lammin Sahti, who has taken Finland's folk beer off the farm, adds another branch of juniper to the *kuurna*.

FOR THE TRIP

- Antialcohol laws forbid the posting of a beer list outside a pub.
- A pub notice reading "After work" lists the times of happy hour discounts.
- Buying a round of drinks is seen as a gift rather than a favor to be repaid.
- Beer in bars is now bought mostly with a bank or credit card.
- A brewery may run a nearby store, but it must also sell groceries.

Above: Finland's 60 or so craft breweries are huddled mainly in the south, where lakes and forests give way to centers of population.

Far left: Helsinki's Spårakoff pub tram runs tours of the city from May to August, the conductor being replaced by a drinks waiter.

Left: Probably the ultimate folk beer, Finnish *sahti* does not travel well. The curious are advised to visit Finland and drink it in situ.

THE BALTIC STATES

On August 23, 1989, over one million people linked hands to create a human chain that ran 404 miles from the Estonian capital Tallinn, via the Latvian capital Riga, to the Lithuanian capital Vilnius. The Baltic States achieved independence from the Soviet Union, and by 2004 were each full members of the European Union.

While the region has strong local cultures and customs, periods of independent self-rule had been rare, the sense of nationhood resting on their distinct languages. The English word "ale" comes via the Scandinavian *øl*, which in turn is predated by the Estonian *ölu*, and *alus* from Latvian and Lithuanian.

All three states have a long history of producing strong porters and stouts, plus different folkloric brewing traditions. However, political and economic instability after World War I and the Russian revolution, followed by lack of investment in Soviet times, meant that, by the early 1990s, brewing throughout the region was in a bad way.

After the Russians left, it fell to Carlsberg, Heineken, and some larger Danish and Finnish independent breweries to fund a beer revival. Since then, progress in the three nations has followed distinctly different paths, jockeying around under a variety of new influences.

FOR THE TRIP

- In Estonia, many bars run beer stores, but local law forbids the stock being shared.
- In Lithuanian bars, look for powerful local cheeses, sliced pig's ear, and other delicacies.
- The consumption of beer in Latvia halves in the winter.
- Scandinavian beers are usually a lot cheaper here than in their home countries.
- For tips on Lithuanian beer, try www. alutis.lt/aludariai.

Below: The arrival of Põhjala in Estonia brought big-league craft beer to the Baltic States.

Estonia

Estonia is seen as the most advanced of the Baltic States. With Scandinavian groups controlling its largest breweries—Saku (Carlsberg), A. Le Coq (Olvi of Finland), and Viru (Harboe of Denmark)—there was little room for innovation. Others were needed for that.

A visit in 2011 found local beer lovers despondent at the lack of other brewers. Sillamae produced good *Müncheners*; the elusive Oü Taako marketed Pihtla Õlu (7% ABV), the only commercial brand of *koduõlu* (*see* The Folk Beers of Northern Europe, p.114); and an Austrian-styled brewpub in Tallinn had opened in 2002. All else was mired in red tape and risk-avoidance.

Then came Põhjala. Confident, careful, creative, led by serious intent, and backed by thoughtful money, this Tallinn-based craft brewery sparked a small revolution that has seen 15 breweries arrive in four years with several more in development.

One refreshing feature of new beer in Estonia is the attention paid to what styles to grow. While all do the necessary by making one or two US-style hoppy pale ales or wheat beers, most also produce at least one beer with brown rye, a traditional Estonian ingredient from way back, plus regional specialties like Baltic porter, imperial stout, and heavy brown ale.

Beyond Põhjala, the ranges to look out for include Õllenaut, Tanker, and Sori, the last run by Finns trying to escape asphyxiating taxation back home. Pühaste shows promise but has yet to open its own brewery, or for gentler beers, including some lagers, try Vormsi or Lehe.

The availability of *koduõlu* remains limited, though there are now three authentic farmhouse versions on the market. Try these fresh, though, as the absence of hops shrinks their shelf life and when sour they are not cool.

Dark, sweet, low-alcohol *kali*, the Estonian take on *kvass* (*see* p.148), also appears occasionally, tasting of liquid burned toast.

Above: The rooftops of the Old Town, Tallinn, Estonia.

Latvia

Latvia once had hundreds of breweries, most exporting beer to Imperial Russia. However, between 1915 and 1950, two wars, the Russian Revolution, a bungled effort at independence, antialcohol laws, and Soviet-style nationalization conspired to close all but two.

Above: Ornamental wooden casks from Latvia's brewing heyday in Riga Old Town.

When the Russians left, three new large breweries were created —Aldaris, Cēsu, and Lāčplēša-Līvu—each funded by foreign investment to produce mainly industrial beers. Additionally, a dozen or so smaller brewers opened to supply a healthy 13 percent of the market thanks to tax breaks for smaller producers.

The best draft beers are those marked *nefiltrētais* ("unfiltered"). Other words worth knowing are *tumšais* (dark), *gaušais* (pale), and *medalus* (literally mead but meaning honeyed), the last playing to a tradition found in Lithuania, Belarus, and parts of Central Europe. Sweet also dominates the two Brenguļu brands from the Abula brewery. For a more folksy style, try brews from the Krāslava and Madonas breweries.

By the end of 2015, the only new Latvian brewery to have mastered both creativity and consistency was Malduguns, from Raunas, 37 miles northeast of Riga, though half a dozen others had managed one or the other. Brewing experimental sour beers before you have mastered the art of keeping sourness out of your other brews is optimistic.

More positive is the creation of a small brewery within the larger Valmiermuižas lager brewery and the replacement by Carlsberg of its industrial plant at Aldaris with one that brews just 528 gallons per run.

Given the clear enthusiasm among younger Latvians for imported craft and traditional beers demonstrated by the fabulous ranges of handpicked beers at the Alus Celle and Beer Fox beer stores in Riga, the current trend among longer-established brewers to dumb down some brands and fail to build on the quality of others is inexplicable.

Lithuania

For those with the adventure gene and time to explore, we recommend Lithuania. Do not expect miraculous hopping, new grains, the latest sourness, or flavors from your childhood. Rather settle on challenging authenticity, sometimes in a plastic bottle.

The country has its usual share of new brewpubs, particularly in its capital, Vilnius. But it is in the more rural northeast that an old culture of farmhouse and small-town brewing is starting slowly to reemerge from the shadows (*see* The Folk Beers of Northern Europe, p.114).

The Aukštaitija region is called the Highlands, though its peaks fall short of 320 yards. Here are found a strongly accented local dialect, a traditional singing style called *sutartinės*, and earthy beers termed *kaimiskas*.

The breweries that make *kaimiskas* are threatened. Five have been absorbed into one producing beers that are compromising with the mainstream, and while the transition from PET to stoppered bottles has benefited the aesthetic, it has increased costs and more subtly the expectation that what flows from it will be the equal of more exotic ales—which is not their point.

The dilemma for Lithuanian brewing is how to start making the styles of other countries, as occurred in the 1920s and 1930s, while preserving a unique homegrown beer culture that is downbeat and hard to assimilate when extreme and obvious tastes are the dominant trend.

When Belgian lambics reached their nadir in the 1970s, it fell to new producers not only to spot their potential but also to sort out major flaws. For *kaimiskas*, which hops and in what concentration make the best hop tea? Should the yeast really be that mucky? What grains work best and in what forms? For some this is sacrilege, for others simply best practice.

The country's best newer brewers are Dundulis (correctly Širvėnos Bravoras), whose brewer knows his beer history; Apynys of Kaunas; and new boys Sakiškių. We expect many more to follow.

Above: Vilnius, capital of Lithuania—one of the last unexplored frontiers of traditional brewing.

CENTRAL & EASTERN EUROPE

Oddly, the separate geographical concepts of Central and Eastern Europe seem to match the extent and nature of their beer cultures. Poland and Czechia are heartlands of creative brewing, with Hungary and Slovakia ever keen to learn. Further east, things are more difficult.

Beer across this side of Europe derives from an odd mix of heritages, ranging from the lightly fermented leftovers of the *kvass* tradition to the strong porters and stouts absorbed from the Baltic rim, incorporating the idea of pan-European brown beers, the residual habits of the wheat-beer belt, and the emergence of the original modern lagers.

If the Soviet times saw little investment, this was not entirely a bad thing. Brewers condemned to use outmoded methods at a time when the fashionable new ones brought beers of wilting interest may have been inadvertently advantaged.

In the post-Soviet era, local consumers and their surviving brewers alike made assumptions about the rejuvenation of their regular beers that industrial brewers neither understood nor were able to deliver.

A quarter of a century later, there is a pervasive sense across lands once said to lie behind the Iron Curtain that today's brewers want to create beers that demonstrate the sort of self-respect one would expect from the part of the world where hop brewing originated, the first town breweries began, and the literal brilliance of pale lager first saw the light of day.

Above: The early success of two rival beer festivals in St. Petersburg foretold the development of craft brewing there. Now Moscow has spawned 40 breweries.

Right: Banská Bystrika, home of Urpina beers, the best of the Slovak Republic's established breweries.

CZECHIA

During the four decades that the Soviet Union governed Czechoslovakia (1948–89) precious little investment was made in its breweries. Despite this, most managed to continue producing well-crafted beers in the styles Bohemia had perfected in the previous century and a half.

Czechs are among the world's most dedicated beer drinkers, still consuming around 37 gallons per head each year. Their preferred style appears on menus as *světly ležák* or pale lager. This is the land of Plzeň (Pilsen) and České Budějovice (Budweis), where Pilsner Urquell and Budweiser Budvar are respectively produced, and until recently 90 percent of the beer consumed was blond and beauteous. The history of Czech brewing on the other hand is less conservative.

In Bohemia, the western half of Czechia, hops were being farmed in the seventh century and by 1089 were subject to taxation. By the thirteenth century, numerous towns had their own brewery, beginning a tradition of public ownership that survives in some form to the present day.

By tradition Czech beers are named for their town, type, and strength, the last of these defined by the Balling scale, an expression of malt density measured in degrees Plato, roughly the percentage of brewing sugars in the mash. There are four categories, although the lightest, *lehké* (less than 8°) has virtually disappeared. *Výčepni* (8–10.99°) means "tapped" even when it is bottled; *ležák* (11–12.99°) translates as "lager" even when it is ale; and stronger beers are *speciál*.

Classically Czech beers are brewed with soft water, use decoction mashing (*see* p.24), feature Saaz hops, and are cool-fermented before being lagered at 32–37°F for a couple of months.

When the Velvet Revolution saw off Soviet influence in 1989, there were around 100 breweries left. All were in public ownership, most nursing elderly equipment used to make delicate beers on a shoestring.

The return of market economics brought foreign companies keen to set up in a nation of habitual beer drinkers and gain a foothold in the new Europe. They bought breweries by the cluster, closed many, and fitted others with new equipment to make lagers the international

Below: Grand townhouses in Plzeň, the Bohemian town where blond lager first appeared.

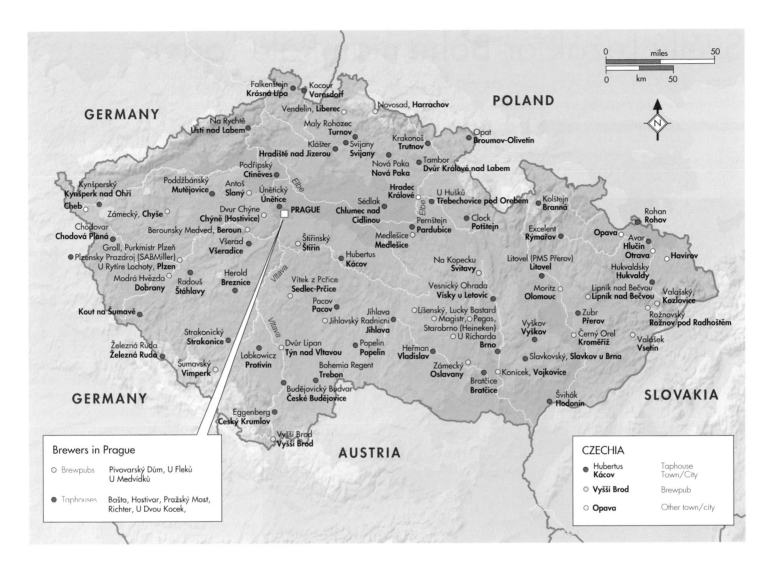

POLAND

GERMANY

Falkenstejn
Krásná Lípa

Kocour
Varnsdorf

Vendelín, **Liberec**

Novosad, **Harrachov**

Na Rychtě
Ústí nad Labem

Maly Rohozec
Turnov

Klášter
Svijany

Krakonoš
Trutnov

Opat
Broumov-Olivetín

Svijany

Hradiště nad Jizerou

Tambor
Dvůr Králové nad Labem

Poddžbánský
Mutějovice

Podřipský
Ctiněves

Antoš
Slaný

Nová Paka
Nová Paka

Hradec
Králové

U Hušků
Třebechovice pod Orebem

Kolštejn
Branná

Kynšperský
Kynšperk nad Ohří

Cheb

Únětický
Únětice

PRAGUE

Sédlak
Chlumec nad
Cidlinou

Pernštejn
Pardubice

Clock
Potštejn

Rohan
Rohov

Zámecký, **Chyše**

Dvur Chýně
Chýně (Hostivice)

Medlešice
Medlešice

Excelent
Rýmařov

Opava

Avar
Hlučín

Chodovar
Chodová Planá

Berounsky Medved, **Beroun**

Štiřinský
Štiřin

Otrava
Havířov

Groll, Purkmistr Plzeň
Plzensky Prazdroj (SABMiller)
U Rytíre Lochoty, **Plzen**

Všerad
Všeradice

Hubertus
Kácov

Na Kopecku
Svitavy

Litovel (PMS Přerov)
Litovel

Hukvaldský
Hukvaldy

Modrá Hvězda
Dobrany

Radouš
Štáhlavy

Herold
Breznice

Vítek z Pcříce
Sedlec-Prčice

Vesnický Ohrada
Vísky u Letovic

Moritz
Olomouc

Lipník nad Bečvou
Lipník nad Bečvou

Valašský,
Kozlovice

Kout na Šumavě

Pacov
Pacov

Jihlava
Jihlavský Radnicní
Jihlava

Lišenský, Lucky Bastard
Magistr, Pegas,
Starobrno (Heineken)
U Richarda
Brno

Vyškov
Vyškov

Zubr
Přerov

Rožnovský
Rožnov pod Radhoštěm

Železná Ruda
Železná Ruda

Šumavský
Vimperk

Lobkowicz
Protivín

Dvůr Lipan
Týn nad Vltavou

Popelín
Popelín

Heřman
Vladislav

Zámecký
Oslavany

Černý Orel
Kroměříž

Slavkovský, **Slavkov u Brna**

Valášek
Vsetín

Bohemia Regent
Trebon

Budějovický Budvar
České Budějovice

Bratčice
Bratčice

Koníček, **Vojkovice**

GERMANY

Eggenberg
Cesky Krumlov

Švihák
Hodonín

SLOVAKIA

Vyšší Brod
Vyšší Brod

AUSTRIA

Brewers in Prague

○ Brewpubs   Pivovarský Dům, U Fleků
U Medvídků

● Taphouses   Bašta, Hostivar, Pražský Most,
Richter, U Dvou Kocek,

CZECHIA

● Hubertus
Kácov   Taphouse
Town/City

○ **Vyšší Brod**   Brewpub

○ Opava   Other town/city

way, which is to say cheaper and faster. When the low point was reached around 1997, fewer than 50 breweries remained.

These new beers were often perceived as poor, and normally uncomplaining Czech drinkers turned against them, state-owned Budvar taking the role of national hero by adamantly refusing to cut corners or sell out to a global buyer.

There has followed a slow revival, begun by some adventurous brewpubs, followed by a few innovative or revivalist microbreweries. One of the biggest problems was lack of distribution around the country, though this has improved in recent years, such that smaller breweries now hold a majority of the taps on bar tops—Czechia is a draft beer culture.

More recently, the fortunes of the longer-established regional companies have improved, driven by a general increase in the demand for local beers,

and there are even signs of reevaluation in the largest, with Pilsner Urquell regaining panache under SAB Miller and Heineken reviving its Krušovice brands.

BREWERIES TO DISCOVER IN CZECHIA ▲
The most rewarding way to explore the brewing culture of Bohemia and Moravia is to seek out the taphouses that have been a feature of the local landscape for more than a millennium. Those featured here cover all types of Czech brewery, from ancient and splendid beer emporia to tiny front-of-house operations.

Left: Pilsner Urquell and Budweiser Budvar as seen from abroad. Czechia is a draft beer culture.

Darker Czech Lagers

The ruler of Bohemia taxed hops in the eleventh century because they were being used to brew ales, so it is likely that some form of dark beer has been part of the Czech brewing landscape for over 1,000 years.

Most are now lagers, coming—as with paler beers—in the lighter *výčepni* and regular *ležák* formats, although there are numerous *speciál* versions at 14° and upward (*see* p.134). In many ways, their production matches that of their blond counterparts, though only double decoction is deployed, a third cycle adding little.

Dark lagers vary hugely in sweetness, color, clarity, and quality. The designations *cerné* (black) and *tmavé* (dark) are largely interchangeable, though stronger examples (15° and higher) are more often branded the latter, with the occasional porter, such as the Pardubický 19° classic, tracing its roots to the Baltic tradition.

For the most historic Czech dark lager, visit U Fleků the 500-year-old brewpub on Křemencova in Prague, where roughly the same brew—times and techniques allowing—has been served over eons, with no variation in the past 145 years, accounting perhaps for why the waiters look so bored.

For a journey of discovery that will introduce you to a different and changing world of Czech beer and to a historic and beautiful country at the heart of Central Europe that, outside Prague at least, is not yet awash with visitors, plot your way round the nation's brewery taphouses (*see* map, p.135), which are often sited in towns on the rail system that have other reasons to be visited.

Back in 1985, several years before the Velvet Revolution, the first organized tour by British beer lovers to small breweries in Czechoslovakia, as it then was, heard

Above and right: There has been a brewhouse and tavern at U Fleků in Prague for five centuries. Through Soviet times its single dark 13° beer seemed to keep getting better, while since craft beer came along it has waned. In reality it has remained constant—a steady marker by which to measure the relative merits of our times.

a brewery director and head brewer complain that local government overseers would not let them brew a dark beer unless local customers requested it. How, they huffed, could local people make a request for something they had never seen or tasted, declaring that such nonsense would never be allowed in the West. The reply from their visitors amused them— different uniform, same mindset; different logic, same outcome.

Three decades on, the confidence of local brewers across Czechia has come full circle, with many following a singular path in pursuit of what they think is right. A lot will now offer a plush restaurant to bring local customers and tourists to

Below: Adam Matuska, pictured in 2010 when aged just 20, already a master brewer with his own brewery and the up-coming radical voice of new Czech brewing.

their brewery gate, some have hotels and maybe even a spa, offering their products as the natural backdrop to a tour of their beautiful town, region, mountain range, or whatever. Others just concentrate on making better beers.

In general, a Czech brewery's blond lagers pepper a narrow range of specifications. It is in the darker brews that they express their variety and where the differentiation from their neighbors is seen, expressed in strength, character, seriousness, and positioning in the market.

With the Czech Tourist Authority putting its Belgian, Bavarian, and British equivalents to shame in adopting the nation's beer as one of its most promotable tourist attractions, there has been no better time for visitors to venture out into the regions of Bohemia and Moravia to observe a culture reinventing one of its great traditions.

FOR THE TRIP

- A gentleman enters a pub ahead of a lady—to check for brawling.
- Toast *na zdraví*, clink glasses, and tap them on the table before drinking.
- Most Czech bars remain the haunt of inveterate smokers.
- Find brewpubs and brewery news by taking a translation tool to www.pivni.info.
- Take a bath in beer at Chodovar brewery's U Sládka Hotel, near Plzeň (Pilsen) and several other brewery hotels.

POLAND

For our first edition, we looked at the new Polish beer scene and concluded that while it had potential, it was not yet vibrant enough to warrant a section to itself. A visit to Kraków just before it was published, when four beer bars yielded 150 different Polish-made ales, made us question that call.

Last time, we wrote that Poland, "might be considered worthy of more space for its variations on Baltic porter and various Germanic styles" but were put off by the rapid assimilation of its larger brewers by global companies, the lack of distinctive products from its independent companies, and virtual absence of brewpubs.

Well the brewpubs have arrived, the global folk have behaved, and the country's better brewers have added variations on virtually every other type of stout or porter, enthusiastic takes on robust IPA and strong brown ales, and more.

Brewers have also started to make a wide variety of smoked beers, a favorite with Polish brewers for centuries. This began around 2010 with new versions of a light beer made with oak-smoked malted wheat, called *grodzišz* or *grodziškie*. Known as *Grätzer* in German, from 1922 its production was confined to the town of Grodziskisz Wielpolski until it died out completely in 1990. Since its successful revival, smoked stouts, pale and brown

ales, rye beers, bocks, and even barley wines have appeared.

Currently Poland has between 150 to 200 breweries, of which around a quarter are brewpubs. The number is hard to pin down because of the large number of beer commissioners and brewery hirers.

The leading places for beer are Kraków, Gdansk, Wrocław, and the capital, Warsaw.

Above: Piwo Grodziszkie Specjalne, one of several true and original re-creations of this ancient and modern folk beer.

THE ORIGINS OF BALTIC PORTER

Our era is not the first to be taken with the excellence of strong black beers. The Imperial Russian Court was also quite smitten, and by the early 1800s trade between British brewers and importers in St. Petersburg was lucrative. However, in quick succession the British government imposed tax on malt, used by the cartload in imperial stout; Empress Catherine (the Great), a woman whose appetites included strong stout, ordered her newly acquired Baltic territories to brew strong dark beers, then added a hefty import tax on beers from beyond her empire.

The first dedicated porter brewery in the region was Sinebrychoff of Helsinki, which opened in 1809. Brewers in Vilnius were producing by

1820, and in 1826 they were joined by Albert Le Coq, who moved his London brewery to the Estonian university city of Tartu. Exports from Britain continued until the war with Russia in the Crimea in 1853, when Le Coq and others upscaled. Within a decade they had brought in lagering techniques to create a sweeter, ruddier, cleaner brew: the first true Baltic porter, different not just by being lagered but for the use of different barleys and hops.

In the Polish beer renaissance, Baltic porter has featured strongly, as production had continued even throughout Soviet times. With stouts of all strengths now trending, the Imperial Russian variety is also returning.

Above: Pracownia Piwa Mr. Hard's Rocks Russian Imperial Stout (9.5% ABV)—one of Poland's top beers.

Above: The Polish capital, Warsaw, now has two dozen specialist beer bars and stores.

Above top: The Baltic port city of Gdansk, one of the first centers of the Polish beer revival and much else.

BREWING WITH ZIP

Hungary's biggest contribution to craft brewing sits in the old steel city of Miskolc, halfway between Budapest and the Tokaj wine region.

Zip Industries employs over 100 skilled engineers to design, manufacture, and assemble breweries, mainly for export to parts of the world unfamiliar with smaller-scale brewing—including Eastern Europe, Russia, the Caucasus, and "the Stans," as well as Sweden, Iceland, London, and California.

Their appeal for brewpub and craft brewery owners is that they specialize in supplying bespoke breweries ranging in size from 58 to 1,320 gallons, plus their equipment comes with observation windows into each part of

the brewing and conditioning process, precise computer monitoring of each part of the brew run, and a remote problem-solving diagnosis and repair service that can operate via the Internet.

To top it all, at their showcase brewpub in Miskolc (1 Arany János tér) they serve their own beers, some via a tabletop dispense system that charges for beers by the milliliter.

Right: At Zip's brewpub in Miskolc they have self-serve dispensers that can charge by the milliliter.

HUNGARY

Hungary is one of the few countries where wine, beer, and spirits each account for roughly one-third of all alcohol consumed. Yet this is not an even playing field, as only the latter two are subject to excise duty.

The Austro-Hungarian Empire did not end until 1918, when Viennese brewer Anton Dreher moved to Budapest to open a brewery. Hungarian brewing was influenced strongly by his descendants, pale lagers becoming the beer of the people.

After the Russians left in 1989, there was an explosion of short-lived breweries. A loophole in the law made unfiltered beer exempt from excise duty. Inexperienced banks lent liberally to entrepreneurs who set up over 300 small breweries in a couple of years, only to go out of business when the loophole was closed a few years later.

With order restored, the three largest state-owned breweries—Dreher, Borsodi, and Soprony—were bought, respectively, by SAB Miller, Molson Coors, and Heineken.

Perhaps 20 of the post-Soviet breweries remain, joined since the late 1990s by small breweries intent on making more beers of greater interest to their local market. There are roughly a dozen brewpubs, too.

Since 2012, a new generation of entrepreneurial younger brewers has also arrived, intent on making "craft beers" that are Hungarian takes on Austrian-style lagers, German *Hefeweizen*, northern European porters and stouts, and US-style pale ales. Other beers include a plethora of herb-infused, spiced, and fruit-laden beers that would not be out of place in Italy.

Around 20 now have their own brewery, with as many borrowing facilities while they save up for one. From a standing start in 2012, more than 150 regular Hungarian craft beers can be found in the capital that would not be out of place in local beer stores anywhere.

At the Cistercian abbey of Zirc, Abbot Sixtus has allowed the creation of a small brewhouse in the cellars, to test the potential for beers brewed of what might be termed a new order. The starter brews were gentle but flawless and we will watch their development with interest. This may yet prove to mark Hungary's entry to serious beer brewing.

Above: Anton Dreher (1810–63), the Austrian brewer whose Budapest brewery passed to grandson Jenó.

Opposite: The Hungarian capital, Budapest, on the Danube, home to many junk-filled "ruin bars" and the local craft beer movement.

Left: The design of Zíp's brewery allows the brewer to see the beer at every point, both literally and via a series of digital measurements that can be monitored remotely.

SOUTHERN EUROPE

Not that long ago it was possible to divide Europe into beer-drinking and nonbeer-drinking sections by tracing a line through France from the Loire estuary to Lake Geneva, across Switzerland, along the Austrian border with Hungary, and off toward the Russian border. Then Italy discovered craft beer, and everything changed.

Although in truth that line was never fixed—who could possibly suggest that Paris was anything but a wine-drinking city?—today it is farcical to imagine any sort of reasonable divide. Some 800 breweries in Italy have been joined by several hundred more in Spain and dozens of other nascent operations in emerging craft beer markets in Portugal and the Balkans.

Simply put, the nations of Southern Europe—not historically beer-loving lands—have now discovered the joys of beer beyond pallid, thirst-quenching lager.

Italy was the first of the wine-centric nations to tumble, with breweries sprouting first in the country's north, then migrating toward Tuscany, and finally covering the entirety of "the boot," to the point that *birra artigianale* is now produced in each of Italy's twenty *regioni*. Further, Italian craft beer is now sufficiently well-traveled that it has started to influence brewing not just elsewhere in Southern Europe, but across the continent's north, into North and South America and Asia.

While we still wait for craft beer to show the sort of explosive growth in the rest of Southern Europe, as it has already in Italy and Spain, there is a sense of inevitability about it all, as though everyone accepts that it's only a matter of time before yet another part of the world rises up to put its own distinctive stamp on craft brewing.

And, indeed, it may not be long before the Greeks are tempting our palates with their own interpretations of pale ales, the Portuguese are trotting out port barrel-aged *Doppelbocks*, and distinctly Balkan strong ales have become part of the global beer dynamic.

Right: A Tuscan afternoon, a little cheese, and a bottle of *birra artigianale*. What could be better?

Modern Italian brewing

Prior to the 1990s, if you were in search of Italian beer beyond pale lager, you needed to rely principally on two words: *doppio malto*. These malty, higher-alcohol darker lagers not dissimilar to *Doppelbocks* (*see* p.93) were one end of the spectrum, with mass-market lagers light of hue and palate at the other. In between lay very little.

Small wonder, then, that Italians were in general unenthusiastic beer consumers. The first changes to this state of affairs began in the 1980s when "birrerias," featuring brands imported from Belgium, Germany, and the UK, began to appear, redefining how Italians viewed beer.

The first homegrown craft brewers were anchored primarily in the country's gastronomically obsessed north, taking their inspiration not from the lagers of Germany but from the ales of Belgium and, increasingly thereafter, the USA.

The Belgian connection, although seemingly remote, made and continues to make sense on multiple levels. The Low Countries are popular vacation destinations for Italians and, in part for this fact, Belgian specialty beers sold well in Italy. Further, Belgian ales are fairly food-friendly and the benefits of adding culinary utility was not lost on new Italian brewers.

Perhaps most significantly, however, Belgians have long placed a great deal of emphasis on the aesthetics of beer drinking, from proper pouring rituals to glassware and bottle design, which appealed to the ever-fashionable Italians.

As craft brewing took hold in Italy in the early years of the twenty-first century, its expansion was dependent on style as well as substance, featuring often extravagantly stylized and cork-finished bottle design, emulating wine bottles in size, and creating elegant glassware. A strong embrace of the Belgian and American "anything goes" brewing attitude did not hurt, either, although, as in the USA, while the more unusual beers are the ones that achieve notoriety, most Italian craft brews are more conventional ales and lagers.

The early days were not without their problems. At the national Birra dell'Anno

Above: Enjoying beer in Chianti country. The annual beer festival at the TNT Pub near Buonconvento—the Villaggio della Birra, or "Village of Beer."

Opposite: Agostino Arioli, head brewer at Birrificio Italiano, cleans out the spent grains after the mash and lauter. Local farmers use them to feed livestock.

ROME—ITALIAN CRAFT BEER CENTRAL

Although the majority of Italy's craft breweries are found in the north, including many of its best known and most highly regarded, the beating heart of Italian craft beer consumption is Rome.

It was not always thus. In the early days the trend-conscious Milanese led the way, supporting pioneering outlets such as the Birrificio Lambrate brewpub and beer-friendly restaurant La Ratera.

But as the years passed and *la birra artigianale* became less of a curiosity and more a fixture in urban bars and restaurants, Rome assumed the role of craft beer capital, anchored by the outstanding beer pub Ma Che Siete Venuti a Fà; its across-the-street restaurant neighbor, Bir&Fud, an early outlet

of Theo Musso's bar chain Open Baladin; and the shop/pub hybrid Birra+.

In 2016, the Italian capital not only abounds with worthy beer destinations, but craft beer is also widely available in many nonspecialty bars, restaurants, and bottle stores, to the point that it is doubtful that anywhere else can supply as encompassing a view of Italian beer culture. The city now even has its own Trappist brewery, Tre Fontane, which makes a eucalyptus-flavored take on the *tripel* style.

Right: The modest and unassuming frontage of Ma Che Siete Venuti a Fà, aka "The Football Pub," belies the wonderful beer bar that resides within.

awards in 2006, judging the best Italian beer was a task with mixed rewards, as a youthful craft brewing industry worked through its teething pains of uninspired flavors, technical flaws, and misguided recipes.

That situation had changed dramatically by 2015, with brewers and beers flowing far more consistently, their innovatively spiced beers joining traditionally-styled ales and lagers and, arguably the new jewel in the Italian craft brewing's crown, its wine-beers (*see* 156).

Led by the always experimental Baladin, alongside other pioneering and/ or innovative breweries like Panil (officially Birrificio Torrechiara), Birrificio Grado Plato, Lovebeer, Birrificio Extraomnes, Birrificio Lambrate, and Birrificio Montegioco, Italian craft brewers have taken an "us against them" approach and with gleeful irreverence transformed the country into one of Europe's newer and very different sort of brewing nations.

Italy's brewing terroir: spices and wine

As much as Italian brewers can be challenged when it comes to crafting hoppy beers (*see* p.156), change the

SPAIN & PORTUGAL

At the start of the second decade of the twenty-first century, there were many (your authors included), who picked Spain as Europe's next new home of creative craft brewing. With its demonstrable devotion to all things epicurean, it was tipped to follow Italy as a wine land that would embrace creative and flavorful beer.

Those pundits have since been proved right and also wrong. Craft beer is now certainly a fact of Spanish life, with breweries and beer bars appearing all across the country, especially in Catalonia and its capital, Barcelona. We have seen a brewery and contracting beer company count for 2015 that exceeds 500, and there is little doubt these have firmly embraced the craft beer ethos. However, what proportion of them actually brew is debatable. Maybe half?

The country also has some of Europe's most interesting new beer destinations, most having sprung up in the past four years, including BierCaB, Homo Sibaris, and Cat Bar in Barcelona and Irreale in Madrid.

The problem is that the dynamism and originality many of us expected from Spain has not yet materialized. Instead, Spanish brewers have for the most part followed in the footsteps of American (and, to a slightly lesser degree, Belgian, Italian, and English) brewers, producing beers of rather predictable style and character. As a result, the Spanish beer market has become populated primarily by solid yet unsurprising brews.

This is not to say that El Bulli-style inventiveness has been entirely absent from the Spanish craft beer scene, or that it won't be seen in greater abundance in the future. Toledo brewery Cerveza Domus created its Greco as an homage to both the painter and the flavors of the local marzipan, successfully so in both regards. Mallorca brewery Sullerica uses local ingredients such as orange blossoms and even olives in its line of beers; and contracting brewer Guinea Pigs is, as its name suggests, consistently experimenting with new and unusual brews. Time will tell as to how influential these and other breweries like them will become.

We will continue to watch with interest.

Above top: Increasingly, glasses of beer are replacing wine and Sherry when the Spanish enjoy their early evening tapas.

Above: The Toledo brewery Cerveza Domus is one of Spain's leading lights in terms of consistency, quality, and creativity.

Opposite: Catalonia boasts not only one of Spain's two highest-level wine regions, in Priorat, but may also soon be styling itself as the country's craft brewing capital.

In neighboring Portugal, while beer is quite popular, the market is utterly dominated by two breweries: Unicer, which is co-owned by Portugal's Viacer Group and Carlsberg—maker of the mainstream Super Bock brands; and Heineken-owned Central Cervejas e Bebidas: brewers of the equally mass-market Sagres line.

There is a proliferation of *cervejarias* in major cities, though such places are rarely breweries; their literal translation suggests atmospheric beer halls or restaurants without brewing facilities. However, a raft of breweries and beer firms has appeared since 2014—maybe 80 in total by the dawn of 2016, with possibly half actually brewing.

The first, Sovina, arrived in Porto in 2009. Of the first two dozen, some 80 percent are based in the northwest and coastal areas around that city, including Post Scriptum, helmed by celebrated Portuguese brewer Pedro Sousa, and Faustino, which makes the respected Maldita line of beers.

The recent splurge is, however, more evenly spread across the country, with increasing development of breweries in the capital, Lisbon, which may yet turn into the nation's beer capital.

GREECE & SOUTHEASTERN EUROPE

The beer scene in southeastern Europe was always underdeveloped, and with the economic woes afflicting Greece, its leading proponent, we feared it might disappear altogether. But brewing is not like that.

Greece has over 20 craft breweries and a couple of brewpubs, scattered all across the mainland and on some islands, with few recent closures. While Greek brewers tend to share the eastern Mediterranean preference for restrained, lighter beers, all the major styles can be found, with Corfu even boasting a cask ale brewery.

The consistent top performer is Septem, at Avlonari, northeast of Athens, on the not-quite-island of Euboea. Meanwhile, the US-influenced Donkey, on the island of Santorini, and up-and-coming all-rounder Siris, near northern Thessaloniki, are getting bolder.

Greek beers featured at the first Balkan beer festival, held in the Bulgarian capital Sofia in 2015, along with beers from Bulgaria that are starting to irrigate the country. These include British-influenced Glarus, from the Black Sea coast at Varna, and local start-up Divo Pivo.

In the former Yugoslavia, now styled Adriatic Europe, even more remarkable changes are occurring.

Some of the 30 mostly German-style brewpubs in Slovenia date back 20 years. In 2008, these were joined by a single craft brewery, HumanFish, now in Vrhnika, southwest of the capital, Ljubljana. The last couple of years have seen this lone wolf joined by a pack of newer brewers that include Mali Grad, from Kamnik, north of Ljubljana, Tektonik in the capital itself, and 1713 of Kobarid, which is close to the Italian border and clearly influenced by Italian brewing. More will come thanks to the Vizir brewery near Črnomelj in the south, itself no slouch at ale brewing, which has opened its facilities to adventuresome brewers.

Croatia has had reliable but numerous cautious brewpubs for over a decade, but since 2013 some proper craft brewers have arrived. Most impressive are two in the capital of Zagreb: Zmajska, which has rapidly gained a regional reputation, and Nova Runda, which shows great promise. Of the dozen or so wannabes, at least two will open plants shortly.

Above: The beer revival in Greece is still in its early days.

Opposite: Although still young, the "Dragon's Brewery," Zmasjka Pivovara in Zagreb, has impressed with its pale ale, IPA, and porter.

THE SMALL STATES OF EUROPE

Europe's smaller nations and semi-independent enclaves often specialize in tax efficiency, although even accountants need good beer.

Liechtenstein led with its small German-style *Brauhaus* Liechtensteiner in 2007, which was joined in 2011 by a second, Prinzenbräu. Monaco's brewpub followed in 2008, since when San Marino got Titanbräu (2010) and Andorra acquired the Alpha brewery (2014).

Among the EU's smallest members, Malta now has Lord Chambray, an interesting craft brewery on the island of Gozo, while Luxembourg has Capital City Brewing, which joins the Simon family's brewery and its smaller offspring. Meanwhile, brewers in

Cyprus need to decide how to respond to beer firm Hula Hops' sharp, lemony IPA shaking up its scene.

The British colony of Gibraltar thus far produces hops only for an exclusive bottled ale executed in the Isle of Man. The Vatican remains beer deprived; Trappists, please apply.

Right: Each brand of Andorra's Cervesa Alpha is named for a feature of one of the principality's seven parishes.

Opposite center: Liechtenstein's Prinzenbräu concentrates on German beer styles.

Opposite right: Brewing at San Marino's Titanbräu takes place at the base of Monte Titano.

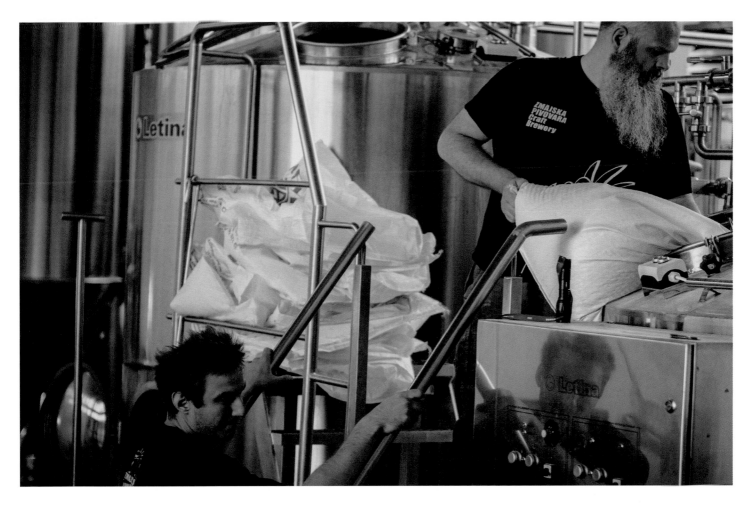

Serbia has a dozen new breweries to date. Thus far, only Kabinet of Nemenikuće, south of Belgrade, has attracted regional attention, though the capital's recent start-up, Tron, should be worth watching.

While Macedonia imports good beers, it has no homegrown craft producers

yet, while Albania and Montenegro each have just a single German-style *Hausbrauerei*. Surprisingly, perhaps, Kosovo has a pretty uncompromising US-style craft brewery called Sabaja, enjoying popularity in the capital Prïstina, though for overcoming adversity we tip our hats

to the Olbridž (Old Bridge) brewery at Mostar in Bosnia & Herzegovina and the spirit behind it.

THE AMERICAS

At the end of 2015, the USA claimed more breweries than ever before seen with 4,144 in operation. With a much smaller population base, Canada is, on a per capita basis, even more brewery-rich, with an estimated national brewery count of over 550.

As impressive as these numbers may be, they are dwarfed by the influence that North American breweries, particularly those of the United States, have exerted on the global craft brewing community in general and emerging markets like Latin America in particular. Its effect has been to inspire significant brewery development all the way from the California Baja region of Mexico to Tierra del Fuego.

These emerging Latin American craft breweries must face off against global corporations determined to protect their massive share of what remains a growth market for beer consumption, and so far they have had some success. The key to their future growth may lie in their ability to develop indigenous beer styles not easily replicated by the big brewing companies.

THE UNITED STATES OF AMERICA

When Jack McAuliffe first opened the doors of California's New Albion Brewing Company in Sonoma in May 1976 he could not have possibly imagined the movement he was about to ignite. For even though the first American craft brewery of the modern age failed to survive more than a few years, like the biblical Adam, its offspring grew to populate the whole of the USA, from Key West, Florida, to Fairbanks, Alaska.

In 2015, with literally thousands of breweries and brewpubs scattered across all 50 states, the story of craft brewing in the USA shifted from one of growth, both potential and realized, to a dual, if rather contradictory, narrative. On the one side, proponents laud its continued expansion with a 20 percent overall market share the goal, while on the other, more pessimistic industry watchers warn of a possible craft beer "bubble" set to burst soon. It is our view that the former is more likely than the latter.

While there is little doubt that the growth rate of American craft brewing over the past decade is unsustainable, neither is there much evidence to suggest that a large-scale contraction is imminent. At the time of writing, the United States can boast a remarkable number of small-scale brewing operations, however the nation's brewery-to-population ratio remains smaller than that of many other countries, including Canada, the UK, and large swathes of mainland Europe. None of these other nations appears to be suffering as a result of a higher brewery concentration.

American craft brewers are not only producing more beer but also producing different beer, sometimes radically so. To the delight of some and the bemusement of others, America's craft brewers have proved, time and again, true to the culture of excess that often appears to define the society. If a beer style is strong and well hopped, as in a traditional India pale ale or even a paler and hoppier American-style IPA, then it is deemed worthy of becoming yet more hoppy and more potent, as witnessed by the development and popularity of the so-called "double," "triple," and even "quadruple" IPAs. Similarly, a malty and warming barley wine or imperial stout can easily be made more intense by aging it six months in a former bourbon barrel or dramatically increasing its malt content so that it ferments to close to 20% ABV.

Most of these style-twisting experiments have resulted in a body of brews that has greatly increased the range of flavors and aromas available to beer connoisseurs worldwide, while others, it should be said, bring to mind the old chestnut: "Just because you can doesn't mean you should." Still, at their best, they have even served to inspire brewers in distant lands, from Belgium to Northern England and Italy to Japan.

Forty years is not such a long time, but it has proved long enough for American craft brewers to make an indelible and expanding mark on their own culture and that of many others, and change the way their fellow citizens drink, probably forever.

BREWERIES PER STATE IN THE USA ▶

With in excess of 4,100 breweries scattered among all 50 states near the end of 2015, some wonder if the craft brewing "bubble" is set to soon burst. We think not.

Above: Stickers adorn even sophisticated machinery at Chicago's Off Color Brewing, reflecting the "punk rock" ethos of many craft breweries.

Top left: Jack McAuliffe pioneered craft brewing in the USA with his New Albion Brewing Company in Northern California.

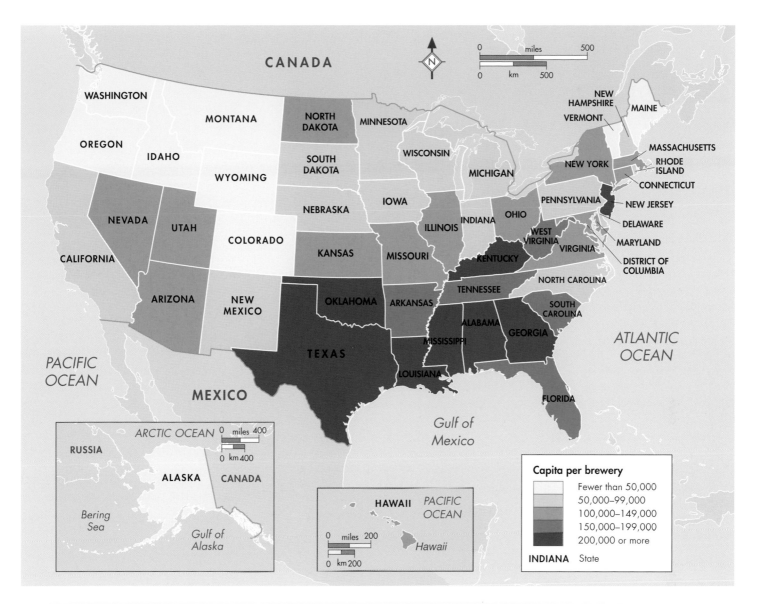

STATE	BREWERIES	CAPITA/BREWERY
Vermont	40	15,664
Oregon	216	18,381
Colorado	235	22,791
Montana	44	23,263
Maine	52	25,579
Wyoming	22	26,552
Washington	256	27,584
Alaska	22	33,488
Idaho	43	38,011
New Hampshire	26	51,031
New Mexico	36	57,933
Nebraska	32	58,797
Wisconsin	97	59,356
Michigan	159	62,326
Iowa	46	67,546
South Dakota	12	71,098
Minnesota	73	74,756
District of Columbia	8	82,362

STATE	BREWERIES	CAPITA/BREWERY
Indiana	80	82,461
Delaware	11	85,056
California	431	90,029
Pennsylvania	136	94,024
Rhode Island	11	95,925
North Carolina	101	98,455
Ohio	110	105,401
Virginia	78	106,747
New York	181	109,095
Missouri	55	110,247
Massachusetts	61	110,580
Nevada	25	113,564
North Dakota	6	123,247
Illinois	103	125,054
Arizona	53	127,009
Kansas	22	132,001
Connecticut	27	133,210
Hawaii	10	141,956

STATE	BREWERIES	CAPITA/BREWERY
Utah	20	147,145
Maryland	40	149,410
South Carolina	31	155,887
Arkansas	19	156,125
Tennessee	39	167,932
West Virginia	11	168,211
Florida	111	179,219
Texas	117	230,401
Kentucky	18	245,192
Georgia	40	252,434
Alabama	19	255,230
New Jersey	32	279,318
Louisiana	15	309,978
Oklahoma	10	387,805
Mississippi	7	427,726

Sources: The Brewers Association, State Craft Beer
Sales & Production Statistics, 2014 and U.S. Census Bureau,
Population Division, December 2014

California

From almost the moment it joined the union in 1850, California has been enshrined in the collective American consciousness as the land of milk and honey, where opportunity awaits and possibilities abound. So it is particularly appropriate that consensus places the roots of modern American craft brewing firmly in the north of the state.

The story begins with a young man named Fritz Maytag, part of the famous appliance manufacturing family, pursuing his graduate studies while living in San Francisco during the 1960s. Partial to a beer called Anchor Steam, enjoyed with friends at a local institution known as the Spaghetti Factory, Maytag was dismayed to hear from a bartender there that the Anchor brewery was nearing closure. A visit was quickly organized.

Touring the decaying regional brewer, Maytag was struck by the opportunity it afforded and speedily secured a deal to assume partial ownership. As he fought to resuscitate the aging plant, the fledgling entrepreneur became increasingly enamored with his purchase and, as the 1960s gave way to the next decade, obtained full ownership.

By the mid-1970s, Maytag had not only turned around the fortunes of Anchor, but he had also begun to introduce new brands into the brewery's lineup, including a porter in 1974 and, in 1975, Liberty Ale and Old Foghorn, the latter labeled a "barleywine-style ale" as a sop to perplexed authorities who could not understand how a wine could be made from barley.

Maytag's commitment to crafting intensely flavorful beer during a time when American breweries seemed caught in a race to produce the blandest and most inoffensive lager possible served as inspiration to other would-be brewing entrepreneurs, including Sonoma's Jack McAuliffe (New Albion Brewing), Chico's Ken Grossman and Paul Camusi (Sierra Nevada Brewing), and Ted DeBakker of Novato (DeBakker Brewery), each of whom had opened a new brewery prior to 1980.

Craft brewing—then known as microbrewing—spread across California and the rest of the USA during the 1980s, stronger in some regions than in others, but always with the Golden State at the forefront, the north dominating the south. In 1982, the brewpub, defined as a brewery with the ability to sell directly to the public through a restaurant setting, was formally recognized in the state, and thereafter two opened in rapid succession, beat to the title of America's first modern brewpub only by Bert Grant's Yakima Brewing in Washington State.

Craft beer continued to grow in popularity throughout California during the 1990s, but the state really hit its stride with the dawn of the new millennium, most notably through the dramatic transformation of the southern region from

SAN FRANCISCO'S BREWERIES ▶
The spiritual home of American craft brewing, San Francisco is known not just for its breweries but also its beer bars, beer-friendly restaurants, and gastronomic lifestyle.

Left: With its assertive, Cascade-fueled hoppiness, it's hard to believe that Anchor Brewing's Liberty Ale was first brewed in 1975.

Center: Founded in 1987, Full Sail has been brewing an IPA since long before it became the juggernaut style it is today.

Far left: Perhaps no other beer in the United States has inspired more brewery launches than Sierra Nevada Pale Ale.

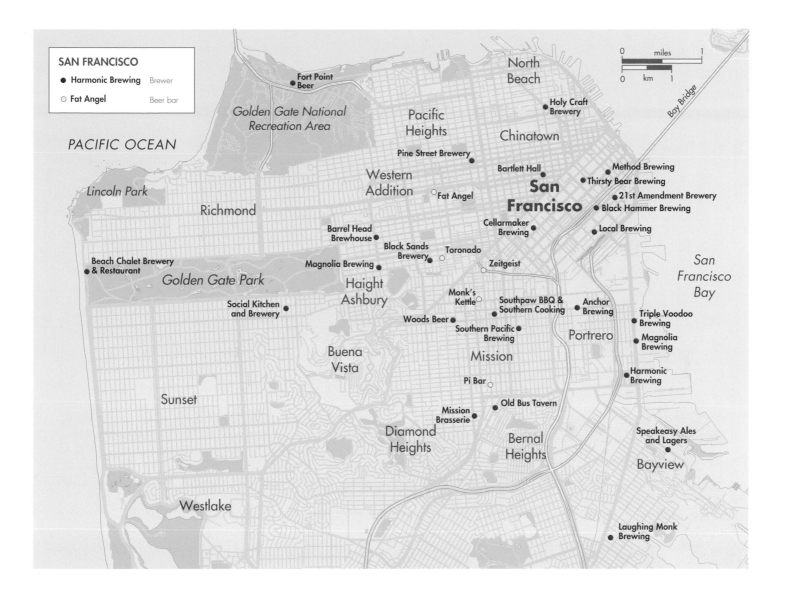

SAN FRANCISCO

● Harmonic Brewing   Brewer
○ Fat Angel   Beer bar

THE RISE AND RISE OF AMERICAN IPA

Looking at today's plethora of India pale ales, it's hard to imagine that the style was once on the verge of extinction. Sure, a handful of examples remained in the UK, and Ballantine India Pale Ale was still in production in the US, albeit in a much-toned-down version, but by the mid-1970s, if you were looking for a beer style to bet on as a potential juggernaut, IPA would have been among the most foolhardy of picks.

Around this time, Fritz Maytag decided to brew a bicentennial beer called Liberty Ale at his Anchor Brewing Company. It was light in color and, at 5.9% ABV, slightly stronger than the norm at the time. Most importantly, it was hopped, and heavily so, with an American variety known as Cascade.

Although not labeled as such, Liberty was effectively an IPA for the times and an influence on budding brewery builders Ken Grossman and Paul Camusi, who were soon to open the Sierra Nevada Brewing Company. Sierra's now-iconic pale ale is a beer that makes extensive, though not exclusive, use of Cascade hops and was a trailblazer for a new breed of American-style pale ales and IPAs.

Liberty and Sierra Nevada Pale took the first two important steps toward the spread of the modern American-style IPA, but it was several more years before the next wave appeared. While early efforts were made to establish the IPA market by the likes of Full Sail Brewing Company in Oregon,

Breckenridge Brewery in Colorado, and Brooklyn Brewery in New York, it was not until the end of the century that a sort of collective palate-shift began to propel IPA toward its current popularity.

Today, IPA is available more widely and in more permutations than any other beer style on earth, from more conventional US and UK interpretations to white, red, and black iterations and strengths up to or even exceeding 12% ABV. And although its origin is unassailably British, its current global reach can be attributed only to the brewers of the United States, beginning with Anchor and Sierra Nevada.

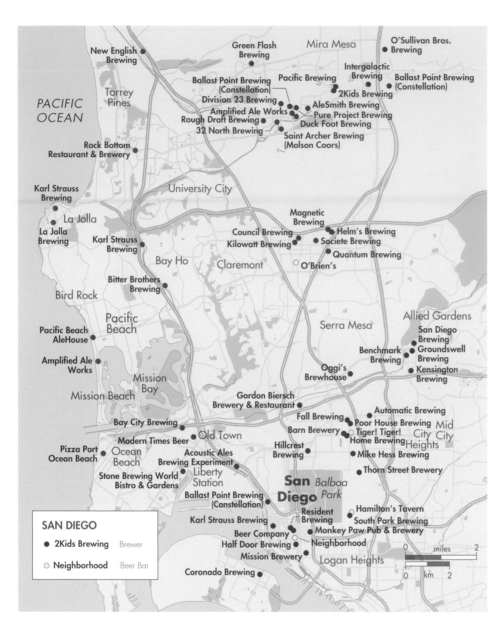

PACIFIC OCEAN

New English Brewing
Torrey Pines
Green Flash Brewing
Mira Mesa
O'Sullivan Bros. Brewing
Ballast Point Brewing (Constellation)
Pacific Brewing
Intergalactic Brewing
Ballast Point Brewing (Constellation)
Division 23 Brewing
2Kids Brewing
Amplified Ale Works
AleSmith Brewing
Rough Draft Brewing
Pure Project Brewing
32 North Brewing
Duck Foot Brewing
Saint Archer Brewing (Molson Coors)
Rock Bottom Restaurant & Brewery
University City
Karl Strauss Brewing
La Jolla
Magnetic Brewing
La Jolla Brewing
Karl Strauss Brewing
Council Brewing
Kilowatt Brewing
Helm's Brewing
Societe Brewing
Quantum Brewing
Bay Ho
Claremont
O'Brien's
Bitter Brothers Brewing
Bird Rock
Pacific Beach
Serra Mesa
Allied Gardens
Pacific Beach AleHouse
San Diego Brewing
Benchmark Brewing
Groundswell Brewing
Amplified Ale Works
Oggi's Brewhouse
Kensington Brewing
Mission Bay
Mission Beach
Gordon Biersch Brewery & Restaurant
Automatic Brewing
Fall Brewing
Poor House Brewing
Mid City
Bay City Brewing
Barn Brewery
Tiger! Tiger!
Home Brewing
City Heights
Modern Times Beer
Old Town
Hillcrest Brewing
Pizza Port Ocean Beach
Ocean Beach
Acoustic Ales Brewing Experiment
Mike Hess Brewing
Stone Brewing World Bistro & Gardens
Liberty Station
Thorn Street Brewery
San Diego
Balboa Park
Ballast Point Brewing (Constellation)
Karl Strauss Brewing
Resident Brewing
Hamilton's Tavern
South Park Brewing
Beer Company
Monkey Paw Pub & Brewery
Half Door Brewing
Neighborhood
Mission Brewery
Logan Heights
Coronado Brewing

SAN DIEGO
● 2Kids Brewing Brewer
○ Neighborhood Beer Bar

0 miles 2
0 km 2

craft beer wasteland into brewery-rich nirvana (*see* below).

Nowadays it is difficult to find any city or town in the state, no matter how small, that does not boast at least one brewpub of its own.

Along the way, California's brewers have proved themselves to be, if not necessarily the instigators of certain creative brewing movements, then certainly some of their most successful early adopters. Vinnie Cilurzo is widely credited with the creation of the double IPA at Blind Pig Brewing Company in Temecula, which some feel he perfected at Russian River Brewing Company in Santa Rosa. In San Marcos, Tomme Arthur at The Lost Abbey was among the first to pursue the conditioning of beer in a variety of differently conditioned wooden barrels. The North Coast Brewing Company popularized the imperial stout, as Anderson Valley did with oatmeal stout; and Berkeley beer veterans John and Reid Martin were among the first to recognize the growing popularity of so-called sour beers by hosting a sour-themed festival at their Triple Rock brewpub and Jupiter beer bar.

◀ SAN DIEGO'S BREWERIES
Although a late developer in craft beer terms, San Diego is now considered one of America's prime brewery hotspots.

THE BLOSSOMING OF SAN DIEGO

During the 1990s, while northern California was enjoying the fruits of Anchor Brewing and Sierra Nevada Brewing Company's labors, the state's southern regions were, well, a bit of a beer wasteland. There was some craft brewing activity, though—Pizza Port and AleSmith were already active, as were Stone, Craftsman, and several others—but the beer was mostly small batch and difficult to find.

The new millennium saw the emergence of Southern California, in particular the San Diego area, as a major force in craft brewing.

In only a scant few years, the breweries of Southern California became the ones to watch. Pizza

Port, a small chain of brewpubs with remarkably creative beers, spun off a full-production brewery that gave us Port Brewing and The Lost Abbey; Stone launched into a period of almost exponential expansion, which even in 2016 shows little sign of slowing; Ballast Point, now owned by Constellation Brands, outgrew its tiny home-brew store location and graduated to a much larger production facility; and new groundbreaking breweries such as Green Flash and The Bruery were born.

These burgeoning operations were joined by many others, from Coronado near the Mexican border to Angel City in Los Angeles, with San Diego at the epicenter. Today, in any survey of the best beer cities in America, California's southernmost

Perhaps the only thing that might prevent California's forward progress in craft beer, it seems, is a force of nature, which, at the time of writing, seems an ominous possibility. Since breweries require considerable amounts of water to operate and California is experiencing a long-running drought, this could indeed pose a definite threat to further brewery expansion. Conservation techniques and, hopefully, a lessening of the drought conditions will be necessary if the state is to continue its long-running pattern of brewery growth and expansion.

Above: Sit at the Anderson Valley Brewing Company bar, and you might just hear some "Boontling," an esoteric dialect spoken only in Boonville.

city must be considered not only among the most brewery-rich, but also among the very finest for enjoying beer, whether in a brewery tasting room, bar, or fine-dining restaurant.

Opposite: Filling barrels for the much-admired Cuvée de Tomme at The Lost Abbey brewery.

Left: Odd ingredients like yams and maple syrup somehow work together well in The Bruery's Autumn Maple.

Right: Some may argue San Diego's claim to the title of craft beer capital, but there is little doubting the city's impressive craft beer culture.

Pacific Northwest, Alaska & Hawaii

While California can rightly lay claim to both the inspiration and first commercial application of the American craft-brewing ethos in, respectively, Anchor Brewing and New Albion, it is in the Pacific Northwest that it has for three decades thrived as nowhere else. Throughout Washington and Oregon and even into Alaska and the Hawaiian islands, most cities, towns, or villages can boast a nearby brewery, brewpub, or, at the very least, one or two decent beer bars.

It should come as no surprise, really. Residents of Oregon and Washington State are notoriously unconventional, preferring to bicycle or take public transport where others would drive and embracing the culture of the "locavore" long before it was fashionable to do so. Additionally, America's most fertile hop fields sit on their doorstep, in Washington's Yakima Valley, providing a ready source of seasoning for the hoppy ales they so adore.

Indeed, even prior to Bert Grant's founding of America's first modern brewpub in Yakima, Washington, and the 1982 opening of Seattle's Red Hook Brewery, Cascadians, as the locals sometimes like to call themselves, were a contrary bunch where beer was concerned. In the late 1970s, as mainstream beer brands grew increasingly bland, Portland's Blitz-Weinhard brewery called attention to itself by producing what the late beer writer Michael Jackson deemed "perhaps the most distinctive lager in the United States"—Henry Weinhard's Private Reserve. It was, it almost goes without saying, especially notable for its hop character.

As was the case for most of America's fabled regional breweries, however, the final decades of the century were far from kind

Right: For more than a century, Washington's, Yakima Valley has been the heartland of US hop cultivation.

WORTHY SIDE TRIPS IN WASHINGTON AND OREGON

While beer destinations abound in many of the Pacific Northwest's major cities, you will also find plenty of exceptional beer experiences well off the beaten track.

• **Bend, Oregon:** Three hours southeast of Portland by car, Bend is home to a trio of impressive breweries, including the always experimental Crux Fermentation Project, seasonal beer stalwart Bend Brewing Company, and Deschutes Brewery, creator of perhaps the finest porter in the USA as well as other impressive ales.

• **Columbia River Gorge, Oregon:** Enthusiasts of outdoor sports from windsurfing to snowboarding

can combine their passions with great craft beer in Hood River, Mosier, and Troutdale, all just a short drive from Portland.

• **Newport, Oregon:** Iconoclasts and rebels will not want to miss the home of Rogue Ales, long-established brewer of impressive beers like Hazelnut Brown Nectar, Old Crustacean Barleywine, and Shakespeare Oatmeal Stout as well as such oddities as Voodoo Doughnut Lemon Chiffon Crueller Ale.

• **Bellingham, Washington:** While there are many worthy beer destinations in this smallish city close to the Canadian border, visitors could

be forgiven if they never saw the outside of the Boundary Bay and Chuckanut brewpubs.

• **Spokane, Washington:** Worth the trip for the No-Li Brewhouse alone, Spokane is also home to seven other breweries and laudable beer bars such as the Manito Tap House and the Viking Bar & Grill.

• **Yakima, Washington:** Yes, there are breweries in Yakima, including Yakima Craft Brewing and Bale Breaker Brewing, but the real reason to make this pilgrimage is to experience the largest hop harvest in the United States—and maybe visit the American Hop Museum down the road.

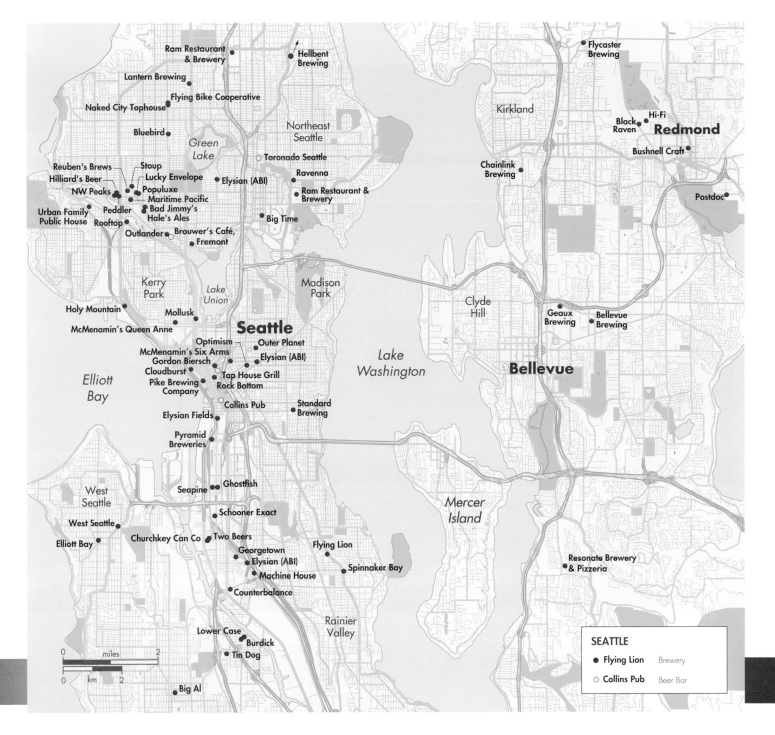

Ram Restaurant
& Brewery

Hellbent
Brewing

Flycaster
Brewing

Lantern Brewing

Flying Bike Cooperative

Kirkland

Black
Raven

Hi-Fi

Redmond

Naked City Taphouse

Northeast
Seattle

Chainlink
Brewing

Bushnell Craft

Bluebird

Green
Lake

Toronado Seattle

Reuben's Brews
Hilliard's Beer
NW Peaks

Stoup
Lucky Envelope
Populuxe
Maritime Pacific
Bad Jimmy's
Hale's Ales

Elysian (ABI)

Ravenna

Ram Restaurant &
Brewery

Postdoc

Urban Family
Public House

Peddler
Rooftop

Big Time

Outlander

Brouwer's Café,
Fremont

Kerry
Park

Lake
Union

Madison
Park

Clyde
Hill

Geaux
Brewing

Bellevue
Brewing

Holy Mountain

Mollusk

Seattle

Lake
Washington

Bellevue

McMenamin's Queen Anne

Optimism
McMenamin's Six Arms
Gordon Biersch
Cloudburst
Pike Brewing
Company

Outer Planet
Elysian (ABI)

Tap House Grill
Rock Bottom

Elliott
Bay

Collins Pub

Standard
Brewing

Elysian Fields

Pyramid
Breweries

West
Seattle

Seapine

Ghostfish

Mercer
Island

West Seattle

Schooner Exact

Elliott Bay

Churchkey Can Co

Two Beers

Flying Lion

Resonate Brewery
& Pizzeria

Georgetown
Elysian (ABI)
Machine House

Spinnaker Bay

Counterbalance

Rainier
Valley

Lower Case
Burdick
Tin Dog

Big Al

0   miles   2

0   km   2

SEATTLE

● **Flying Lion**   Brewery

○ **Collins Pub**   Beer Bar

SEATTLE'S BREWERIES ▲
Known as the Emerald City, pretty much every one
of Seattle's neighborhoods has at least a couple of
breweries to call its own.

Left: Opened as a pub brewery in 2010, the
Breakside Brewery has since expanded to a
production facility in nearby Milwaukie, Oregon.

Rocky Mountains

The Rocky Mountain states, specifically Colorado, achieved brewing infamy long in advance of craft beer. Well before Coors became a national brand, it had cult status in the East thanks to its scarcity outside a jumble of western states—easterners were known to "bootleg" home cases of the stuff at a time—and a clever ad campaign that touted the purity of the mountain-stream water with which the beer was brewed.

More substantial fame arrived in 1979, when two former Colorado University professors founded the Boulder Brewing Company, now Boulder Beer, in a goat shed outside Denver. Around the same time and in the same town, an association of homebrewers was set up by Charlie Papazian, who probably did not realize that what he was doing was sowing the seeds for a national organization of small-scale breweries.

The American Homebrewers Association eventually spun off several wings, including the Brewers Association, a now vital craft brewing trade group, a publishing house, and the largest beer event in the Americas: Denver's annual Great American Beer Festival (GABF). Along the way, craft beer spread from Boulder all the way up and down the Rockies, from Montana to Arizona and New Mexico.

The heart of mountain brewing today remains Denver, Colorado, where at the helm of the city's beer aristocracy sits Wynkoop Brewing Company, founded by John Hickenlooper, who went on to become state governor; the over-twenty-year-old Great Divide Brewing Company; and a beer bar, Falling Rock, which at GABF time becomes the nucleus of the swirling, sweaty, Denver-wide beer-festival experience.

Craft beer radiated westward from Denver and Boulder. Declaring its inspiration in their name, New Belgium Brewing early on found itself with a modern cult favorite in the form of its Fat Tire Amber Ale, while, in the unlikely bastion of Salt Lake City, Squatters Brewing and Wasatch Brewery proved that Utah's 4% ABV limit for "beer"—anything higher is "liquor"—need not be a limit to flavor. Farther still, Montana's Missoula Brewing Company, and Four Peaks from Tempe, Arizona, were among the early influencers in their respective states.

Today, although many have relatively small populations, four of the eight Rocky Mountain states—Colorado, Montana, Wyoming, and Idaho—rank among the top ten in the United States in terms of breweries per capita, with New Mexico only one position out at 11th.

THE GREAT AMERICAN BEER FESTIVAL

Founded in 1982, the Great American Beer Festival, or GABF, is without question the most prestigious beer event in the United States, drawing 60,000 ticket holders, volunteer pourers, and brewery staff to downtown Denver every year. It was not always thus.

In the early days, the GABF was held in Boulder, not far from Denver, and hosted a mere couple of dozen breweries. It moved to Denver in 1984 and grew steadily, drawing 7,000 people to the Denver Merchandise Mart on the outskirts of town in 1992, yet even after it was firmly established downtown in the late 1990s, its effect on tourism was, according to local tourist authorities, minimal.

Today, tickets for the GABF sell out in only slightly over an hour, and hotels get fully booked early on. At the 2015 festival, 750 breweries offered their brands, making for a total of 3,800 different beers, poured in samples limited to one ounce in size—a frustratingly small quantity for someone seriously trying to taste the beer. With so many from which to choose, though, perhaps this is not such a bad thing.

Above: Coors once launched an effective advertising campaign based on the water from the Rocky Mountains.

Right: The Great American Beer Festival draws thousands to Denver every year, usually selling out months in advance.

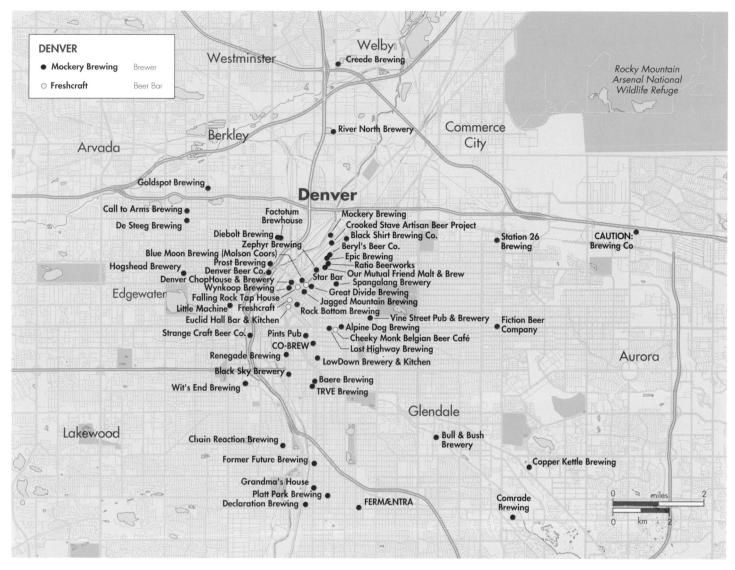

DENVER

● Mockery Brewing   Brewer
○ Freshcraft   Beer Bar

Westminster

Welby
Creede Brewing

Rocky Mountain
Arsenal National
Wildlife Refuge

Berkley

Arvada

River North Brewery

Commerce
City

Goldspot Brewing

Denver

Call to Arms Brewing
De Steeg Brewing

Mockery Brewing
Crooked Stave Artisan Beer Project
Black Shirt Brewing Co.

Station 26
Brewing

CAUTION:
Brewing Co

Factotum
Brewhouse
Diebolt Brewing
Zephyr Brewing
Blue Moon Brewing (Molson Coors)
Hogshead Brewery
Prost Brewing
Denver Beer Co.
Denver ChopHouse & Brewery
Wynkoop Brewing
Falling Rock Tap House
Little Machine
Freshcraft
Euclid Hall Bar & Kitchen
Strange Craft Beer Co.
Pints Pub
CO-BREW
Renegade Brewing
Black Sky Brewery
Wit's End Brewing

Beryl's Beer Co.
Epic Brewing
Ratio Beerworks
Our Mutual Friend Malt & Brew
Star Bar
Spangalang Brewery
Great Divide Brewing
Jagged Mountain Brewing
Rock Bottom Brewing
Vine Street Pub & Brewery
Alpine Dog Brewing
Cheeky Monk Belgian Beer Café
Lost Highway Brewing
LowDown Brewery & Kitchen

Fiction Beer
Company

Edgewater

Aurora

Baere Brewing
TRVE Brewing

Glendale

Lakewood

Chain Reaction Brewing

Bull & Bush
Brewery

Former Future Brewing

Copper Kettle Brewing

Grandma's House
Platt Park Brewing
Declaration Brewing

FERMÆNTRA

Comrade
Brewing

0   miles   2
0   km   2

DENVER'S BREWERIES ▲

Other cities may boast more breweries, both in total
and on a per capita basis, but Denver is the only
American city that can brag about a craft brewery
owner going on to become governor.

FOR THE TRIP

- Beer bars and brewpubs in the USA vary widely, from screen-festooned sports bars to casual but upmarket venues with white tablecloths. When planning a visit, first read some reviews online so that you know what you're getting into.
- Unless you are stationed at the bar, ordering is normally directed through the waiter.
- While most establishments will place the emphasis on their draft taps, don't overlook the bottled beer menus, which may list much-sought-after rarities.
- As most serious beer destinations hire people who are enthusiastic about beer, discovering a great beer you have never heard of can be as simple as asking the bartender for advice. Do not be dissuaded from this course simply because you find yourself in a chain bar, as many such operations have effective training programs for their staff.

Above: The Brewers Association is the voice
of craft brewing in the USA.

The Midwest & Great Lakes

The Midwest was once America's brewing heartland. Immortalized in song and story, Milwaukee was its capital, home at one time or another to such celebrated breweries as Schlitz and Blatz, Pabst and Heileman, and—still standing today—Miller.

Farther south, the brewing anchor was provided by St. Louis, Missouri, in which were rooted Falstaff, Anheuser-Busch, and the latter's fierce rivals, the Griesedieck Brothers. Cincinnati laid claim to Hudepohl-Schoenling, while St. Paul, Minnesota, had Hamm's, and Detroit, Michigan, boasted the "fire-brewed" flavor of Stroh.

Over time, of course, that list shrank, as brewery after brewery was absorbed by larger and stronger competitors, until eventually all that was left were the foreign-owned conglomerates AB InBev and SABMiller, since merged into one entity with the old Miller side spun off to Molson Coors. Also a survivor is Pabst, although it has done so as a brewing company without a brewery, instead having all of its beer brewed under contract by others, largely Miller breweries.

Then modern craft brewing arrived, and with it, a Midwestern brewing revival.

Phase one of the craft brewing renaissance started slowly, with breweries

Below: Motor City, Detroit, appears to be on the cusp of a comeback following years of hard times—and craft beer is there to toast its recovery.

ST. LOUIS' BREWERIES ►
A surge in brewery openings since the start of the twenty-first century has seen St. Louis returned to its former status as a major Midwestern brewing center.

THE TRADITION OF MIDWESTERN LAGERS

When American craft breweries—widely referred to as "microbreweries"—first began appearing in force over the last two decades of the twentieth century, the styles they chose for their beers were almost uniformly ales: pale ales, brown ales, blonde ales, IPAs, and so on. A lager was rarely seen, much less a pale lager, because the breweries sought to disassociate themselves from the utterly dominant big breweries that produced pale lagers exclusively.

There were exceptions, of course. Boston Beer's Samuel Adams Boston Lager and Brooklyn Lager from the Brooklyn Brewery were the most notable, along with lesser-known but impressive bottom-fermented jewels from the likes of Stoudts

Brewing Company in Pennsylvania, Full Sail Brewing in Oregon, and the now-defunct Baltimore Brewing Company.

The one region that countered this always-ale trend, however, was and remains the Midwest. From Madison, Wisconsin, to St. Louis, Missouri, the area that was once the heartland of early American brewing refused to turn its collective back on its bottom-fermented heritage, resulting in some of the finest lagers of the American craft beer renaissance.

In Middleton, Wisconsin, the 30-year-old Capital Brewery built its success largely on the back of lagers like the just off-dry Pilsner and the honeyish

springtime blonde Doppelbock. Cleveland's Great Lakes Brewing Company, another early entry, has long offered an exceptional Dortmunder Gold Lager and the sweet-to-bitter Eliot Ness Amber Lager. Newer Missouri operations like the Kansas City Bier Company and Urban Chestnut Brewing Company in St. Louis both specialize in lagers that wear their German heritage on their sleeves. Milwaukee's Sprecher Brewing is noted for its Black Bavarian: the picture of balance in a black lager.

And those are just a few of a sizable number of lagers from the American heartland, a number that continues to grow with each passing year. Proof that while Midwesterners enjoy a porter or IPA as

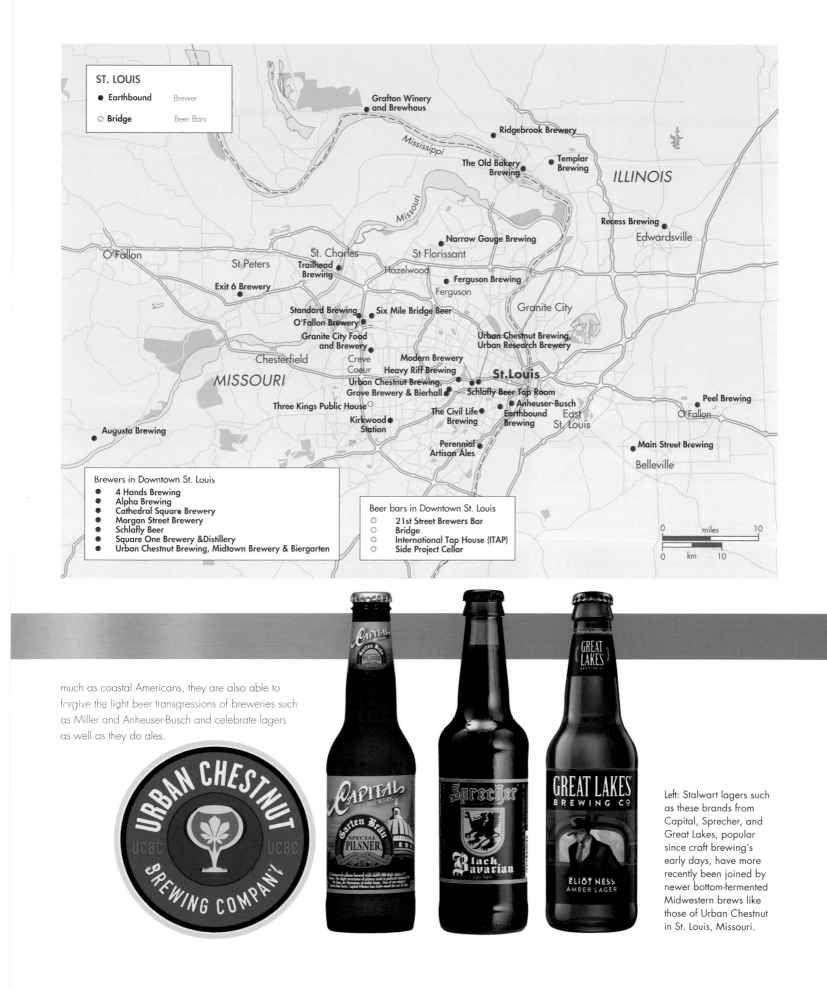

ST. LOUIS

● **Earthbound**   Brewer

○ **Bridge**   Beer Bars

Grafton Winery and Brewhaus

Ridgebrook Brewery

The Old Bakery Brewing

Templar Brewing

Mississippi

ILLINOIS

Missouri

Recess Brewing

Edwardsville

Narrow Gauge Brewing

O'Fallon

St Peters

St. Charles

Trailhead Brewing

St Florissant

Hazelwood

Ferguson Brewing

Ferguson

Exit 6 Brewery

Standard Brewing

Six Mile Bridge Beer

Granite City

O'Fallon Brewery

Granite City Food and Brewery

Urban Chestnut Brewing, Urban Research Brewery

Chesterfield

Creve Coeur

Modern Brewery

Heavy Riff Brewing

St.Louis

MISSOURI

Urban Chestnut Brewing, Grove Brewery & Bierhall

Schlafly Beer Tap Room

Peel Brewing

Three Kings Public House ○

Anheuser-Busch

The Civil Life Brewing

Earthbound Brewing

East St. Louis

O'Fallon

Kirkwood Station

Augusta Brewing

Perennial Artisan Ales

Main Street Brewing

Belleville

Brewers in Downtown St. Louis

- 4 Hands Brewing
- Alpha Brewing
- Cathedral Square Brewery
- Morgan Street Brewery
- Schlafly Beer
- Square One Brewery & Distillery
- Urban Chestnut Brewing, Midtown Brewery & Biergarten

Beer bars in Downtown St. Louis

○ 21st Street Brewers Bar
○ Bridge
○ International Tap House (ITAP)
○ Side Project Cellar

0   miles   10

0   km   10

much as coastal Americans, they are also able to forgive the light beer transgressions of breweries such as Miller and Anheuser-Busch and celebrate lagers as well as they do ales.

Left: Stalwart lagers such as these brands from Capital, Sprecher, and Great Lakes, popular since craft brewing's early days, have more recently been joined by newer bottom-fermented Midwestern brews like those of Urban Chestnut in St. Louis, Missouri.

The Northeast

Being the birthplace of the USA, it is inevitable that the Northeast would hold a considerable amount of brewing history within its borders. George Washington brewed here, or at least we think he did, as did Thomas Jefferson, or at least his wife, Martha. The oldest operating brewery in the country, Yuengling, still also stands proudly in Pottsville, Pennsylvania.

Somewhere along the line, however, New England and the mid-Atlantic states were marginalized where beer and brewing were concerned. Sure, Ballantine had some outstanding years in New York and New Jersey, as did Narragansett in Rhode Island and Rheingold in New York. But as the brewing industry became more of a national concern, it also grew increasingly centralized, not in the Northeast but in the industrial and increasingly German-influenced Midwest. Until, that is, the Boston Beer Company came along (*see* pp.184–5).

While Jim Koch's company was not the first craft brewery to bloom in the Northeast—it was beaten to the punch by the since-closed Newman Brewing Company in Albany, New York, and a small handful of others—it certainly became the most significant over time.

PHILADELPHIA'S BREWERIES ►
Although perhaps better known among beer aficionados for such outstanding beer bars as Monk's Café and the Standard Tap, Philadelphia has also quietly evolved into a first-rate brewing city.

Left: Portland, Maine, just minutes from picturesque Cape Elizabeth (pictured), has become one of the Northeast's most interesting cities for craft beer.

ONES TO WATCH

As the American craft brewing movement continues to grow and thrive, certain young but notable breweries are rising to the top of the ranks, proving themselves possible heirs to many of the icons denoted on p.178. Here are 18 breweries worth watching.

- Bluejacket Brewery, Washington, D.C.
- Central Standard Brewing, Wichita, Kansas
- Community Beer Company, Dallas, Texas
- Community Beer Works, Buffalo, New York
- Crooked Stave Artisan Beer Project, Denver, Colorado
- Crux Fermentation Project, Bend, Oregon
- Hill Farmstead Brewery, Greensboro, Vermont
- Jack's Abbey, Framingham, Massachusetts
- Kansas City Bier, Kansas City, Missouri

- La Cumbre Brewing Company, Albuquerque, New Mexico
- Lift Bridge Brewing, Stillwater, Minnesota
- Maine Beer Company, Freeport, Maine
- Perennial Artisan Ales, St. Louis, Missouri
- Prairie Artisan Ales, Tulsa, Oklahoma
- Silva Brewing, Paso Robles, California
- Societe Brewing Company, San Diego, California
- Wicked Weed Brewing, Asheville, North Carolina
- Wiseacre Brewing, Memphis, Tennessee

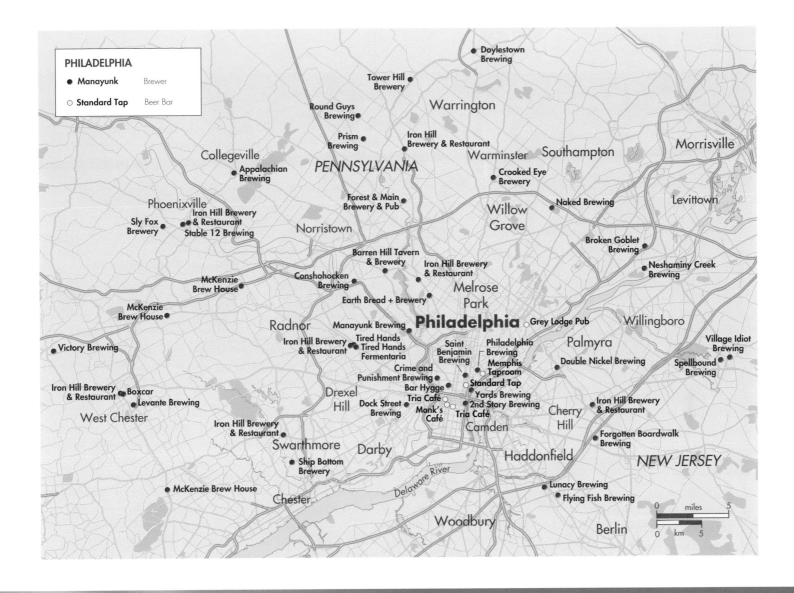

PHILADELPHIA

● Manayunk   Brewer

○ Standard Tap   Beer Bar

Doylestown Brewing

Tower Hill Brewery

Round Guys Brewing

Warrington

Morrisville

Collegeville

Prism Brewing

Iron Hill Brewery & Restaurant

Warminster

Southampton

PENNSYLVANIA

Appalachian Brewing

Crooked Eye Brewery

Levittown

Phoenixville

Forest & Main Brewery & Pub

Willow Grove

Naked Brewing

Sly Fox Brewery

Iron Hill Brewery & Restaurant

Stable 12 Brewing

Norristown

Broken Goblet Brewing

McKenzie Brew House

Barren Hill Tavern & Brewery

Conshohocken Brewing

Iron Hill Brewery & Restaurant

Neshaminy Creek Brewing

McKenzie Brew House

Earth Bread + Brewery

Melrose Park

Philadelphia

Grey Lodge Pub

Willingboro

Radnor

Manayunk Brewing

Tired Hands

Saint Benjamin Brewing

Philadelphia Brewing

Palmyra

Village Idiot Brewing

Victory Brewing

Iron Hill Brewery & Restaurant

Tired Hands Fermentaria

Crime and Punishment Brewing

Memphis Taproom

Double Nickel Brewing

Spellbound Brewing

Iron Hill Brewery & Restaurant

Boxcar

Levante Brewing

Drexel Hill

Bar Hygge

Tria Café

Standard Tap

Yards Brewing

2nd Story Brewing

Iron Hill Brewery & Restaurant

West Chester

Dock Street Brewing

Monk's Café

Tria Café

Cherry Hill

Iron Hill Brewery & Restaurant

Camden

Forgotten Boardwalk Brewing

Swarthmore

Darby

Haddonfield

NEW JERSEY

Ship Bottom Brewery

Delaware River

Lunacy Brewing

Flying Fish Brewing

miles 0–5

McKenzie Brew House

Chester

km 0–5

Woodbury

Berlin

Opposite and above: Northwestern craft beer veteran Larry Sidor designed Crux Fermentation Project in Bend, Oregon, to explore the experimental side of brewing.

Right: Societe Brewing brews beers in styles from straight-up hoppy ales to tart brews aged in wine barrels and delivers them all at their San Diego tasting room.

The South

For any number of varied reasons—economic, cultural, historic, and legislative—the South lagged badly for years in the development of its craft brewing industry. With few exceptions, notably the Spoetzl Brewery in Texas, there was no great tradition of brewing in the region, and the hot weather often experienced in the southern states tends to have people reaching for ice-cold and light-bodied lagers: precisely the sort of beer the major breweries specialize in.

Above: Not all breweries make it. Some, like Nashville, Tennessee's Market Street Brewery, succumb to commercial pressures but leave their trademark behind.

What might have played the biggest role in the suppression of southern craft brewing was the web of odd and arcane regional laws that governed states from North Carolina to Texas. Regulations capping the percentage of alcohol allowed in beer were relatively commonplace, for example, and one of the most bizarre alcohol laws must have been that which once required all bottles of beer sold in Florida to have the letters "FL" inscribed on the side of their caps.

As those laws fell by the wayside, prosperity arrived in the South, and craft beer boomed. Led by North Carolina,

RALEIGH-DURHAM'S BREWERIES ►
The area known as "The Triangle," loosely bound by Raleigh, Durham, and Chapel Hill, is home to a diverse mix of breweries and beer destinations.

ASHEVILLE: THE UNEXPECTED BEER CITY

In early 2012, California's Sierra Nevada Brewing Company announced plans to build a new facility in Asheville, North Carolina. A lot of people connected to the US brewing industry responded, "Where?" The small city at the foot of the Smoky Mountains was not exactly shining brightly on the craft beer radar.

It is now. Since that day in January, Asheville has blossomed as a beer destination, attracting investment also from New Belgium and, outside town in nearby Brevard, the Oskar Blues Brewery. This comes in addition to roughly 30 local area breweries, including some, such as Wicked Weed and Green Man, that number among the most admired in the region. Best of all for visitors, a great many local breweries may be visited on foot.

Water quality and abundance have something to do with Asheville's popularity among brewers, as does access to major north–south and east–west transportation routes. But a lot has to do with quality of life, the community of brewers, and a general passion for beer among the local citizenry. All of which have made Asheville a beer city that is as praiseworthy as it is unexpected.

Right: When California's craft beer icon, Sierra Nevada Brewing, decided to build a brewery in Asheville, the industry took notice.

Opposite left: The Asheville Beer Festival brings almost all of the region's breweries together.

Opposite right: The opening of the Sierra Nevada Taproom was a great boon to the growth of Asheville's now-burgeoning beer tourism industry.

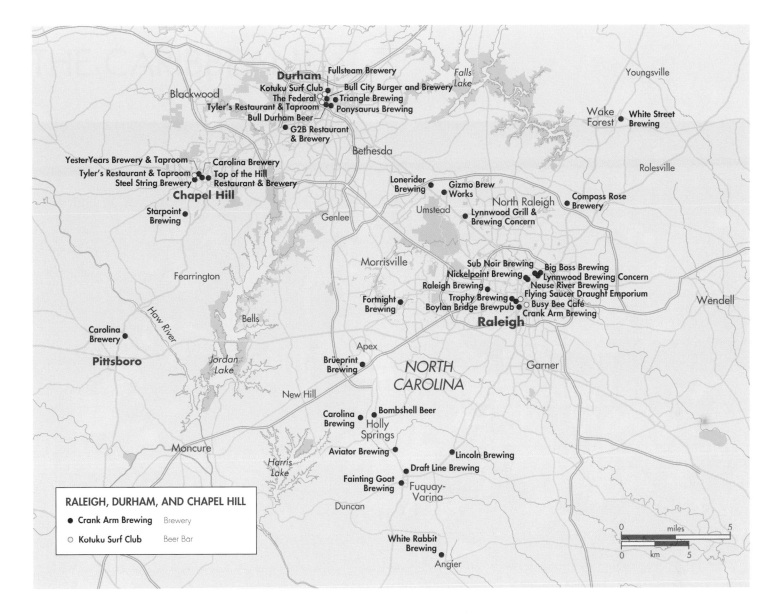

RALEIGH, DURHAM, AND CHAPEL HILL

● Crank Arm Brewing   Brewery
○ Kotuku Surf Club   Beer Bar

CANADA

Canada's iconic twentieth-century prime minister Pierre Trudeau famously promoted the "cultural mosaic" to define his model of Canada, providing contrast to the "melting pot" approach of the USA. He could equally have been describing his nation's history of brewing.

The primary influences on brewing in Canada were first British and then, with westward expansion, German, augmented by twentieth-century Belgian success in Québec. With increased influences from the USA and elsewhere, plus the mingling of cultures and rise of an indigenous approach to brewing in French Canada, the map is becoming much more complicated.

Beer drinkers born near the middle of the last century will recall when the great national beer divide was Toronto's central Yonge Street, to the east of which, it was said, citizens drank predominantly ales, while lagers held sway to the west. It was a theory with some validity, since the ale-centric British and French immigrant cultures could be found largely in eastern Ontario, Québec, and the Atlantic provinces, while the Germans and Eastern Europeans, who favored lagers, led the county's westward expansion.

Since the dawn of craft brewing in the 1980s, a similar though more complex divide has continued to define beer in Canada,

albeit based less on immigration patterns than on regional cultures. In the Atlantic provinces of Nova Scotia, New Brunswick, Prince Edward Island, and Newfoundland, where hospitability is held in high esteem and beer drinking is arguably more of a purely social act than anywhere else in Canada, "sessionable" English and Irish beer styles—those with a lower-alcohol content—have long held sway. From Halifax to St. John's, pale ales and best bitters, porters and stouts dominate, the arrival of higher-alcohol contents, elevated hopping rates, and unconventional styles being but a recent development.

Travel westward to Québec, and the French embrace of gastronomy and *joie de vivre*, coupled with a small brewery-friendly taxation policy, have resulted in what has until very recently stood as the country's most innovative brewing culture. Beer aficionados in search of oddball ingredients, mixed fermentations, and barrel aging, all frequently employed to

BREWERY CONCENTRATION IN CANADA ▶
Groupings of breweries in Canada largely reflect where the major populations are based, with majorities concentrated in Ontario and Québec.

delectable results, are advised to begin in Montréal and circle outward from there.

Canada's most populous province, Ontario, for many years boasted the nation's most firmly conservative traditions, save perhaps for much smaller Alberta and slow-to-develop regions like Newfoundland and Manitoba. This has resulted in a craft-brewing market in which the dominant styles have, until very recently, been European standards from Bavarian *Weissbier* to Bohemian pilsner and northern English brown ale. More unusual efforts, from strongly hopped, US-influenced double IPAs to ales fermented with *Brettanomyces* and *Doppelbocks* conditioned in bourbon barrels, are generally newer creations of sometimes less predictable quality and consistency.

Saskatchewan boasts the country's greatest per capita number of brewpubs. This is due to legislation allowing packaged beer sales on site and has resulted in a slew of generally mediocre beers, although this is now changing. Elsewhere on the Prairies, a methodical, practical approach to brewing has resulted, with a few notable exceptions, in generally solid though unexciting beers from Manitoba to the Rockies.

Finally, in British Columbia, a long-lasting loyalty to British brewing traditions is finally giving way to influence from the province's "Cascadian" neighbors to the south, manifesting in a new generation of boundary-stretching beers from highly hopped and potent IPAs to a miasma of seasonal specialties. Although brewing continues to be concentrated in the population centers of greater Vancouver and the capital region, a surprising number of breweries is now appearing in areas far more remote, such as upper Vancouver Island and the Kootenays.

Opposite: There are strong genealogical and emotional ties between Scotland and Nova Scotia and ample Celtic influence in many of the province's craft ales.

Right: The O'Keefe name now belongs to MolsonCoors, although the Pilsner Lager and Special Extra Mild Ale are but distant memories.

Breweries per Province

	Fewer than 5
	5–20
	20–30
	30–125
	125–150
	150 or more
MANITOBA 4	Province with number of breweries

ARCTIC OCEAN

YUKON 2

NORTHWEST TERRITORIES 1

NUNAVUT 0

BRITISH COLUMBIA 125

ALBERTA 32

SASKATCHEWAN 18

Vancouver

ONTARIO 168

QUÉBEC 145

NEWFOUNDLAND AND LABRADOR 3

NEW BRUNSWICK 26

PRINCE EDWARD ISLAND 5

NOVA SCOTIA 30

Québec

Montréal

OTTAWA

Toronto

miles 500

km 500

AMERICA

ATLANTIC OCEAN

O'Keefe's

PILSENER LAGER SPECIAL EXTRA MILD ALE

Ontario & the Prairies

With the onslaught of operations that have opened since the start of the new millennium, the craft breweries of central Canada are finally beginning to shed their conservative, Eurocentric approach to beer making. But oh, what a long road it has been!

Without exception, all of Ontario's first-generation craft breweries began with beers firmly founded on the traditions of the British Isles, Czechia, or Germany. These habits persisted with little variation through the second generation of breweries and into the new millennium, and when they finally began to give way to innovation and experimentation, most of the initial results left a considerable amount to be desired.

In Manitoba and Saskatchewan, meanwhile, with few exceptions, early craft breweries operated in a climate of disinterest and general apathy, resulting in a number of failures, and even more lamentable brewpubs operated mainly for the lucrative beer store license that accompanied their brewing permit.

On a cheerier note, Ontario, Manitoba, and Saskatchewan today offer a patchwork of brewing styles that combines the practical traditionalism of brewery flagships like the pale ale and nut

brown of Toronto's Black Oak, the *Kölsch*-style Lug Tread of eastern Ontario's Beau's All-Natural Brewing Company, and the Czech Mate Pilsner of Saskatoon's Paddock Wood Brewing Company, with the increasingly commonplace adventurism of breweries such as Toronto's Bellwoods and Great Lakes, Niagara's High Road, and Regina's Rebellion Brewing.

With an estimated brewery count of well in excess of 150 in Ontario in 2016, a few dozen more in relatively sparsely populated Saskatchewan and four active and several more planned for Manitoba, it would seem that the future for middle Canadian craft brewing is indeed quite bright.

Right: Like many North American brewpubs, Toronto's Granite Brewery offers tasting flights of all its beers.

TORONTO'S BREWERIES ►
As little as 15 years ago, a brewery crawl of Canada's largest city would have been a short trip. Recent years, however, have seen rapidly accelerated growth.

THE BEER BARS OF TORONTO

While brewing has recently returned in force to Toronto, the greatest craft beer strength of the city still resides in its beer bars, a tour of which will satisfy even the most particular of beer aficionados.

Depending upon who you ask, the best beer bar in the city is either Bar Volo on Yonge Street, home to dozens of kegs, casks, and bottles of often hard-to-find beers (and also the tiny House Ales brewery), or King Street's Bar Hop, with 37 taps complemented by a studious selection of bottled brews. The latter has a second location just up John Street, a ten-minute walk away.

Other contenders, each impressive in its own right, include: C'est What on Front Street, the elder

statesman of Toronto beer bars; Craft Brasserie & Grill, a newcomer in Liberty Village; the Germanic beer hall, Wvrst, on King Street, not far from Bar Hop; Trinity Common, another recent arrival on the scene, in Kensington Market; the beer cuisine restaurant and bar, beer-bistro, at the intersection of King and Yonge streets; three locations of the beer-centric chain the Bier Markt; The Loose Moose, across from the Convention Centre; and Danforth Avenue perennial The Only Café.

Coupled with over a dozen brewpubs and brewery tasting rooms, this wealth of beer destinations makes it difficult to go thirsty in Canada's largest city.

Above: Bar Volo is one of Toronto's best beer destinations.

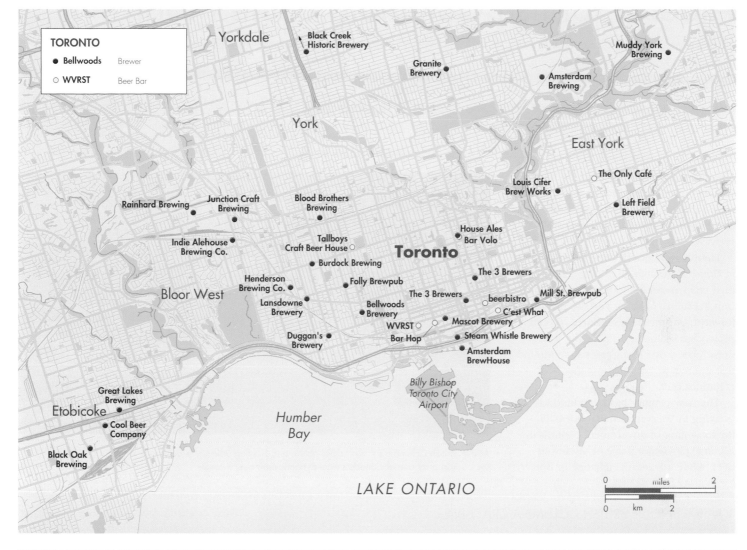

TORONTO
● Bellwoods   Brewer
○ WVRST   Beer Bar

Yorkdale

Black Creek
Historic Brewery

Muddy York
Brewing

Granite
Brewery

Amsterdam
Brewing

York

East York

The Only Café

Louis Cifer
Brew Works

Left Field
Brewery

Rainhard Brewing

Junction Craft
Brewing

Blood Brothers
Brewing

House Ales
Bar Volo

Indie Alehouse
Brewing Co.

Tallboys
Craft Beer House

Toronto

Burdock Brewing

The 3 Brewers

Bloor West

Henderson
Brewing Co.

Folly Brewpub

The 3 Brewers

beerbistro

Mill St. Brewpub

Lansdowne
Brewery

Bellwoods
Brewery

C'est What

WVRST

Mascot Brewery

Bar Hop

Duggan's
Brewery

Steam Whistle Brewery

Amsterdam
BrewHouse

Billy Bishop
Toronto City
Airport

Great Lakes
Brewing

Etobicoke

Cool Beer
Company

Humber
Bay

Black Oak
Brewing

LAKE ONTARIO

0   miles   2

0   km   2

Above: Grain elevators like this one in Saskatchewan are familiar sights on the Canadian Prairies, processing up to about 2 million tons of malting barley per year.

LATIN AMERICA

Along with much of Asia, Latin America came late to the modern good beer movement, arriving in force only around the time that the first edition of this book was published. Since then, however, large parts of the territory have been making up for lost time in a considerable hurry.

Leading the charge has been Brazil, the biggest and most populous nation of Latin America and also the one that gave birth to the South American brewing giant known as Ambev, which grew and grew before ultimately merging into the international colossus known as AB InBev. Led by a strong Germanic heritage and ample curiosity, Brazilian craft brewers have countered the megabrewery's progressively blander take on lager with beers of ever-growing substance and style, even establishing their own uniquely Brazilian take on craft beer.

Second to Brazil is the craft brewing industry of Mexico, which, over a remarkably short time, battled against the duopoly of AB InBev–owned Modelo and Heineken-owned FEMSA Cerveza to establish itself a legitimate and credible alternative. So great has been its advance that 2015 saw not just a beer festival and competition held in the capital but a well-organized craft beer conference.

Next in line come Argentina and Chile, followed by Colombia and Costa Rica, and then a mix of hopeful craft beer

development in places like Nicaragua, Uruguay, and Paraguay.

The road ahead is steep and fraught with peril—the big breweries still enjoy over 99 percent market share throughout Latin America and, as it remains a growth market for them, are loathe to cede sales to other newcomers. But the continent's craft brewers can hardly be faulted for lack of enthusiasm, dedication, and, in some instances, sheer nerve.

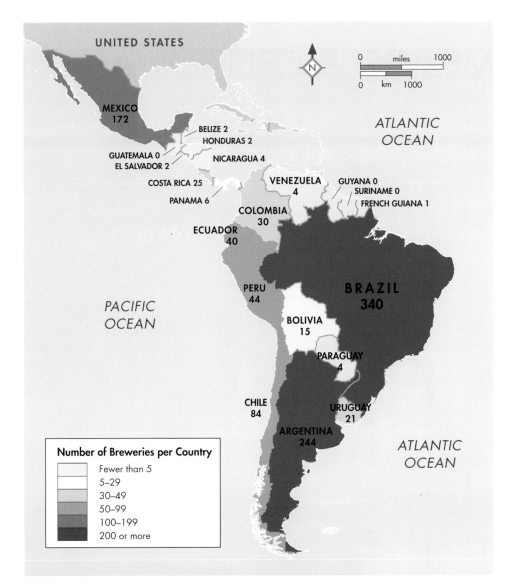

Number of Breweries per Country

- Fewer than 5
- 5–29
- 30–49
- 50–99
- 100–199
- 200 or more

CRAFT BREWING IN LATIN AMERICA ▶
After a slow start, craft brewing has now arrived in most Latin American nations and is experiencing rapid growth in the vast majority of the places where it has taken hold.

Opposite: Bottling remains very much a hands-on process at the Szot brewery in Santiago, Chile. Along with neighboring Argentina and Brazil, Chile is poised for great craft-beer growth in the coming years.

Left: Tequila is the traditional drink of Mexico, but sometimes it must take second place to the refreshing nature of a cold beer.

BRAZIL

Brazil is the third-largest beer-producing nation in the world, after China and the USA. It is also one of the rare places where both production and consumption have continued to increase in recent decades, the former growing by 158 million gallons between 2013 and 2014.

The bulk of this production, however, is of pale and bland lager designed to be served at ice-cold temperature, the creation of which has been perfected by AB InBev, which controls over two-thirds of the market. Of the remainder, the bulk belongs to Brasil Kirin and Heineken-owned Kaiser, with but a tiny portion left for the country's craft brewers.

That said, even a minute portion of a massive market is worth fighting for, which is exactly what the estimated 340 or more Brazilian craft breweries are doing. Having seen some of their number sell to the larger concerns—Eisenbahn went early to what is now Brasil Kirin, followed more recently by Wäls and the pioneering Cervejaria Colorado, both

to AB InBev—the craft segment seems emboldened rather than cowed and is growing rapidly not just in number but also quality and consistency.

Challenges, of course, remain. The country lacks a cold chain of distribution, meaning that beer remains at warm or, during summer, quite hot temperature from brewery to consumer. An affinity for rather crude pasteurization techniques persists among some breweries, although that is changing. And further, as with all youthful craft beer cultures, there is a tendency to run before being able to walk when it comes to beer styles and brewing techniques.

On the positive side, brewing schools and institutes are well-attended (we

Above: The coastline of Rio de Janeiro. Spurred by a growing middle class, craft beer is poised to take off in the cities and towns of Brazil.

Left: These beer-drinking Brazilian farmers trace their ancestry to Germany's Baltic coast.

particularly admire the Instituto da Cerveja in São Paulo) and the availability of craft beer in major cities is becoming much more prevalent than it was even a few years ago.

Most common among Brazilian craft brews remains the pilsner, which may denote anything from a mild-mannered *Helles*-style lager intended to wean drinkers off Brahma and Antarctica to a strongly hopped, Czech-, or German-influenced refresher. Also popular are pale ales and IPAs, the hoppiness of which seems to suffer from the expense and scarcity of quality hops, and various, sometimes quite loose, interpretations of Belgian styles.

Without doubt, the trend most encouraging in Brazil is the use of indigenous ingredients in the creation of beers loosely based on traditional styles. Included in this mix are breweries such as Cervejaria Colorado, which makes use of everything from local coffee to the hard sugar known as *rapadura*, and beers like Cervejaria Way's Amburana Lager, aged in exotic Amazonian wood, Falke Bier's limited edition Vivre pour Vivre,

ARGENTINA & THE REST OF SOUTH AMERICA

After the Argentine economy went into meltdown in 1989 and the peso had to be replaced for trading purposes by the US dollar, a new government determined to encourage entrepreneurs. There followed an explosion of microbreweries, which have come and gone with dizzying frequency ever since, although some are now well into their second decade.

Above: The garden patio at the Berlina pub brewery provides breathtaking views of the Andes to accompany its India pale ale, authentically hopped with imported East Kent Goldings.

Since 2002, at any one time there have been between 75 and 250 craft breweries extant in Argentina, with a couple of dozen consistently found around Bariloche and the hop-growing region of El Bolsón, in the spectacularly beautiful Lake District of northern Patagonia.

The further development of hop cultivation could bode well for the future of craft brewing, although Argentina's hop farms were originally created to supply those large South American breweries that eventually agglomerated to become the AmBev brewing group, the leading lights of which provide a driving force within the world's largest brewing group, AB InBev.

The varieties historically grown are regarded by many northern hemisphere brewers as of inferior quality and woefully lacking in aromatics. Argentine Cascade, for example, rather than being fresh and citrus-spicy, is herbaceous and subtle, unsuited to

THE HOPS PROBLEM IN CHILE

It doesn't take a lot of beer-drinking in Santiago to recognize a flavor profile that seems to cut across different brands and even different breweries. That flavor is old hops.

It is an all too familiar problem to Chilean brewers. Many will complain that it takes too long for American hops to make their way from the USA's Pacific Northwest all the way down the Pacific coast and that the fragile plant is not at all well treated en route. Three-week travel times in unrefrigerated cargo holds are cited, as is warehousing under equally detrimental conditions.

If Argentine hop growers develop better, craft beer–friendly hop varieties, as we predict will

eventually happen, that will go a long way toward advancing the quality of Chilean craft beer, of course. Otherwise, brewers must hope and petition for refrigerated shipping and shorter travel times—or grow used to the taste of stale hops.

Right: Whether shipped in pelletized or whole cone form, the flavors of hops can suffer when subjected to difficult conditions, such as prolonged exposure to hot temperatures.

Opposite top: Even in the face of the country's recent economic challenges, the Antares chain of brewpubs continues to draw crowds and expand to new locations.

creating American-style pale ales and IPAs. However, new hybrids, suited to the soil and climate, are being cultivated that should assist in the growth of those styles and others like them.

Meanwhile, the roller coaster that is the Argentinian economy has not exactly paved the way for the nation's craft breweries, although some, such as the 25-outlet Cervecería Antares chain, have managed to thrive despite the difficulties. Others beating the odds include Buller and Buena Birra Social Club in Buenos Aires, Berlina and Jerome in the west, and the Fuegian Beverage Co., makers of Beagle and Cape Horn beers, the world's southernmost brewery in Ushuaia.

After Argentina, the next most advanced is Chile, where Santiago has become established as the hub of the nation's craft brewing community. Dominated by a handful of older, familiar names, Szot, Kross, and Tübinger among them, Chile's second wave of breweries shows much promise if they can manage to overcome several obstacles, chief among them the quality of the hops available to them (see opposite).

Next in the Latin American hierarchy come Peru, Ecuador, and Colombia, where the leading light Bogota Beer

Company was purchased by AB InBev not long before their tie up with SABMiller. Bolivia and Uruguay are making tentative steps forward, and elsewhere the building blocks of the future are in place. Home brewers, always vital to the development of new craft beer cultures, are active throughout the continent, particularly in the capital city regions.

Hurdles remain to be overcome. The absence of a so-called "cold chain," for instance, in which beer is kept refrigerated during the entirety of its journey from brewery to consumer—essential in hot weather—results in the overuse of pasteurization. Equally, the lack of experience in many breweries leads to far too many technically flawed examples of the brewing arts.

Competition should also speed the beer education of producers and consumers alike. Both The Great South Beer Cup in Buenos Aires and the Concurso Internacional de Cervezas en Chile have, since 2011, challenged professional brewers in the rest of South America to overturn the craft beer hegemony of the Brazilians, and soon they might do just that.

If consumers increasingly demand characterful beer, as they appear to be doing with growing regularity, it will be

up to the brewers to supply it. And if the south follows the lead of the north, there could be a considerable amount of catch-up going on throughout Latin America in the very near future.

Above: Starting life as a sort of brewpub speakeasy, the Buena Birra Social Club is among the must-see beer destinations in Buenos Aires.

Overleaf: Chilean gauchos ride up a thirst, with the Cuernos del Paine mountains in the backdrop.

AUSTRALASIA & ASIA

The global renaissance of flavorful beer over the last half century or so may be tracked from a handful of centers—the United States, Great Britain, and Belgium, mainly—radiating slowly outward toward northern, western, and central Europe and up and down the Americas. The western Pacific Rim, with its great distance from these western heartlands, was slower to take up the cause than were these other, more proximate regions.

New Zealand and Japan were first to embrace the crusade, with the former stumbling badly at the outset and the latter embracing craft beer with boundless enthusiasm once legislative constraints were lifted, followed by Australia and, in lesser degree, elsewhere.

Since about 2010, however, there has been a blossoming of brewing interest in the East and Oceania, with even the pariah state of North Korea now claiming some small breweries—not that we have had the chance to visit in person. We note in particular the unfettered growth that has occurred in Australia and New Zealand, the sensible development of the Japanese market, and the rapidly emerging potential of Vietnam, South Korea, and, though in equal parts ominous and intriguing, China.

AUSTRALIA

For many years, Australia's contribution to the world of beer was limited to Foster's Lager and, for those with a bit more insider knowledge, Castlemaine XXXX and Victoria Bitter, better known as VB. Beer aficionados admired the remarkable staying power of the family-owned Coopers Brewery and, more recently, the rise of Little Creatures, but beyond that there was little.

Since the publication of the first edition of this book, that situation has changed dramatically, beginning with the Galaxy hop, which now threatens to do for Australian beer what the Shiraz grape did for Australian wine.

Australia came relatively late to the global expansion in craft brewing, to the point that Lion Nathan, now owned by the Japanese brewers Kirin, plus Carlton & United Breweries, part of SAB Miller, supply between them over 90 percent of the beer drunk in a nation that by tradition prefers its beer ice-cold, its brand names familiar, and its advertising campaigns on the wry side.

The oddity is Coopers Brewery of Adelaide, a family-owned firm that for decades produced Australia's only unconventional beers—easily clouded ales that tasted of their yeast and drew scorn from mainstream drinkers, while nurturing the generation that has spearheaded a new brewing scene and running a tidy sideline as home-brewing suppliers. The "little brewery that could" grew by an impressive 8 percent in 2014 and today accounts for a full 4.4 percent of the Aussie beer market, more than the rest of the craft brewing community combined.

It is estimated that there were between 300 and 400 brewing companies operating in Australia in 2015, a number impossible to calculate accurately due to the numerous families of sub-brands developed as spin-offs by existing breweries, as well as an indeterminate number of operations that are breweries in name only, relying on real brewers to create the product. The latter includes entrepreneurs and ambitious amateur brewers who dabble in the industry until it proves profitable, fails wretchedly, or they grow bored.

What threatened to become a brewing movement in the country (but as yet has not) is wineries branching out into brewing. In 2012–13, several wine companies did try their hands at brewing, but few made a lasting impression. It remains to be seen if this trend will raise its head with greater significance in the future.

At the heart of Australian brewing today, and potentially its calling card for the near future, is the Galaxy hop, a variety developed in-country and cited by some as one that helped inspire the term "flavor hop" with its high alpha content and robustly fruity, even pungent character. Though popular among experimentally inclined brewers worldwide, it is, like the

Opposite left: Developed in-country, the Galaxy hop has the potential to become Australian craft brewing's calling card to the world.

Opposite right: The family-owned Coopers Brewery has operated in Adelaide since 1862 and at its Regent Park location since 2001.

Above: The sometimes intense heat Australia experiences fuels the national appetite for ice-cold, thirst-quenching lagers, although other beer styles are now making significant inroads.

unique species grown in neighboring New Zealand, employed best by the brewers of its native land, who have more recently been gifted with two others to play with: Vic Secret and Enigma.

Another of Australia's brewing strengths harks back to the developing days of modern British brewing. As in the early part of the twentieth century in the UK, beer taxation in Australia is based upon alcohol content, a situation which, on the negative side, has discouraged the development of impressive higher-strength beers, such as IPAs of 7% ABV and beyond. On the plus side, however, Australian brewers have become particularly adept at producing beers of 3.8–4.4% ABV, in particular golden ales, beers that mimic *Kölsch*, and so-called English summer ales.

Aside from these lower-strength brews, Australian Galaxy-hopped pale ales and IPAs, and the standard craft beer assemblage of black, brown, and "white" beers, more is happening in Australian brewing. This constitutes what top Australian beer writer Matt Kirkegaard

ISLANDS IN THE SUN

Those who seek an island paradise as a suitable backdrop to their beer need to travel to that part of the western Pacific styled locally as Oceania, though be warned—if the global brewers are planning a fightback, the recent changes in this tropical backwater might mark the first victories of a cunning plan.

The islands of Fiji are down to hosting just one brewery, a boutique lager maker, the Island Brewing Company, while Solomon Islands and Tonga waste craft-sized breweries on making wannabe industrial lagers.

Not far away in Pacific terms, the Cook Islands are now down to the Matutu Brewing Company of Rarotonga, which makes a couple of ales. Farther north on the American dependency of Guam, long-established brewpub Great Deep Brewing has been joined by the Ishii Brewing Company, while the Micronesian island of Yap supports the more hobbylike Stone Money Brewing, matched for its absurdity by the Red Rooster brewery in the tiny island republic of Palau.

Vanuatu had been matching Guam by having a brewpub and a microbrewery, until chummily named Cyclone Pam hit in March 2015. The last online review we can find dates from 2014 and since then we have heard nothing. If either revives, we are going to claim that better made beer is indeed invincible.

Right: Vonu Pure Lager by Island Brewing provides an alternative to the ubiquitous and not-very-bitter Fiji Bitter.

characterizes as "the terrible teens of brewing," referring to a host of *saisons*, *Brettanomyces*-influenced ales, barrel-conditioned beers, and other assorted and unusual styles, which are attempted by many yet mastered by few.

It is our bet that once the teenager matures a bit more—perhaps helped along by a change in taxation law and even better understanding of the local hops—great things might be expected of Australian craft beer.

BREWERIES IN AUSTRALIA ▶

From a small, mainly southern base, craft brewing has spread throughout Australia to all of its six states and two mainland territories.

---

0 miles 500
0 km 500

INDIAN OCEAN

Coral Sea

Darwin ○

NORTHERN TERRITORY
1

Alice Springs ○

QUEENSLAND
29

WESTERN AUSTRALIA
45

SOUTH AUSTRALIA
27

Brisbane ○

NEW SOUTH WALES
69

Perth ○

Adelaide ○

CANBERRA

VICTORIA
74 ○Melbourne

○Sydney

AUSTRALIAN CAPITAL TERRITORY
4

Number of Breweries per State

Fewer than 5	30–50
5–20	50–70
20–30	70 or more

QUEENSLAND   State

TASMANIA
17
○Hobart

Tasman Sea

FOR THE TRIP

- The top reference is Matt Kirkegaard's website Australian Brews News, www.brewsnews.com.au.
- Most Australian beer is served way below tasting temperature.
- With friends, buy rounds of draft beer in 2-pint (1-quart) jugs that serve five pot glasses ("midis" in New South Wales).
- As you go north it gets hotter, so glasses get smaller to prevent the beer from warming up.

Opposite top: Now a subsidiary of Lion Nathan, which is in turn owned by Japan's Kirin, Little Creatures in Western Australia was one of the country's craft beer pioneers.

Left: Hop growing in Australia is mainly centered in Victoria and, pictured here, Tasmania.

NEW ZEALAND

From beery also-ran to rising star to flagging market to poster child for New World craft brewing, New Zealand's recent brewing history has certainly been one of peaks and valleys. Recent years, however, have seen nothing but ascent.

Of the over 60 breweries listed in the 1999 book *Kerry Tyack's Guide to Breweries and Beer in New Zealand*, roughly half had shut down operations a mere decade later. This high rate of attrition, Kiwi brewing insiders suggest, was due in part to the rather mundane offerings of some of the earliest small breweries but also to the country's modest population coupled with its celebrated remoteness and isolation.

With a scant 4.5 million people scattered over two islands stretching roughly 1,250 miles north to south, New Zealanders are not only isolated from the nearest major land mass—Australia is a farther 1,250 miles away—they are also to an extent isolated from each other.

Kiwi brewers, however, have proved themselves equal to this challenge. New Zealand's craft brewing industry has thrived in the second decade of this century, with an estimated 120 to 140 beer companies operating in the country in 2015, split roughly 50/50 between brewers with breweries and contracting beer firms. Furthermore, New Zealanders have figured out a third approach to brewing for their small and scattered audience. This is brewery cohabitation, in which two completely separate brewing companies share a single brew kit: an unorthodox but functional approach that has proved popular in recent years.

Hops remain at the forefront of Kiwi brewing, and no wonder. Absent from the influence of foreign strains or diseases, New Zealand's hop industry has thrived in recent years, notably with organic varieties but also with homegrown variants such as the fruity, tangy Nelson Sauvin, passion fruity Riwaka, and lime-citrus Motueka. It is in these hops that we continue to believe the future of Kiwi craft brewing may well be writ.

The New Zealand pilsner, Czech in approach but made with New Zealand

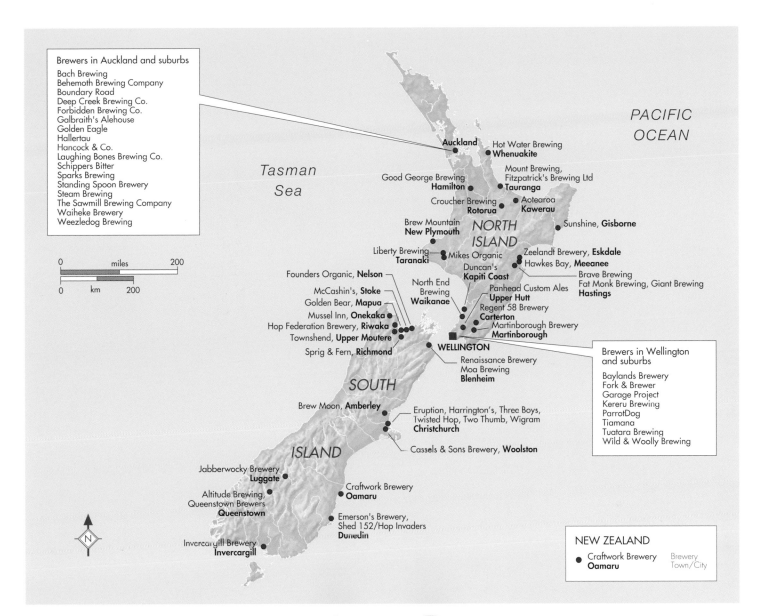

Brewers in Auckland and suburbs

Bach Brewing
Behemoth Brewing Company
Boundary Road
Deep Creek Brewing Co.
Forbidden Brewing Co.
Galbraith's Alehouse
Golden Eagle
Hallertau
Hancock & Co.
Laughing Bones Brewing Co.
Schippers Bitter
Sparks Brewing
Standing Spoon Brewery
Steam Brewing
The Sawmill Brewing Company
Waiheke Brewery
Weezledog Brewing

Tasman Sea

PACIFIC OCEAN

Auckland
Hot Water Brewing
Whenuakite

Good George Brewing
Hamilton
Mount Brewing, Fitzpatrick's Brewing Ltd
Tauranga

Croucher Brewing
Rotorua
Aotearoa
Kawerau

NORTH ISLAND

Brew Mountain
New Plymouth
Sunshine, Gisborne

Liberty Brewing
Taranaki
Mikes Organic
Duncan's
Kapiti Coast
Zeelandt Brewery, Eskdale
Hawkes Bay, Meeanee

Founders Organic, Nelson
North End Brewing
Waikanae
Panhead Custom Ales
Upper Hutt
Brave Brewing
Fat Monk Brewing, Giant Brewing
Hastings

McCashin's, Stoke
Golden Bear, Mapua
Mussel Inn, Onekaka
Hop Federation Brewery, Riwaka
Townshend, Upper Moutere
Sprig & Fern, Richmond
Regent 58 Brewery
Carterton
Martinborough Brewery
Martinborough
WELLINGTON
Renaissance Brewery
Moa Brewing
Blenheim

Brewers in Wellington and suburbs

Baylands Brewery
Fork & Brewer
Garage Project
Kereru Brewing
ParrotDog
Tiamana
Tuatara Brewing
Wild & Woolly Brewing

SOUTH ISLAND

Brew Moon, Amberley

Eruption, Harrington's, Three Boys, Twisted Hop, Two Thumb, Wigram
Christchurch

Cassels & Sons Brewery, Woolston

Jabberwocky Brewery
Luggate

Craftwork Brewery
Oamaru

Altitude Brewing, Queenstown Brewers
Queenstown

Emerson's Brewery, Shed 152/Hop Invaders
Dunedin

Invercargill Brewery
Invercargill

NEW ZEALAND
● Craftwork Brewery   Brewery
  Oamaru   Town/City

miles 0—200
km 0—200

N

hops, was the first local take on beer style, pioneered by the now Kirin-owned Emerson's Brewery. It's New Zealand pale ale that seems set to become the standard-bearer, though, along with New Zealand IPA; both replace the more familiar American varieties with Kiwi hops. Advanced practitioners of both include Tuatara Brewery, Epic Brewing Company, Panhead Custom Ales, mike's Organic Brewery, and Liberty Brewing Company.

When global demand means they can't get supplies of their own country's hops, which happens from time to time, Kiwi brewers have also proved themselves adaptable. While production will simply stop on some hop-dependent brands—an action consumers now understand, says

NEW ZEALAND BREWERIES ▲

Craft breweries have appeared and disappeared with regularity through the three-plus decades of New Zealand craft brewing, although consistent growth has been the rule in recent years.

Opposite top: Richard Emerson, MD and brewer at the Emerson Brewing Company of Dunedin, New Zealand.

Opposite bottom: Expatriate Danish brewer Søren Eriksen was one of the earliest proponents of the use of exclusively New Zealand hops.

Left: Perhaps the first bottled IPA made from 100 percent New Zealand malt and all-Kiwi hops was Hopwired IPA from 8 Wired Brewing, pictured here with the brewery's chardonnay barrel-conditioned Saeson.

local beer writer Neil Miller—the other option is the brewing of nonhoppy styles, like the various barrel-conditioned and otherwise soured ales of breweries such as Hallertau, 8 Wired, and Fork & Brewer, many of which have received generous accolades from international visitors.

In a country where "small batch" simply means that the beer doesn't travel quite as far as it might otherwise, the edge that New Zealand brewers have is the ability to experiment with near-impunity. It is an opportunity they have utilized very much to their advantage in the recent past, and something that might very well spell great things for their future.

Left: Ripples of sand on Pohara Beach at sunset, Golden Bay, South Island, New Zealand.

Right: Filling a growler at Auckland's Hallertau Brewery.

Below left: An early New Zealand contract brewing success story was the Yeastie Boys, who still farm out the production of their beers to breweries such as Renaissance Brewing in Marlborough.

Below right: The Nelson Sauvin hop is so named because it is grown in Nelson and possesses flavor and aroma characteristics similar to those of Sauvignon Blanc grapes.

FOR THE TRIP

- For the best New Zealand brewery and beer bar information, go to www.beertourist.co.nz.
- You can mail order beer within New Zealand from www.beerstore.co.nz.
- Getting served at the bar ahead of someone who arrived before you is a sure-fire way to see easy-going attitudes freeze.

EASTERN ASIA

Those who promote craft beers and the people responsible for steering international brewing groups often have little in common, but they agree on one thing, which is that Eastern Asia, and China in particular, is extremely important to the future of beer, not for what its peoples do now but for how they choose their future.

In Europe, through the traditions of the ages, and across the Americas, for their colonization by Europeans, beer is a part of the cultural furniture. In the countries on the northwestern Pacific Rim and in Southeast Asia, this is not the case. Here, peoples of similar ancestry have acquired beer as an add-on to a Western lifestyle.

There is an attraction to brands by their association to economic and social success, but this largely holds only so long as the West is economically dominant. The rival thread is an attraction to food and drink that have their own character, whether so subtle as to elude some palates or brutal enough to strip the lining off others. The street food of the region tends to make the burger stand look lame.

When the global brewers realized, a couple of decades ago, that they were rapidly heading toward saturation point for their brands in their Western homelands, the game plan became to grow new markets—and the eastern side of Asia was the biggest target.

Yet the game plan did not give proper consideration to what would happen if local people came to like beer for its range of possibilities. We love the fact that for all the emphasis on processed fast blond lagers with designer labeling, even the world's biggest brewers are continuing to supply local markets with strong stout—where does the terroir for that originate?

Above: Tabletop beer dispensers that allow patrons to serve their own "draft" are a common sight in some parts of Asia.

Additionally, many Southeast Asian cultures have their own types of alcohol with which to ease human interaction—and until the last two centuries few of these featured either malted barley or hops. Japan has sake, Indonesia arak, and Laos a rice spirit called Lao.

Right now we reckon the future of beer in the region is up for grabs. Meanwhile the import-export beer merchants of Singapore have our blessing to keep spreading awareness of beer's possibilities in the most practical way of all by sending it to whoever needs it.

Below: Traditional junk in Halong Bay, Vietnam.

JAPAN

Until the last couple of years, imported ales and locally made *ji-biru*, known collectively as "special beers," were niche products accounting for less than 2 percent of the Japanese beer market. However, by playing to the love of new and distinctive flavors, their share has doubled and is growing year on year despite most costing several times the price of ordinary beers.

The traditional drink of Japan is sake, made for over 2,000 years by boiling milled rice and fermenting the extract with pitched yeast. Often referred to as rice wine, for its alcohol content and lack of carbonation, as a fermented grain drink it is closer to beer, a beverage virtually unknown on the Japanese archipelago before the nineteenth century, as neither barley nor wheat grew there.

On July 8, 1853, the experienced US naval commander, Commodore (later Rear-Admiral) Matthew C. Perry docked four frigates in the port of Uraga, at the entrance to Tokyo Bay, engaged his guns in a little target practice, and then invited the Japanese authorities to open their country for trade, a perfectly timed act of gunboat diplomacy that is credited with provoking Japan's gradual and bumpy transition from being an isolated empire run by local warlords to a modern democratic state engaged in a global community.

There had been Europeans living in Japan since the mid-sixteenth century, although the interaction of cultures was minimal. The gap seemed unbridgeable, even when it came to that most universal of social lubricants, alcohol.

The first mention of beer in Japan comes from the Oranda Mondo, a record of dealings with the early Dutch traders, penned in 1727. It did not bode well, the author noting that, "The Dutch ... make *sake* from barley .... It was absolutely horrible. It has no flavor at all, and they call it bier."

After 1853, political and economic change progressed rapidly. The country's first definite beer brewery was Spring Valley—later to become Kirin— established at Yokohama in 1869. Around the same time, barley, wheat, and hops were introduced to the northern island of Hokkaido, where in 1876 the government established the Kaitakushi brewery, at Sapporo.

When the Sapporo brewery was sold to private interests in 1889, the money raised was invested in creating hundreds of smaller breweries in the Kansai region around Osaka and Kyoto, including Osaka Bakushu, later renamed Asahi.

Government-sponsored expansion did not last long, though, and by the end of the century, the state was demanding amalgamation. In 1908, a law was passed stipulating that no new brewery could be properly licensed unless it sold 5,000 gallons in its first year—an unlikely target in a largely agrarian society where beer was drunk mainly by the urban middle classes and foreigners.

By 1940, beer brewing had condensed to just two companies.

JAPANESE *JI-BIRU* MAKERS ▶
Around half of Japan's 280 breweries aim to make beers that capture their customers' imagination in styles that vary from mainstream German to distinctive local and international variations on craft brewing. We consider that those represented here usually succeed in that aim.

Left: Beer was a late arrival in the Land of the Rising Sun.

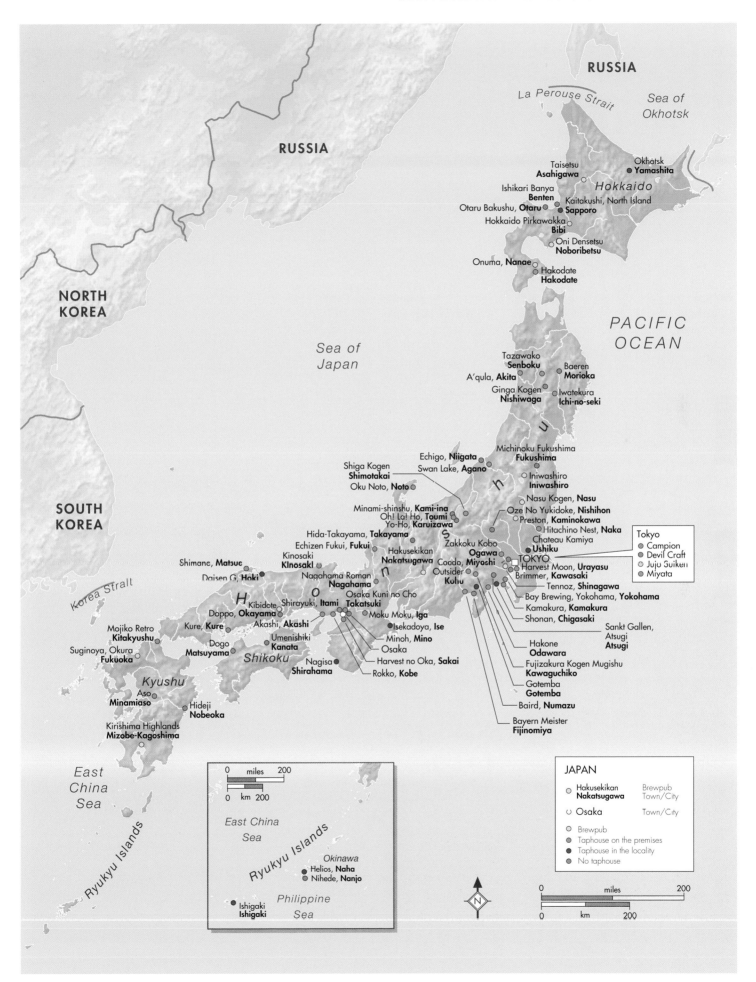

RUSSIA

La Perouse Strait

Sea of Okhotsk

RUSSIA

NORTH KOREA

Okhotsk **Yamashita**

Taisetsu **Asahigawa**

Hokkaido

Ishikari Banya **Benten**

Kaitakushi, North Island

Otaru Bakushu, **Otaru**

Sapporo

Hokkaido Pirkawakka **Bibi**

Oni Densetsu **Noboribetsu**

Onuma, **Nanae**

Hakodate **Hakodate**

Sea of Japan

PACIFIC OCEAN

Tazawako **Senboku**

Baeren **Morioka**

A'qula, **Akita**

Ginga Kogen **Nishiwaga**

Iwatekura **Ichi-no-seki**

SOUTH KOREA

Michinoku Fukushima **Fukushima**

Echigo, **Niigata**

Swan Lake, **Agano**

Shiga Kogen **Shimotakai**

Oku Noto, **Noto**

Iniwashiro **Iniwashiro**

Nasu Kogen **Nasu**

Minami-shinshu, **Kami-ina**

Oh! La! Ho, **Toumi**

Yo-Ho, **Karuizawa**

Oze No Yukidoke, **Nishihon**

Preston, **Kaminokawa**

Hitachino Nest, **Naka**

Hida-Takayama, **Takayama**

Echizen Fukui, **Fukui**

Chateau Kamiya

Zakkoku Kobo

Ushiku

Hakusekikan **Nakatsugawa**

Ogawa

Coodo, **Miyoshi**

Outsider

Koliu

TOKYO

Tokyo
● Campion
● Devil Craft
○ Juju Suiken
● Miyata

Shimane, **Matsue**

Kinosaki **KInosakI**

Harvest Moon, **Urayasu**

Brimmer, **Kawasaki**

Daisen G, **Hoki**

Nagahama Roman **Nagahama**

Tennoz, **Shinagawa**

Bay Brewing, Yokohama, **Yokohama**

Osaka Kuni no Cho

Shirayuki, Itami **Takatsuki**

H

Kibidote

Doppo, **Okayama**

Moku Moku, **Iga**

Kamakura, **Kamakura**

Shonan, **Chigasaki**

Mojiko Retro **Kitakyushu**

Kure, **Kure**

Akashi, **Akashi**

Isekadoya, **Ise**

Sankt Gallen, Atsugi **Atsugi**

Suginoya, Okura **Fukuoka**

Dogo **Matsuyama**

Umenishiki **Kanata**

Minoh, **Mino**

Hakone **Odawara**

Shikoku

Osaka

Fujizakura Kogen Mugishu **Kawaguchiko**

Nagisa **Shirahama**

Harvest no Oka, **Sakai**

Gotemba **Gotemba**

Kyushu

Aso

Rokko, **Kobe**

Baird, **Numazu**

Minamiaso

Hideji **Nobeoka**

Bayern Meister **Fijinomiya**

Kirishima Highlands **Mizobe-Kagoshima**

Korea Strait

East China Sea

Ryukyu Islands

Ryukyu Islands

| 0 | miles | 200 |
| 0 | km | 200 |

East China Sea

Ryukyu Islands

Okinawa
Helios, **Naha**
Nihede, **Nanjo**

Philippine Sea

Ishigaki **Ishigaki**

JAPAN

○ Hakusekikan **Nakatsugawa** — Brewpub Town/City

○ Osaka — Town/City

● Brewpub
● Taphouse on the premises
● Taphouse in the locality
● No taphouse

N

| 0 | miles | 200 |
| 0 | km | 200 |

In the period of economic regeneration that followed World War II, these became three (Kirin, Asahi, and Sapporo), but start-up regulations were significantly toughened, ensuring that by 1970 only two further brewers had joined them: Suntory, adding brewing to its wines and spirits interests, and Orion, created to supply beer to the US military bases around Okinawa.

It was only when the Japanese economy began to deflate alarmingly in the early 1990s that legislators determined to open the market to new businesses, lowering the sales stipulation in 1994 from an absurd 5 million gallons in year one to a much more achievable 15,850 gallons per annum by the end of year three. The door to evolution opened.

Above: Specialty craft beer bars have steadily gained in popularity throughout Japan.

ON TAXING MALT

Governments are fond of offering tax breaks to those who earn their living by continuing trades or traditions that are seen as part of the shared cultural heritage. So it was historically that beer is taxed more heavily in Japan than fermented grain drinks made from other cereals, particularly sake.

Then clever brewery companies began to exploit this loophole by inventing drinks called *happoshu* (literally "bubbly alcohol"). These are fermented typically from, say, 25 percent malted barley mixed with rice, corn, sorghum, soybeans, and other sugars. A more recent variant, called Third Category or "3C," is made entirely without malt.

Happoshu and 3C contain the same amount of alcohol as regular beer but are, of course, significantly cheaper. Grainy flavors are added by use of aromatizing additives, which add a hint of stale flower-vase water. Routinely they are branded in ways that suggest that they are beers, and grocery store will happily stack them on the beer shelves.

Dubbed "Frankenbeers," in 2010, these monster brews took one-third of the market in regular beers, prompting the large brewery groups who mostly make them to look at ways of reducing their popularity. Selling them at the same price as beer and labeling them "imitation" has yet to be tried.

Above: While craft beer is expanding in Japan, 95 percent of the market is in industrial lager.

Two decades on, Japan has just short of 300 breweries, with at least one in each of the country's 47 prefectures. These vary in type and purpose. Some are brewpubs run by one of the larger companies, a few are kit breweries making cheap beer for retail stores, and a number are eccentric outfits making beers to fit with new health fads. However, from within the group there emerged a steadily growing number of top-quality craft brewers, including a few sake makers seeking to increase the use of their brewhouses outside the traditional sake brewing season of late October to early April.

Tellingly, however, Japan's preferred collective term for these new beers derives not from craft or small, but from *jizake*, which translates as "local sake" and gives us *ji-biru*, implying locally made beers. Interestingly not all new, smaller breweries are considered to be worthy of this category, some being seen as creators of cheaper beer rather than beer in more distinctive styles.

It comes as no surprise to those who know Japan that many producers honed their products and their business skills rapidly and at an early stage began exporting to the growing beer markets on the Pacific Rim and in North America.

More recently, Europe has come into their sights also. The expansion has been impressive enough to persuade Kirin, thus far the most entrepreneurial of Japan's traditional brewers, to take a stake in one of the most active newcomers, Yo-Ho.

What we have noticed is that several Japanese brewers of *ji-biru* were early adopters of the current global movement toward putting an indigenous spin on established beer styles, experimenting with sake yeast and rice, even in one instance cultivating an almost extinct variety of local barley. We look forward to tasting how this trend will progress in the future.

Above: Specialist sake stores, like this one in Okinawa, remain far more common in Japan than beer stores.

Left: *The Japan Beer Times*, invaluable reading for expatriates and visitors.

FOR THE TRIP

- Most Japanese craft breweries operate a bar on site.
- In many bars, the glasses are small, so you can share your beer with friends.
- Most *ji-biru* breweries have online stores and will send beer by mail.
- Mark Meli's *Craft Beer in Japan* and its publisher's magazine the *Japan Beer Times* are both invaluable resources.

CHINA

For several years now, the elephant in the global brewing industry's fermenting room has been China. It may not be long before its feet are heard padding into the craft brewing world's personal space as well.

China more than doubled its output between 2000 and 2010. Since 2010, the country has produced more beer than the second-, third-, and fourth-largest global brewing nations combined—that is, the USA, Brazil, and Russia from 2010 to 2012, with Germany replacing Russia in the years since. With the exception of slight dips in 2014 and 2015, it still shows signs of growing larger.

The vast majority of the country's roughly 1.3 billion gallons of beer production fits a single flavor profile, that being fast-fermented lager light in color, flavor, and strength. An overwhelming percentage is consumed domestically. Only small amounts of popular brands like Tsingtao are exported, while top brand Snow—the world's number-one selling beer—is virtually unknown outside of the country, as are Yinjang and Gold Star, two of the world's top 15 breweries.

In terms of global impact, China's daunting potential may be found in its beer consumption patterns to date. In global terms, China's per capita beer consumption is still low at roughly 9 gallons per year: less than half that of even nontraditional beer lands such as Spain. Couple that with the growth of the Chinese beer market over the past quarter-century, from 2 billion gallons to more than six times that, and you begin to understand the effect China could have internationally.

Simply put, if the Chinese increase their annual consumption of beer by only 1.75 quarts per person, for an overall production growth of just 4.4 percent, the volume added would be greater than the entire output of the USA's craft brewing sector today.

Still, with Chinese beer production having leveled off of late, that might be an unlikely scenario. Far more probable is a surge in the country's craft brewing scene.

Thus far, the majority of China's small brewery development has taken place in or near major cities, particularly Shanghai, Hong Kong, and Beijing. Most has also come at the behest of expatriate brewers, principally Americans such as Michael Jordan, Chinese craft beer's spiritual leader, who owns Shanghai's Boxing Cat.

Largely thanks to Jordan's inspiration and leadership, Shanghai remains at the forefront of the country's craft beer scene, although there are signs that Beijing may soon challenge that status. In particular, we are encouraged by the rise of Chinese-owned and -operated breweries like NBeer and Panda Brew in the capital. Along with expatriate-owned Jing-A, the latter has made significant advances in the use of indigenous Chinese ingredients in brewing, using the bitter herb *kuding* as a hop substitute in Panda's Kuding Pale Ale, just as Jing-A employs Sichuan pepper and osmanthus flower for its floral Full Moon Farmhouse Ale.

Hop availability may yet pose considerable challenges to the seemingly inevitable growth of craft brewing in China (*see* below), but the further use of herbs like *kuding* and others used in traditional Chinese medicine may go at least some way toward mitigating that impact.

HOPS IN CHINA

We have written elsewhere how the hop-growing industry has faced a series of challenges since the arrival of the new millennium, but these may in time seem minor compared to what could happen in China.

Although most Chinese beer is very lightly hopped, 1.3 billion gallons of even the most gently seasoned lager still requires an enormous quantity of this basic ingredient. Which is why it is significant that, since 2002, when China first superseded the USA as the world largest beer-producing nation, the country's hop industry has more than halved in terms of acreage, production, and percentage of contribution to the world's hop supply.

In fact, the year 2014, the last for which figures were available prior to the publication of this book, marked a postmillennium low for China in terms of both hop acreage and production. Given that the agricultural consensus is that it takes a minimum of three years to establish a viable hop field, either a return to growth by Chinese industrial brewing or, to a lesser degree, a suddenly explosive Chinese craft beer market could signal severe difficulties for the global hop industry.

Right: It is possible that bitter herbs such as kuding could reasonably stand in for hops should Chinese craft brewers be faced with shortages of the latter.

Above: With beer production almost twice that of the second-largest brewing nation and a low per capita consumption, China remains the biggest wild card in the emerging beer market deck.

Left: Expatriate North Americans Alex Acker and Kristian Li are behind Jing-A Brewing, one of Beijing's most exciting breweries.

Right: Snow Beer, virtually unheard of outside of China, is the world's bestselling brand of beer.

VIETNAM

It surprises many that Vietnam might be of any interest to beer lovers, but in truth we can only scratch its surface here, as the evidence of an even greater history has been slipping, disregarded and unrecorded, from the scene.

Brewing is said to have been introduced to the country in the 1870s by French colonists. The best documented is the 1895 Hommel brewery, which became the Hanoi brewery in 1954, when French Indo-China became Vietnam.

Records from 1995 suggest that Vietnam had over 300 small breweries, mostly elderly, ramshackle concerns that had somehow survived from French colonial times to serve local bars with often unlabeled beers, likely in the *bia hoì* tradition (*see* below). Locating these today is difficult, and many have been replaced, we assume with some form of government approval, by larger modern plants producing international-style blond lagers of little distinction.

More recently, a few dozen new brewpubs—45 by the end of 2015—have appeared, often serving a small chain of air-conditioned beer halls and large paved gardens, where polished copper vessels are displayed behind well-staffed bars. Beer

may or may not be made on the premises, using ingredients typically imported from Australasia and expertise from, of all places, Czechia.

In Communist times, Vietnamese people were welcomed in Czechoslovakia as guest workers, and following the end of Soviet

BIA HOÌ

The most authentic Vietnamese drinking experience is found most commonly in the north, around the capital Hanoi and out along the coast toward Hạ Long Bay. *Bia hoì* refers to freshly made draft blond beers made from malt, rice, and sugar, fermented typically to around 3% ABV. It is served by gravity dispense, from vertical metal kegs that arrive each morning from a local brewery, into notoriously brittle blue-tint glasses.

From morning till night, small groups of laborers, office workers, students, or travelers squat on upturned plastic crates in shacks, also called *bia hoì*, the fanciest of which may have rough-shaded terraces to share a glass or two of ultrafresh beer, swap news, and complain about the heat. It is not

unusual to see some of these simple places, many with barely a dozen places to sit, get through ten or more kegs a day.

The additional attraction for a tourist is that a dollar, euro, or pound should buy several of these light, refreshing beers.

Right: A a simple but delicate *bia hoì* in its equally simple and delicate glass.

BREWERIES IN VIETNAM ▶

Starting in the major cities and gradually spreading along the length of the country, brewpubs in a variety of European traditions are slowly being assimilated into Vietnamese brewing culture and challenging larger breweries to make more interesting beers.

rule many remained. However, disillusionment with the climate and positive developments back home led many to return, bringing with them respect for Bohemian ideas about brewing. The taste can be disconcerting, but there is no question that a freshly krausened Vietnamese *světlý ležák* (*see* p.136) goes really well with eel and banana flower hotpot.

Czech influence is obvious in over 30 brewpubs the length of the land from Hanoi to Saigon, now Ho Chi Minh City, where the original Hoi Vien brewpub doubles as the official consulate of Czechia.

A smaller number of German-style brewpubs developed in parallel with the Czech ones, and more recently a handful of ale breweries—like Louisiane in Nha Trang and Pasteur Street Brewing in Ho Chi Minh City—have joined a tentative new clutch of retail craft brewers.

The best source of up-to-date information is www.beervn.com, the website of blogger Jonathan Gharbi, the Swedish author of the comprehensive if improbable *Beer Guide to Vietnam and Neighbouring Countries*.

Brewers in Hanoi
- Bia Thuoi
- Cientos
- Eresson
- Gammer Beer
- Goldmalt
- Hoa Vien
- Lacvieen Brewery
- Legend
- Mai Vien Brauhaus
- Pho Beer
- Pilsner Urquell
- Plzen
- Truc Vien
- Windmill

Brewers in Ho Chi Minh City
- Big Man Beer
- Brauhof
- Gammer Beer
- Golden Pargue
- Goldmalt Nguyen Thi Tap
- Hoavien
- Legend Beer
- Lion Brewery

VIETNAM
- Tulip
  Da Nang   Brewer
               Town/City

Opposite top left: Rice is an obvious and plentiful substitute for malted barley in Asian brewing, but it makes for less full-bodied beers.

Opposite top right: International beers share shelf space with high-end spirits at this streetside Vietnamese bottle store.

Right: This up-market *bia hoí* bar spoils its customers by providing small chairs instead of up-turned crates.

THE REST OF SOUTHEAST ASIA

In Singapore, off the southern tip of Malaysia, perhaps the world's most entrepreneurial trading state, they have specialist import-export companies for beers from different regions: the UK and Ireland, Germany and Central Europe, the US West Coast, Australia and New Zealand, and, of course, Japan.

Founded in the late 1990s, the brewpub culture has evolved little, unless you count the arrival of Level 33, the world's highest brewpub on the 33rd floor of the Deutsche Bank building. As a trading center, however, Singapore's place in the regional distribution of craft beers is pivotal, and its 50 or so specialist beer bars get a staggering choice of stock.

In South Korea, changes in 2013 to the laws that held back the development of new breweries led by the end of 2015 to the creation of no fewer than 25 small breweries and brewpubs. Feedback on quality is generally positive, but we stop short of making recommendations not least because the big local brands with which they have gone into competition are so bland that fermented noodle soup might be hailed as an improvement.

Bizarrely, North Korea too has a nexus of small local breweries about which we know little. A handful of brewpubs in the capital Pyongyang, and a couple of breweries produce beers mostly in German and Czech styles. Best of luck getting there.

We understand that Taiwan has seen six microbreweries open since 2014 in addition to a small chain of Gordon Biersch brewpubs sneaking in from the USA. Local contacts assure us it is about to burgeon.

We apologize if we make a harsh judgment, but of the 18 companies in the Phillipines, which, at the end of 2015, were claiming to be breweries, we would be surprised if more than five actually brew their beers. Nonetheless, spurred on by importers of good beers from Europe, North America, and elsewhere, they are exploiting (with varying degrees of honesty) a desire to drink beers that are more interesting than the country's famed San Miguel.

Above: With the sale of beer allowed in most stores, deliveries in the Cambodian capital, Phnom Penh, can appear disorganized.

After several years of cranking up, Cambodia now has a couple of small commercial breweries growing out from the half-dozen brewpubs found mainly in the capital, Phnom Penh, plus a new US-owned craft brewery, Cerevisia, pushing the longer-established Kingdom to greater imagination.

In neighboring Laos, a centralized economy enables a delightful light lager, Beerlao, to be made in several breweries around the country, though little else is memorable.

We know of no interesting breweries yet in Malaysia or Myanmar, though the latter may be one to watch. Military rule may be giving way slowly to democracy, but this has not prevented both Heineken and Kirin from buying majority stakes in its two largest breweries. Meanwhile, in Indonesia progress is limited to three or four lackluster brewpubs on the vacation island of Bali.

The bigger question across the whole of Southeast Asia is whether new indigenous styles and preferences will evolve. Is it possible to create beer styles of character

that are more attuned to the climate, or should we take the traditional regional attraction to strong stouts—like Guinness Foreign Extra, Carlsberg's local Malaysian and Cambodian labels, or Heineken's four versions of ABC Extra—as indicating that there is more to beer appreciation than such simple truths?

Above: Advertisements for beer in Taiwan still tend to emphasize image over content.

Above top: While tourists may travel to Thailand for its idyllic beaches, the country's best brewing destinations are centered around the urban sprawl of its capital region around Bangkok.

REST OF THE WORLD

Tracking the spread of craft brewing around the globe is like watching the colonization of a new species. In nations where brewers are normally called upon to produce lightly alcoholic, cold, and frothy yellow fluids, the first signs of new life are usually brewpubs, which either expand their operations to serve others or else entice new colleagues to join the entrepreneurial wagon train. Fewer and fewer parts of the world remain untouched by more ambitious brewing.

ISRAEL & THE MIDDLE EAST

That part of the eastern Mediterranean known as the Fertile Crescent is where beer was invented. Now a place where political strife has become endemic, even here you can find the green shoots of beer evolution.

Israel's nascent brewing revival is distinctly west-facing, with 16 companies testing the water since young Israelis brought a taste for beer back from overseas travel and fell on early imports from the likes of Samuel Adams.

The country's best-known craft brewer, Dancing Camel, is based in Tel Aviv, the Mediterranean port city that is Israeli brewing's natural home—Jerusalem being far too intense a place for such relaxed trends. The more experimental Mivshelet Ha'Am a few miles north proved too offbeat to thrive, but in the south of the country surviving pioneers include Isis of Moshav Dekel, Malka of Yehiam, and the prize-winning Negev from Kiryat Gat.

The absence of trade with any neighboring lands may suggest Israeli beer would be culturally eccentric for the region, but remarkably the same soft, light, and southern European-leaning ales are a feature of the small number of new breweries serving Palestine, Jordan, and Lebanon (see map).

Further, the challenges facing brewers across the Middle East are remarkably similar, regardless of which side of the divide they sit on. The supply of raw ingredients is complicated, the taste of local drinkers subdued, and the attitudes of government generally unhelpful—on one side through religious conviction, on the other by cultural prejudice, with the shared expression being ever higher taxation and regulatory ambivalence.

Were these brewers ever to meet on neutral ground we suspect they would find common cause with ease. A regional beer festival is, however, some way off for now.

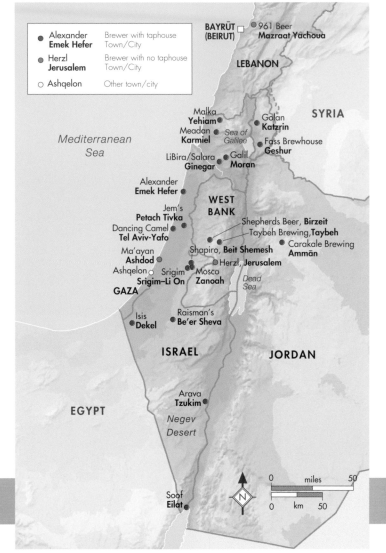

THE REGIONAL ANOMALY

The only multinational brewer based in a Muslim country, albeit a secular one, is the Turkish group Anadolu Efes, currently part-owned by SAB Miller. As well as producing 80 percent of the beer in its growing home market, including a wheat beer and one brewed with coffee, it has expanded into the Balkans and the former Soviet Union. Turkey also has five brewpubs, including the American-leaning Bosphorous Brewery Company.

BREWERY MAP OF THE MIDDLE EAST ▲

In the region where beer was first developed, more recent traditions dictate that brewers must work hard to succeed. This unique map shows all the smaller breweries where beer is made for a new public.

Right: Turkey's Efes brewing group has brought high-tech production to its Moscow plant. But will distinctive flavors follow?

INDIA & SRI LANKA

Waiting for Indians to become beer drinkers is like hoping that Germans will come to love cricket. There is no reason why it cannot happen, and if they did it they would no doubt become great at it. It is just the infrastructure that is lacking.

India is an immature beer market that is showing signs of early development. Because a modern day mogul, Dr. Vijay Mallya of the Bangalore-based UB Group, had invested heavily in craft beer at California's Mendocino Brewing, it was hoped business people would not be averse to seeing such developments in India.

New brewing licenses were banned until 2010, and when they became available, first in Bangalore, then New Delhi and Gurgaon, Orissa, Mumbai, and Pune, massive interest was expressed. Yet to date, only around 65 or so brewpubs have arrived, plus a handful of small breweries—such as Independence and Doolally in Pune and Gateway Brewing in Mumbai. The last of these has managed to source close to 100 percent Indian malt,

which eases the costs associated with imported ingredients.

The home-brewing scene is strong and getting stronger. However, the greatest challenge Indian brewers face is overcoming the long-standing local preference for spirits over beer. This might be the time to create some indigenous India pale ale and East India porter.

Meanwhile in Sri Lanka, where annual beer consumption is under 5½ pints per head and its three breweries are but small parts of larger local businesses, the beer of choice since brewing first began has been strong stout. Lion at Biyagama (part owned by Carlsberg) has Lion Stout (8.8% ABV; known in some export markets as Sinha Stout), Lanka (part owned by Heineken) has Kings Extra Strong (8% ABV), and Millers (Cargills Ceylon plc) has Sando

(8.8% ABV), all routinely sold in large 22-ounce bottles.

While it is tempting to suggest that these beers are hang-ons from the days when strong porter and stout found its way from London to Australia via all ports in between, brewing did not begin here until 1881, at the behest of European tea planters, by which time export strong porter was a distant memory.

Above: Brand name lagers are the norm in India, but brewpubs are springing up to challenge the status quo in urban areas.

Left: Gateway Brewing in Mumbai is one of India's first new small breweries with a more craft-oriented vision.

SOUTH AFRICA

In our first edition, we predicted that the country on the African continent most likely to spawn an interesting new beer culture was South Africa. We had in mind that a dozen or so new breweries might have emerged by now. We were wrong—there are ten times that many.

New South African brewing is an extraordinary story. A decade ago, South African Breweries (SAB) and its descendant companies—most recently SAB Miller—ran South African beer. It still dominates the markets of sub-Saharan Africa.

New blood was rare. Mitchell's opened at Knysna in the Western Cape in 1983 to concentrate on making British-style ales. It was nearly 20 years before a second independent, Birkenhead, set up at nearby Stanford, joined a year later by Gilroy at Muldersdrift near Pretoria.

In Cape Town, 2005 saw the well-equipped Boston making restrained own-brand beers before branching out

into contract brewing for new enterprises like Bierwerk, Jack Black, and Darling, which has gone on to run its own highly successful brewing operation.

Of the 130 or so companies that are now running or intending to run their own brewery, we are guessing that around a quarter have yet to brew in their own kit. Of the rest, around half are brewpubs, and of those around half also sell beer to others. No craft brewer has yet achieved national distribution, though local breweries are now found in most parts of the country.

The main beer style remains blond international lager, though specialist

German and British breweries exist. Porters and stouts are becoming popular, particularly in winter, and, as elsewhere, there is a nascent trend of adding indigenous ingredients such as African fruits and spices to some ales.

BREWERIES IN SOUTH AFRICA ▼

South Africa is one of the most beautiful and fascinating countries on the planet. Experiencing the dramatic expansion to its craft brewing scene can be tagged onto a journey of more general exploration. This map shows more reliable breweries, including those that have taphouses.

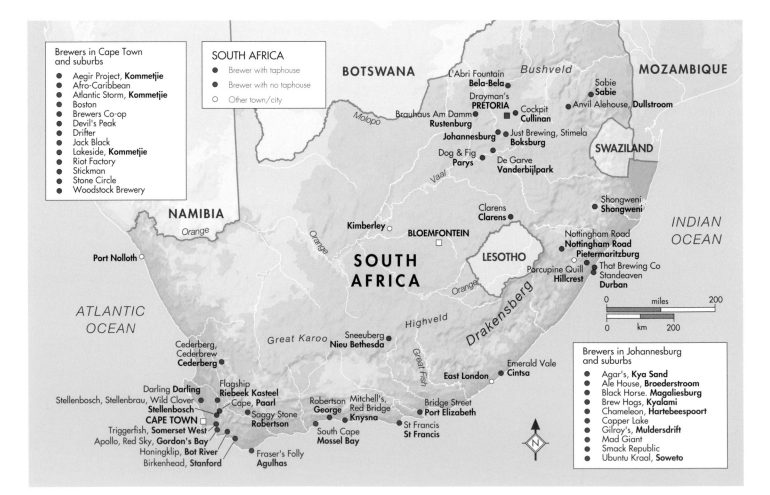

Brewers in Cape Town and suburbs
- Aegir Project, **Kommetjie**
- Afro-Caribbean
- Atlantic Storm, **Kommetjie**
- Boston
- Brewers Co-op
- Devil's Peak
- Drifter
- Jack Black
- Lakeside, **Kommetjie**
- Riot Factory
- Stickman
- Stone Circle
- Woodstock Brewery

SOUTH AFRICA
- ● Brewer with taphouse
- ● Brewer with no taphouse
- ○ Other town/city

Brewers in Johannesburg and suburbs
- Agar's, **Kya Sand**
- Ale House, **Broederstroom**
- Black Horse. **Magaliesburg**
- Brew Hogs, **Kyalami**
- Chameleon, **Hartebeespoort**
- Copper Lake
- Gilroy's, **Muldersdrift**
- Mad Giant
- Smack Republic
- Ubuntu Kraal, **Soweto**

THE REST OF AFRICA

The pace of change is so great at present that it is tempting to believe that interesting beer is available universally. Yet this is not the case. Much of Africa, for economic and agricultural reasons, and its Islamic north, for religious ones, remain inadequately served.

In many parts of Africa, homebrewing traditions have continued into the twenty-first century, employing cereals such as sorghum in West African *shakparo* and South African *chibuku*, millet in Namibian *oshikundu* or *ontaku*, and honey in *tella* from the Horn of Africa. Making these ancient brews often falls to women, preserving an authentic line back to the ale wives of medieval Europe.

Kenya has one small brewery, Sierra Premium Beer, based in the capital, Nairobi, which is also home to a confident brewpub, Big Five.

The most adventurous African brewery outside of South Africa is 1,300 miles out into the Indian Ocean. Flying Dodo of Mauritius is the brainchild of Oscar Olsen, who founded the extraordinary Lambic beer store, café, and restaurant in Port Louis. It uses all glass equipment to make a range of German and US style beers. There are two small independents on neighboring Réunion too—Picaro and L'Ilet—making ales in international and local styles.

Windhoek, the capital of Namibia, was home to a pioneering craft brewery, Camelthorn. This went under in 2014 but may yet be revived by a larger brewer.

Zimbabwe has acquired a British-style "real ale" brewpub, the Harare Beer Engine, whose designers have plans to repeat the feat in Gabarone, the capital of Botswana. Meanwhile, Swaziland has Thunderbolt, near Malkerns, dipping its toe into ale brewing.

Just outside Addis Ababa, the capital of Ethiopia, the Beer Garden Inn produces the remarkably good Garden Bräu Blondy and Ebony. The country's commercial breweries, along with those in Eritrea, retain a more "local" feel, too.

Whether changes in the Arab World will lead eventually to a less restrictive, some would argue more authentically Quranic, attitude to alcohol across the Islamic diaspora remains to be seen.

Meanwhile, the only Muslim countries we know to have interesting local beers are Tunisia, which has three German-style brewpubs, and Turkey (*see* The Regional Anomaly, p.234), though commercial breweries are well established in Morocco.

Above: Oscar Olsen's Flying Dodo *hausbrauerei* in Mauritius mashes in glass to show customers how beer is made.

Left: Ladies selling their freshly made *oshikundu* in a Namibian street market.

ENJOYING BEER

Drinking beer is easy; just order a pint, pop a cap or crack a can, and sip, gulp, or guzzle—simple. Getting the most out of a beer, on the other hand, appreciating all the subtleties and nuances of appearance, aroma, and flavor brewers work so hard to develop ... well, that takes a bit more effort.

Of course, sometimes you're just not that concerned about full appreciation. Sometimes you just want something that is cold, wet, and satisfying, and that's just fine. Yet even in such instances, the choice of beer, selection of glass, technique of pouring, and even the way it does or does not harmonize with the snacks you're idly munching can make the difference between an experience that is merely pleasurable and one that truly marks the occasion. Such is the nature of the remarkable beverage that is beer.

Whether you're in the middle of amassing an extensive beer cellar or just wondering what beer style would go best with your burger, we're betting that the following pages will help you find some answers—and, hopefully, enjoy the beer you're drinking that much more.

BUYING BEER

All beers have enemies, chief among them light, heat, and, for the great majority of mainstream beers, age. Which is why the greatest damage inflicted upon the beer you buy is likely to take place before you even purchase it, making your choice of retailer all the more important.

When shopping for beer, look to buy from a source where stock turnover is apt to be high and where individual bottles are not left gathering dust in the heat or exposed under fluorescent lights. The best will have refrigerated coolers or a beer storage area maintained consistently at something approaching cellar temperature (58°F) with staff who are beer savvy and willing to share their knowledge when asked.

Ideally, as a repeat customer, you will be able to forge a relationship with the store owner or manager or head salesperson, who can help guide you toward unheralded treasures and away from overrated and sometimes overpriced cult beers or contrived rarities.

Purchases that reveal themselves to be "off" in some fashion should be happily refunded or replaced since, with some beer prices approaching the range typically occupied by fine wines, quality assurance should be as good as that found in better wine stores.

If left to your own devices, choose from the middle of a row of the same beer since being farther back will insulate the product from light and any direct heat source.

Reading labels

Beer labels rarely require an extensive education in order to understand them. Sure, they may be written in a variety of different languages, depending of course on their place of origin, but much, if not most, of the information they display will be standard across the board—and, many would say, often inadequate. That said, there are a few key points to note.

ALCOHOL CONTENT

Most labels will list alcohol content in percentage by volume, 4–5.5% alcohol by volume (ABV) being the range for a typical pilsner, pale ale, porter, brown ale, and the like. Some, however, will instead use a number followed by a "degree" sign, as in 15°, which can indeed be a substitute for the percentage sign but can also stand for the original, prefermentation gravity of the wort in degrees Plato. In the latter instance, the number will be much greater than the actual strength, since 15°P will, for example, generally ferment to something close to 6% ABV.

IBU

Short for International Bittering Units and a general indicator of the hop content of the beer. However, few such numbers are tested in a lab, most being theoretical measures calculated by the brewer. Even when exact, a high number does not necessarily equate to high bitterness on the palate, as the bitter impact is reduced by sweet maltiness, although anything over 50 IBU is going to be a fairly hoppy beer.

ORIGINAL GRAVITY

In addition to the degrees Plato outlined above, breweries sometimes list the original gravity of their beer in a measure relative to the density of water (*see* Glossary, p.260). Where lower densities are listed, such as 1,050 or 1,065, an approximation of the alcohol content may be made by inserting a decimal between the final two numbers, so that 1,050 becomes 5% ABV. Where higher numbers are listed, this method yields less exact results.

SRM OR EBC

Two scales that measure the color of a beer, the Standard Reference Method and European Brewing Convention, with a higher number indicating a darker beer. A golden ale will measure 5 SRM or 9.8 EBC, while a jet-black stout can reach 40 SRM or 79 EBC.

AND WHAT'S MISSING

Conspicuous by its absence on many labels is mention of where the beer is made and by whom: usually critical factors by which to judge the likely qualities of the beer. Efforts to make this a statutory requirement will rise the more that evasion is practiced by global brewers feigning local credentials.

Above: Breweries sometimes use their labels to relate useful information to the consumer and sometimes to practice obfuscation.

COMMON SERVING SIZES

While bottle and glass sizes can range widely, several standard volumes are most common. Regardless of where in the world you find yourself drinking beer, the following are the measures you're most likely to see:

ML	CL	US oz	UK fl oz	Other
250	25	8.6	8.8	European small beer
284	28.4	9.6	10	UK half-pint
300	30	10.1	10.6	Dutch bottle
330	33	11.2	11.6	Standard small bottle
341	34.1	11.5	12	Canadian bottle
375	37.5	12.7	13.2	Wine half-bottle, often cork-finished
400	40	13.5	14.1	Scandinavian draft
473	47.3	16	16.6	US pint, draft, and cans, sometimes bottles
500	50	16.9	17.6	Euro draft & German/UK bottles and cans
568	56.8	19.2	20	UK pint
600	60	20.3	21.2	Brazilian bottle
650	65	22	22.9	US "bomber" bottle
750	75	25.4	26.4	Wine bottle
1,000	100	33.8	35.2	German Maß or liter
1,180	118	40	41.5	US malt liquors

Above: With ever-increasing numbers of different brands appearing on beer store shelves, the need for clear, useful label information has become greater than ever.

STORING & CELLARING BEER

Most beer purchases will be brought home, chilled, and then consumed, which is an approach we can cheerfully endorse provided chilled does not mean frozen. Pay heed, however, to those bottle-conditioned beers that require at least a couple of days—sometimes considerably longer—for their live yeast content to settle, and ensure that those beers—mostly ales—intended to be enjoyed at cellar temperature (around 58°F) are not served ice-cold.

For longer-term storage, avoid placing bottles in areas exposed to bright light or extremes of heat and cold, as these are sorely detrimental; avoid exposure to strong odors, too.

A limited number of high alcohol beers, particularly those that are darker and highly hopped by less aromatic strains, or else fermented by multiple wild yeast strains, like *oude gueuze*, will develop enhanced character if allowed to age undisturbed for months or even years in a cool, dark place protected from light, vibration, and dramatic shifts in temperature. Better a warmer spot that stays at a constant temperature than a cooler one that becomes periodically hot, and best of all is a place that is consistently and moderately cool rather than arctic in nature. Optimally, the long-term cellaring of beer should take place at a temperature somewhere between 46°F and 58°F, although most beer should survive shorter periods of storage perfectly well at temperatures between 34°F and 75°F.

Finally, all bottled beer is best stored upright to avoid prolonged contact with the closure. This is also generally true of most cork-finished bottles, which these days mainly feature composite corks sealed with plastic or wax to prevent airflow, or else use poorer quality corks that could cause cork taint.

Right: Matt VandenBerghe, of Seattle's Brouwer's Cafe and Bottleworks beer store, transformed a root cellar in his home into an elegant space for storing his considerable beer collection.

Right: While most beers will endure short-term storage at room temperature without ill effect, long cellaring should take place at much cooler temperatures.

Below right: It is best to store cork-finished beers upright.

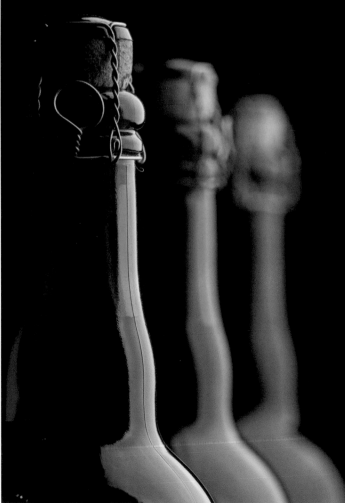

SERVING BEER

Bottled beer requires little specialized equipment to serve it. In most cases, a bottle opener and glass will do the trick, while even the most involved service will only necessitate the addition of a corkscrew to your arsenal. Decanters and aerating funnels need not apply.

Glassware, on the other hand, is where beer takes the realm of specialized design to the extreme. Certain glass shapes and sizes are designed specifically to enhance the tasting experience of the beers that they serve: the oversize tulip for Duvel allowing necessary foaming; the statuesque, vaselike *Weissbier* glass aiding the even distribution of suspended particles; the diminutive cylindrical *Stange* for *Kölsch* helping to retain gas before swift dispatch; and the chalice used for stronger abbey beers enabling the warming of the beer in the palms. Others, though, are employed primarily for the sake of tradition or aesthetics, as with the varieties of British pint glass, German steins, or thistle-shaped glasses for Scotch ale.

Recent years have witnessed the development of numerous new glass shapes, many of which are said to have been designed to showcase the attributes of specific beers or beer styles. Among the first and the best of this is the Teku glass, a general tasting glass developed by a pair of Italians, Teo Musso of the brewery Baladin and beer writer Lorenzo Dabove, which presents an elegant, aroma-friendly shape atop an unconventional—for a beer glass—tall and thin stem. It was followed by many others, a surprising number of which shared the basic design of a stemless, cylindrical base topped by a wider bowl of varying depths. Tastings conducted in many of these have yielded varying degrees of sensorial success, but little in the way of visual appeal.

Since humans are well known to assess their food and drink with all the senses, not the least of which being sight, it strikes us as curious that the aesthetic element of these specialized glasses seems to have not been paid much in the way of consideration. For our money, it is better to have an attractive glass that may or may not funnel the beer's bouquet in a prescribed way than an ugly clunker that perfectly presents the aromatic compounds of its contents.

With this in mind, and until the ultimate all-purpose beer glass is developed, most bottled beers show well and can be enjoyed from stemmed, tulip-shaped, or chalice glasses or even large, balloonlike wine glasses. For optimal enjoyment and presentation, however, we recommend building at minimum a stock of variously sized stemmed glasses for higher-strength, aromatic ales, pint glasses for larger-format "session" beers, and *Weissbier* glasses for beers of that style.

Above: Beer drinkers today have a veritable cornucopia of glass shapes and sizes from which to choose.

The *nonic* British pint glass has bulging sides to assist stacking.

A broad-bowled *chalice* allows stronger ales to be warmed in the palm.

The pinch-topped, stemmed *snifter* works well for barley wine and other strong beers.

Czech lagers glint best in a heavily faceted, thick-walled, half-liter *pull*.

The *Kölsch* beers of Cologne appear in a narrow cylindrical *Stange*.

The beer *flute* traditionally used for pilsners can often be straight-sided.

Helles beer from Munich demands a *Maß*—the ultimate supersized jug.

The ugly *shaker* pint is synonymous with draft beer in the US, although its ubiquity is thankfully on the wane.

A foggy Bavarian wheat beer only reaches full pomp in a puffed-out *Weizen glass*.

A stemmed *wine glass* with a broad bowl is the simplest way to present many styles of beer.

The *Teku glass* delivers both aesthetic appeal and proper channeling of a beer's aromatics.

The *American IPA glass* adds ribs to the common "bowl-topped cylinder" shape.

POURING BEER

THE BELGIAN POUR

Many stronger ales, especially those associated with Belgium, are bottle-fermented, meaning that a sediment is present. Although nutritious, these dead yeast cells can be visually unappealing and will alter the taste of the beer, so careful decanting is necessary. (The sediment can be consumed on its own as a sort of brewer's multivitamin.)

Begin with the glass held at a 45-degree angle, and start pouring the beer slowly down the side.

While continuing to pour, slowly straighten the glass, making sure not too much of a head is allowed to form.

THE HEFEWEIZEN POUR

Unlike most stronger ales, wheat beers are generally intended to be enjoyed in a cloudy state, with the yeast from their bottle-fermentation included in the glass. In the case of the German *hefeweizen* beer style, this involves a somewhat ritualistic pour into a very specific, almost vaselike beer glass.

Start pouring slowly with the glass held at a fairly steep angle, otherwise the beer will immediately generate prodigious amounts of foam.

As the pour progresses, carefully straighten the glass, and let the head form. If too much foam is generated, slow the pour, and increase the angle of the glass, but don't stop pouring altogether.

THE STANDARD BEER POUR

The pouring of a beer into a glass should be one of the simplest actions in the world of food and drink, but it is all too often conducted carelessly or with undue speed, resulting in either a foamy mess or a too-bubbly brew with no head. With a little attention to detail, however, a picture-perfect beer is within easy reach.

A clean glass and a steady hand are key to the perfect pour. Start off by holding the glass at roughly a 45-degree angle, and slowly begin to pour the beer.

Keep pouring the beer down the side of the glass, never toward the middle. If the foam is not rising quickly enough, simply straighten the glass a bit.

Keep pouring in one continuous motion, otherwise the yeast will become mixed with the beer. If too much foam is forming, simply tilt the glass more toward the diagonal.

As the pour is coming to an end, watch for any sediment rising to the neck of the bottle. The goal is to stop pouring just before the yeast escapes.

An expertly decanted beer will boast a rather dense collar of foam atop bright and unclouded beer. The chalice glass is an allusion to monastic brewing traditions—and an elegant one at that.

When about three-quarters of the beer has been poured, stop, and gently swirl the remaining beer so that any residual yeast clinging to the bottom of the bottle might be picked up. Don't swirl too aggressively, or you'll end up with a bottle of foam.

The beer should become cloudier when you add the final few ounces of beer and yeast to the glass. The goal here is a thick layer of dense foam atop the cloudy beer.

No doubt one of the most visually appetizing beers, a well-poured *Hefeweizen* is truly a thing of beauty; no wedge of lemon required!

Pour slowly in a single motion. Part of the enjoyment of a beer is the anticipation of that first sip, so there is no reason to hurry.

As the glass fills with beer, gently straighten it so that a decent-sized head forms. Now you can stop pouring down the side of the glass and begin pouring more toward the center.

When complete, a collar of foam roughly an inch or two in depth should allow for all of the beer's aromatic qualities to present themselves.

TASTING BEER

To appreciate a beer properly, you should always enjoy it from a glass and never swig it from the
bottle or can since doing so deletes the contribution made to flavor by aroma and appearance.
A fine beer is deserving of a more thoughtful approach.

1 Observe
This might seem elemental, but brewers go to great lengths to
give their beers just the right appearance, and besides, if you
look closely enough, your beer could be telling you something.
Clouding can be deliberate or not, excessive or incidental foaming
could be a sign of infection or old age, and, if the color has a
brassy tinge to it, oxidization may be an issue.

3 Taste
Take your time to discern the tastes within your beer, thinking
about what is in your glass and your mouth. Sip slowly, allowing
it to roll over your tongue and around your palate, appreciating
the tones before you swallow. Then, before returning for another
sip, consider the aftertaste—is it bitter or malty, sharp, or warming,
short or lingering? Creating a personal catalog of the flavors you
find in beer takes time, but it becomes easier with experience.
Above all, trying to absorb what it is that you have just tasted will
lead to a better appreciation not only of the beer just finished but
also of all subsequent beers.

4 Consider
Seldom will your first impression of a beer remain unchanged
to the end of the glass. Nor may it be carved in stone by just
one sampling. In the way that a song or piece of music at first
dismissed can, over time, grow on you and become a favorite,
so it is that some beers, unimpressive at first, may after full
consideration become part of your regular repertoire.

2 Smell
Sniffing your beer can draw odd looks in a bar, but appreciating
the aroma is essential. We humans can discern hundreds of
thousands of smells yet only a handful of tastes, so, when our
brain aggregates the two to create flavor, it is the nose that brings
the subtleties. In an ale, try to detect fruity aromas; in a lager, look
for notes of straw, hay, or fresh-cut grass; in a malty beer such as
Bock, hints of toffee or caramel; in hoppy beers, herbal, spicy, or
citrusy notes; and in lambics, musty farmyard scents.

BEER & FOOD

As more flavorful ales and lagers have found their place on the world stage, it is perhaps only natural that in the 1990s many beer aficionados began to turn their attention to where wine has long ruled—the dining table. Good thing, too, because, as it turns out, beer is probably the most versatile beverage there is for pairing with food.

The utility of beer as a dining companion begins with the wealth of flavor possibilities it presents, a result of the almost unlimited number of ingredients and seasonings it may contain, from malted grain, hops, water, and yeast to a panoply of spices, fruits and vegetables, herbs and edible flowers, chocolate, coffee, and even specific, flavor-enhancing varieties of sugar.

As with any other beverage, however, the successful harmonizing of beer with food is largely dependent upon the skills of the person making the pairing. Fortunately, with the assistance of a few handy pointers, the basics are fairly simple to absorb. The rest will come with practice.

Getting started

The first myth to dispel is the one that was perpetuated by innumerable brewery-sponsored beer dinners during the 1990s and early 2000s, specifically that, if you cook with a certain beer, you should also pair the resulting dish with that same beer. While this might initially appear to be a sound principle, it presupposes that the primary flavor of the dish will be that of the beer—and this is very seldom true.

Even when bottle after bottle of brown ale goes into the chili or the steak spends two days marinating in Baltic porter, the taste of those beers will be subjugated by the seasonings and spices involved as well as by the flavor of the cooked and caramelized beef. The perfect pairing, then—if indeed such a thing does exist, taste being as subjective as it is—will depend upon the alchemy of all the ingredients and the ultimate profile of the dish.

Weigh up the dish

Most people at all serious about food and drink will be familiar with the notion of lighter and heavier dishes, such as salads as opposed to stews or broiled red snapper compared to roast beef. Extending this principle to the beverages we drink with our meals, we can conclude that ales, with their bigger, rounder, and fruitier bodies, pair better with heavier flavors such as red meats, while generally crisper and cleaner lagers and quenching and spicy wheat beers better complement lighter flavors such as seafood and poultry. That is, assuming that the pairing being sought is a complementary one.

Such is not always the case. In certain instances, the desire might be to build a contrasting relationship rather than a complementary one, and this somewhat trickier pairing requires thinking that can, on the surface, seem rather contrary.

Right: Although it's a fact sometimes forgotten, beer has long been welcomed at dining tables around the world.

Where contrast is the goal, the weight of the dish and the beer can (and indeed often should) be opposite, providing that other factors likewise work in favor of creating a beneficial relationship. A cream-rich pasta dish, for example, can be effectively contrasted with a crisp, light, and refreshing pilsner because the hoppiness will work with the beer's effervescence to cut through the fat and clear the palate between bites. A similarly bodied *Kölsch*, however, wouldn't work because its relative lack of hops would cause the beer to be steamrolled by the onslaught of fat and flavor from the pasta. And speaking of which …

Mind the spice, salt & fat

Few aspects of food try the vibrancy of a palate more than spicy heat, serious saltiness, and fattiness arising from cream or deep-frying. Beer, however, happens to possess two elements that combine to combat the deleterious impact of these factors: carbonation and hoppiness. The effect of each of these is to wipe away lingering fat, salt, and spice, readying the mouth for another bite of the dish, rather than allowing multiple mouthfuls to accumulate like layers of ice, ultimately obscuring the original taste of the food.

To test this for yourself, sit down with a bowl of salty French fries and two beers: one a hoppy pale ale and the other a malty *dubbel*. As you snack and drink the maltier beer, the salt will slowly erode its flavor to the point that it will taste thin and anemic, even in some instances developing a sort of sourness to its malt profile. Switch over to the hoppier ale, however, and the hops will keep the salt in check, while the salt and fat of the fries will enliven the taste of the beer.

Consider sweetness

Unlike wine, beer offers a world of possibilities when the time comes for dessert, providing that, except in the case of chocolate, the beer selected is sweeter than the dessert. The reason for this is that, in the same way as the residue from sweet, minty toothpaste will make fruit eaten afterward seem tart, a dish sweeter than the beer served with it will cause the beer to seem flat in flavor or even sour.

Where chocolate is concerned, food and drink fall into similar categories since chocolate, like beer, will almost always have a degree of pleasing bitterness to it. With such a common ground in taste, not to mention the mutual bond of fermentation, it becomes a simple matter of playing with flavors—usually those resulting from the use of dark malts, such as roastiness, licorice, stewed fruit, and, yes, chocolate—without needing to be overly concerned with sweetness.

And remember to bear in mind the active flavors

When charting the food affinities of various beers, or the beers that would pair best with specific foods, our tendency is to deal in generalities along the lines of porter and roast beef, extra-special bitter (ESB) and steak, and sautéed red snapper with Belgian-style wheat beer. Unfortunately, things are rarely that straightforward.

Consider the ESB-and-steak partnership, for instance. If the beef is broiled to medium rare and served with a sprinkling of salt and pepper, that pairing makes a lot of sense. Ladle a red wine sauce or demi-glaze on the steak, however, and the dynamics of the marriage change to the point that a Scotch ale would be a much better match. Delete the sauce and add a spicy rub, and you'd be wise to go with an IPA brewed with dark malts. Mix the rub and smoke the steak, and a porter or *Rauchbier Märzen* would be a superior selection.

Turn your attention to the snapper, and the same factors apply. Add a butter-based sauce to the fish, and a *Kölsch* would be a smarter choice, but, if instead you were to season and blacken it in a cast-iron skillet, a pilsner or golden ale with a bit of hoppy bite is more what you'd want at the table—or even a tart *Oude Gueuze*.

All of which serve to illustrate that the flavors being paired with beer can vary significantly even if the main part of the dish —the steak and the snapper in the examples above—remain constant. So it is important when crafting your beer-and-food partnership to consider carefully the elements of taste that you are using as your base for the pairing—the steak or the sauce; the base ingredients or the seasonings in a stew, and in desserts the primary flavor or the secondary modifier—the chocolate or the mint in a chocolate mint ice cream, for instance.

But above all, pair for pleasure

While we remain steadfast in our conviction that the ideal pairing of beer with food can increase the pleasures derived from both, we equally caution that no one likes to dine with an ideologue. Thus the best beer pairing can, in many cases, simply be what you or your tablemates want to drink, so long as it doesn't create a partnership that impacts negatively on the taste of both food and beer.

The bottom line, though, is that it is difficult to go too far wrong when partnering your meal with beer, so the guidelines above should be viewed as exactly that: guidelines rather than absolutes. They exist to elevate the dining experience, but in a sense you already accomplish that simply by bringing flavorful, quality ales and lagers to your table. The rest is simply a bonus.

While generalizations are, as noted, fraught with difficulties, the Food Affinity Chart (*see* pp.252–3) presents some broad suggestions to use as starting points for essays into beer and food pairing.

Left: Beer and chocolate, with their flavor commonalities, can make a most sublime pairing.

Opposite: Whether dining at home or in a pub, alfresco or in a Michelin-starred restaurant, a carefully chosen beer can be every bit as fine a complement to a meal as any wine.

Food Affinity Chart

Food	Key Flavors	Beer	What Makes It Work
Oysters	Delicate, briny	Dry stout, *méthode Champenoise* beer	The boldness of a stout provides cleansing contrast, while the Champagne-style beers offer salt-cleansing bubbles and gentle flavors.
Charcuterie	Meaty, spicy, fatty	Best bitter, nonassertive pale ale, Flemish oak-aged ale, *Altbier*	Fruity flavors to complement the cured meat, with some hoppiness or acidity (oak ages ales) to counter the spice and fat.
Foie gras	Unctuous texture, rich	Belgian-style strong golden ale	The high effervescence will cut through the fattiness of the foie, while the spicy fruitiness of the beer will complement the rich flavors.
Globe artichoke	Sweetens the perceived taste of whatever is served with it	Best bitter, pale ale	The sweetening effect of the artichoke will be absorbed by the hoppiness, allowing the malty qualities of the ale to shine through.
Cream soups	Rich creaminess	Bohemian or German-style pilsner	Crisp hoppiness to cleanse the palate of the fat and refresh the taste buds between spoonfuls.
French onion soup	Beefy, sweet onion, fatty cheese	Hoppy brown ale, *Altbier*, lower-strength barley wine	Sweet malt for the onions, roasty, earthy flavors for the beef, and some hoppiness to balance the fat of the cheese.
Green salad, vinaigrette	Crisp greens and acidic dressing	*Helles*, German-style pilsner, lambic	Fresh malt flavors to complement the greens, with hops or acidity to counter or complement the vinaigrette.
Green salad with fruit	Sweetness from the fruit, regardless of type	*Hefeweizen*, Belgian-style wheat beer	Either style of wheat beer will complement well the fruity sweetness, with their light bodies not overwhelming the flavors of the greens.
Ceviche	Tart, acidic from the citrus juices used to "cook" the fish, salty	*Saison*, dry *Helles*	As tempting as it might be to match acidity with acidity, such as a lambic, better to provide a hoppy foil supported by a firmly malty base.
Oily fish such as salmon, sardines, or herrings	Oily nature combined with assertive fish flavor	Stout, dry brown ale, dry *Dunkel*, *Dunkel Weiss*	Dark and earthy malt flavors to complement the fish, plus some degree of hoppiness or spiciness (*Dunkel Weiss*) to counter the oils.
Delicately flavored fish such as red snapper, black cod, and flounder	Light fish—not too much in the way of fatty oils	*Helles*, *Kölsch*, *Weissbier*, Belgian-style wheat beers	Soft and gentle flavors will harmonize well without overwhelming the flavor of the fish.
Fish and chips	Deep-fried batter, potato	Pilsner, mildly hoppy golden ale, best bitter	A crisp hoppiness will meet the fatty fried batter on its own terms without the flavor of the beer becoming overbearing.
Hamburger	Fatty beef topped with multiple garnishes	Assertive pilsner, pale ale, IPA	Strong flavors and fattiness require equal presence from the beer, plus a fair degree of hoppiness.
Pizza	Tomato sauce, multiple topping variations	Vienna lager, *Bock*	The light sweetness of a Vienna or *Bock* will match the sweetness of the sauce, while the drier yet not bitter finish will cleanse the palate.
Roast beef, cooked to medium-rare	Sweet taste of beef accentuated by caramelization of the outside "crust" of the roast	Brown ale, best bitter, abbey-style *dubbel*	The key is sweet, fruity flavor from the malt without too much hop bitterness, which any of these styles, sagely selected, will provide.
Game meats and birds	Slightly gamey flavors, less fat than beef	*Brettanomyces*-affected brown ales, Flemish oak-aged ale	The mild gaminess of the flesh will be nicely balanced by the tartness from the *Brettanomyces*.

Food	Key Flavors	Beer	What Makes It Work
Fried chicken	Deep-fried batter	Hoppy *Märzen*, golden bitter	Some hoppiness is desired because of the fried nature of the dish, but a firm, gently sweet maltiness will benefit the bird.
Roasted or broiled poultry	Rich poultry, gravy	Pale *Bock*, fruit beer	Relatively simple sweetness is needed to complement the diverse flavors in the dish.
French soft cheeses such as Camembert or Brie de Meaux	Ample creaminess with a touch of acidity from the rind	Oatmeal stout, porter, robust brown ale	The acidity will be well met by the roastiness, while the creaminess of the cheese will accent the richness of the beer.
Firm, aged cheeses like cheddar or manchego	Sharp, fruity, and nutty	British pale ale, best bitter, dry brown ale	Fruity malt and nutty or spicy hop complement similar flavors in the cheese.
Dark, high cocoa-content chocolate (70 percent or higher)	Intense, often fruity or nutty, some bitterness	Almost anything dark and rich: imperial stout, barley wine, strong Trappist and abbey-style ales	Similarly robust and comforting flavors, with modest to mild amounts of bitterness matching that same quality in the chocolate.

Above: Even sommeliers will admit that beer pairs better with a selection of cheeses than does wine.

Above: Often called "liquid bread," a pint of porter is a pleasant companion to hunks of thickly buttered fresh bread.

THE BAD BEER GUIDE

With parts of the world falling headlong for zany beer styles with sour or musty character, with IPAs sometimes considerably hazier than even the cloudiest of *Hefeweizen*, and with highly regarded breweries cranking out ales in under two weeks and lagers in fewer than three, to attempt an across-the-board set of rules that mark out flawed or bad beer is an increasingly awkward task.

The idea that aromas or tastes should conform to an old-fangled set of rules is anathema to many craft beer enthusiasts. They may have a point.

Take haze, for example. Convention accepts it in many styles of wheat beer but frowns on it in most other instances, yet small-production beers of all sorts are increasingly hazy as a matter of course—to the delight of some and the consternation of others. Many such brews approach turbidity in appearance yet are otherwise exemplary of their style.

Then consider serving temperature. In the US, the Brewers Association publishes a "Draft Beer Basics" primer, in which the ideal serving temperature for keg beer is listed as 38°F, while the Belgian norm for ales is "between 46.5° and 53.5°F." In the UK, CAMRA's highly regarded manual, *Cellarmanship*, states that a beer cellar should be kept "at 55.5°F," with no cooling applied before serving.

Expanding into a more complicated area like sourness (perhaps better described as tartness), the same puckering sharpness that defines excellence in an authentic *gueuze* can suggest infection in a pale ale. Even where some tartness is expected, definitions can be exceedingly broad, ranging from a soft, lactic-acid tanginess to an acetic-acid effect similar to that of balsamic vinegar.

Diacetyl (*see* opposite) may be viewed in the same fashion, bringing a smile of benign recognition to the drinkers of certain British cask ales and Czech lagers while rendering other beers undrinkable. The key resides in suitability to the style and degree of persistence since few drinkers would embrace a pale ale that tastes of liquid butterscotch.

In reality, any beer can be subject to bad design, poor method, sloppy transportation, inadequate storage, or just plain bad luck. And while taste is most certainly subjective, overt flaws are not; any that do exist should result in a beer being returned and replaced or refunded. Here is our best shot at offering the universal modern beer drinker a guide to the common flaws that matter.

Left: Tart is good, sour is daring, and fruit essential, but sweet is poor and tight foam suspicious in a *kriek* lambic.

CARBONATION

The amount of carbon dioxide (CO_2) dissolved in a beer is important to its flavor and character. There is no "correct" level; just a set of conventions and personal preferences—the strength of the latter bordering on religious conviction for some. High carbonation can annoy by causing bloating in the stomach, while inadequate carbonation can deaden the taste of a beer.

By tradition, British cask-conditioned ales are best served with carbonation equivalent to around 1.1 liters of CO_2 per liter of liquid, similar to that found in those German and central European beers that are racked bright for serving the same day.

Stronger barley wines share the tendency to low carbonation, as yeast become inactive at higher alcohol strength. A few brewers have experimented with even stronger beers that end up virtually uncarbonated.

Filtered bottle beers and draft beer under gas pressure typically absorb between two and four liters of CO_2 per liter of liquid, the mouthfeel ranging from spritzy to fizzy, while bottle-conditioned beers can display even higher carbonation, most aggressively in a sub-style of beers that use a process inspired by the *méthode Champenoise*.

MAJOR FLAVOR FLAWS

ELEMENT OR COMPOUND	TASTE AND AROMA	CAUSE(S)	NOTE
Acetaldehyde	Green or rotten apples, organic solvent	Too young, partially oxidized, (occasionally) bacterial infection	Never considered normal, major hangover potential
Acetic acid	Vinegar	Advanced oxidation, contamination in draft beer lines	Tolerated in tiny amounts in some oak-aged ales
Butyric acid	Rancid butter or vomit	Nasty microbes in the cellar or storage vessels	Never an asset—even in a "wild" or "sour" beer
Caproic and isovaleiric acid	Cheesy, sweaty, goaty, slightly acidic, (sometimes) deadening	Going stale	Rarely an asset
Cardboard	Soggy paper or cardboard in the aroma and/or flavor	Oxidation, stored too warm, using some dried yeast	Never an asset
Dimethyl Sulfide (DMS)	Boiled corn or vegetables, sea spray when concentrated	Speedy brewing, aggressive pasteurization, (rarely) bacterial	Try drinking an industrial lager at room temperature.
Onion	Onion, chive, or garlic aromas affecting the taste	Oxidation of certain hops, such as Simcoe	Considered normal by some
Ribes	Aroma of cat pee, taste of tomato, gooseberry, or black currant leaf	An unintentional effect of aging, via oxidation	Never an asset
Skunky (sulfurous)	Sulfurous or hydrogen sulfide on the nose	Lightstrike: hop acids reacting with sulfur-containing compounds when exposed to the sun or fluorescent light	Never normal, unless briefly on opening some bottle-conditioned beers

TAKE IT OR LEAVE IT

ELEMENT OR COMPOUND	TASTE AND AROMA	CAUSE(S)	NOTE
Diacetyl	Butterscotch or strong butter	Residual unfermented saccharides, especially with oxygen contact	Normal in some English cask ales and Czech lagers
Lactic acid	Tart or sour, without aroma	The action of lactobacilli, pediococci, and other microorganisms	Deliberate and desirable in lambic, Berliner Weisse, and many types of oak-aged ale, a flaw in most others
Phenols	Aromatic plastic, sticking plaster, or antiseptic	Badly sourced yeast (especially dried), chlorinated brewing water	Some phenols add smoky, spicy, or fruity backtastes
Sherrying	Backtastes of bourbon, caramel, toffee, honey, sherry, or Madeira	The passage of time—even with perfect storage	Considered great attributes in some stronger ales but a flaw in lighter beers such as blond lager

Beer Festivals

Like everything else in the world of brewing, beer festivals vary in their origins, purposes, and traditions. We are not taken with those where sober people make money out of drunk ones. Instead, here is our selection of those where to attend is to learn as well as enjoy. For further suggestions, see the For the Trip sections of our national listings.

JANUARY

BIERFEST SANTIAGO
Chile, second weekend in January, www.bierfest-santiago.cl
Part of a bigger event with food and music, but attracting 30-plus mostly Chilean breweries, outdoing the rowdier national Oktoberfest Fiesta de la Cerveza (www.fiestadelacerveza.cl).

GREAT ALASKA BEER & BARLEY WINE FESTIVAL
Anchorage, Alaska, third week in January, www.akbeerweek.com
The ultimate in beer against the elements. Expect most of the state's 30 breweries and 14°F outside.

FEBRUARY

BEERATTRACTION
Rimini, Italy, mid-February, www.beerattraction.it
Travelers dedicated or foolish enough to head to the Italian coast in the dead of winter will be rewarded with likely the most diverse cross-section of Italian breweries found anywhere. Note that only the weekend portion is open to the public.

CRAFT BEER RISING
London, UK, last week in February, www.craftbeerrising.co.uk
New British beer's top gathering, with all the marketing clatter and lifestyle accoutrements, plus the UK's most interesting beers. Mirrored in Glasgow in September.

MARCH

BARCELONA BEER FESTIVAL
Spain, first weekend in March, www.barcelonabeerfestival.com
Europe's coolest and most educational festival, celebrating the new national scene and showcasing imported beers.

FESTIVAL BRASILEIRO DA CERVEJA
Blumenau, Santa Catarina, Brazil, second weekend in March, www.festivaldacerveja.com
Young and growing beer festival featuring the best of this exciting, fast-developing beer market. Book accommodation well in advance.

APRIL

SALON DU BRASSEUR
St. Nicolas-de-Port, Lorraine, France, second weekend in April, www.salondubrasseur.com
Village festival in the national museum of beer to coincide with a trade fair for new-wave French brewers that is a gathering of the clan.

GREAT JAPAN BEER FESTIVAL
Various cities, early April to late September, www.beertaster.org
Japan's most prestigious beer celebration, split into ten separate events, ending with the largest in Yokohama. Up to 200 Japanese craft beers. The entrance fees are high, but the beers are free.

Above: Few beers to choose from, but mighty volumes at Stuttgart's *Volksfest*, Germany.

Above: Getting a taste for it at Qingdao Beer Festival in Shandong, China.

CRAFT BIER FEST

Linz and Vienna, Austria, second and fourth weekends of April,
www.craftbierfest.at
Strangely enjoyable, garage-style festival with a mix of mostly Austrian
brewers from every background, who often turn up in person with a few
from neighboring nations.

ZBF

Leuven, Belgium, last weekend in April, www.zythos.be
Belgium's consumer-run, brewer-operated national festival, featuring
only Belgian brews, with many brewers present in person on Saturday
afternoon. Regular bespoke bus service from the station.

SOLOTHURNER BIERTAGE

Solothurn, Switzerland, last week of April, www.biertage.ch
The nearest thing to a Swiss national beer festival currently, held in the
German-speaking region between Bern and Basel but attracts some
Francophone brewers among the 40 who attend.

MAY

ØL FESTIVAL

Copenhagen, Denmark, third week in May, www.beerfestival.dk
Well-organized consumer-run festival staffed by brewers, featuring over
700 craft beers served in snifter-sized measures. Nowadays preceded
by the Copenhagen Beer Celebration, a gathering of Eurocraft's finest,
built around its own exclusive but classy beer tasting event.

NEDERLANDS BIERPROEFFESTIVAL

Den Haag, Netherlands, third week in May,
www.weekvanhetnederlandsebier.nl
The centerpiece of Dutch Beer Week. A large tasting event attracting
many dozens of Dutch breweries and lent a large measure of civilized
charm by being held in a former church.

Above: Pints of persuasion at one of a hundred
annual festivals of real ale in Britain.

WEEKEND OF SPONTANEOUS FERMENTATION

Opstal, Belgium, last weekend in May, www.bierpallieters.be
A simple, civilized celebration of lambic beer held in the community
hall of a small Flemish village. Featuring most of the commercially
available authentic beers, with traditional accompaniments. Prebook
a taxi from Buggenhout train station, or take the 25-minute walk
from Heizijde.

JUNE

WROCŁAWSKI FESTIWAL DOBREGO PIWA

Wrocław, Poland, second weekend in June,
www.festiwaldobregopiwa.pl
The nearest thing to a Polish national festival of smaller brewers in the
country's beeriest city.

FESTIVAL MINIPIVOVARŮ

Prague, Czechia, second weekend in June,
www.pivonahrad.cz
The cream of the small breweries in the beautiful setting of Prague
Castle, following on from the more commercial official festival that runs
through May.

JULY

ANNAFEST

Forchheim, Germany, second half of July, www.alladooch-annafest.de
Huge Upper Franconian shindig featuring two-dozen temporary
Bierkellers that operate for a fortnight as part of a beer-based festival
that speaks loudly of its region.

SUURET OLUET

Helsinki, Finland, last weekend in July, www.suuretoluet.fi
Wonderfully natural, open-air event on Rautatientori square, next to the
main station, featuring most of best Finnish craft and sahti brewers. The
largest of four similar events held around the country.

OREGON BREWERS FESTIVAL

Portland, Oregon, last full weekend of July,
www.oregonbrewfest.com
Free admission festival for which each of over 80 participating breweries
is limited to showcasing but a single beer. Recent years have also
featured invited brewers from a chosen foreign land.

AUGUST

INTERNATIONALES BERLINER BIERFESTIVAL

Berlin, Germany, first weekend in August,
www.bierfestival-berlin.de
Two rows of 300-plus stalls taking up 1.4 miles of Karl Marx Allee,
between Strausberger Platz and Frankfurter Tor, attracting a bemused
local crowd eager to try beers of all pedigrees and nations. Just roll up
and get a glass.

GREAT BRITISH BEER FESTIVAL
London, UK, second week in August, www.gbbf.org.uk
The UK's largest celebration of cask-conditioned beers nowadays invites foreign producers and also includes an impressive array of world beers. Take one-third-pint (7 ounces) pours to sample the greatest variety.

BEERVANA
Wellington, New Zealand, mid-August, www.beervana.co.nz
New Zealand's premier beer event, featuring mostly NZ and Australian breweries plus a few elite foreigners. One-hour beer education seminars are highlighted. Free water.

SEPTEMBER

VILLAGGIO DELLA BIRRA
Buonconvento, Italy, first week in September,
www.villaggiodellabirra.com
Cult gathering of Europe's craftiest in a farmstead community in rural Tuscany, increasingly drawing only from among the best brewers and most ingenious beer travelers.

IRISH CRAFT BEER FESTIVAL
Dublin, Ireland, second week in September,
www.irishcraftbeerfestival.ie
A lovely, chatty exhibition of all the best of modern Irish brewing by day, rolling seamlessly into noisier, alcohol-fueled craic by night.

GREAT CANADIAN BEER FESTIVAL
Victoria, Canada, first weekend after Labour Day, www.gcbf.com
Hugely popular two-day outdoor festival, proud of its cask-conditioned beers but boasting more kegs and cases. Originally focused on western Canadian brewers but now drawing as many from the American Pacific Northwest.

GREAT JAPAN BEER FESTIVAL
Yokohama, Japan. (See April: www.beertaster.org)

OKTOBERFEST
Munich, Germany, 17 days ending the first weekend of October,
www.oktoberfest.de
More Bavarian folk fest than beer-tasting event, this 200-year-old celebration—which actually begins in September and ends the first weekend of October—features beer from Munich's "Big Six" brewers and should be attended for the experience rather than for the beer.

BOREFTS BIERFESTIVAL
Bodegraven, Netherlands, last weekend in September,
www.brouwerijdemolen.nl
A funny mix of self-affirmation and beauty contest, drawing trainee rising stars to strut their stuff at one of Europe's most inventive breweries.

STOCKHOLM BEER & WHISKY FESTIVAL
Stockholm, Sweden, last week in September and first week in October,
www.stockholmbeer.se
Lush exhibition of best Swedish and imported beers and whiskies, run in successive weeks. Attracts all breeds of brewer from market leaders to startups, plus other drinks and upmarket food.

OCTOBER

GREAT AMERICAN BEER FESTIVAL
Denver, Colorado, early October,
www.greatamericanbeerfestival.com
Unrivaled variety of over 2,500 American beers from breweries large and small, served in 1-ounce tasting portions. Be warned that tickets sell out within hours of sales opening.

BEERTOPIA
Hong Kong, China, second weekend in October, www.beertopiahk.com
Growing waterfront festival of beer, food, and music with 120-plus breweries from all over the world, including Hong Kong's craft brewers.

CASK DAYS
Toronto, Canada, late October, www.caskdays.com
Likely the largest festival devoted to cask-conditioned beer outside the UK, serving casks of ale from over 130 breweries across Canada, the USA, and the UK. Serves beer in jam jars.

NOVEMBER

CERVEZA MÉXICO
Mexico City, Mexico, first weekend of November,
www.tradex.mx/cerveza/
See p.201.

CAPE TOWN FESTIVAL OF BEER
Cape Town, South Africa, last week of November,
www.capetownfestivalofbeer.co.za
The biggest and best of South Africa's many new craft beer festivals. For others, look at www.craftbru.com.

DECEMBER

PIG'S EAR
London, UK, first week of December, www.pigsear.org.uk
London's local beer festival, aimed at Londoners but welcoming all with an international outlook that typifies the city.

KERSTBIERFESTIVAL
Essen, Belgium, third week of December, www.kerstbierfestival.be
Iconic and popular annual gathering of dedicated fans, featuring every Belgian winter beer. Held in a small town with no hotels—a 20-minute walk from its deserted train station.

Glossary

ABBEY ALE A term used in Belgium to denote particular beers licensed by monastic orders as fundraisers and outside Belgium to represent the styles of sweet, heavy ale associated with monastic breweries. *See also* TRAPPIST BEER.

ABV (ALCOHOL BY VOLUME) The volume of alcohol relative to the total volume of a beverage.

ADDITIVES Collective term for substances added to beer to help present, preserve, or flavor it artificially.

ADJUNCTS Cereals, sugars, fruits, and syrups used as a substitute for malted barley in the MASH.

ALE Beer resulting from warm fermentation by YEAST of the family *Saccharomyces cerevisiae*; sometimes referred to as TOP-FERMENTED.

ALPHA ACIDS Chemical compounds found in HOPS that, when converted to iso-alpha acids in the boil, contribute much of the bitterness to beer.

ALT or *ALTBIER* A style of warm-fermented, cold-conditioned beer, associated with the German city of Düsseldorf.

BARLEY WINE Term used historically to denote the strongest beer in a brewer's portfolio, often of low carbonation or even "flat," with the strength of a light wine. Nowadays it is more often a specific style of strong ale, which is hoppier in the American interpretation.

BARREL (BBL) With HECTOLITER, the most common unit of measure for beer production. In the UK, a barrel is 43 gallons); in the USA, 31 gallons.

BERLINER WEISSE Low-strength, tart style of WHEAT BEER originating from Berlin, now more frequently brewed elsewhere.

BIÈRE DE GARDE Traditional northern-French style of "stored" or brewery-conditioned beers associated with the area between Calais and Strasbourg.

BITTER Often served in CASK-CONDITIONED form, especially in the UK but also elsewhere. Today the standard ale of British pubs, pale, mildly to moderately hopped, and increasing in body and strength as it progresses from "ordinary" to "best" and "extra-special" bitter (or ESB).

BLOND(E) ALE Light-colored ales that emerged in various beer cultures in the 1990s, largely on the premise that lager drinkers would try ale if it looked the same. Indistinguishable from GOLDEN ALE. Despite humble origins this is sometimes a beer of great character and integrity.

BOCK German style of strong LAGER thought to have originated from the city of Einbeck. Stronger and heartier in the *Doppelbock* or "double" version and usually pale of hue in the *Maibock*, springtime version.

BOK Term used in the Netherlands to describe dark, fall beers partially related to German *BOCK*, and also appearing as pale, sweet *lentebok* or *Meibok* in April.

BOTTLE-CONDITIONED Beer that undergoes further fermentation in the bottle.

BOTTOM-FERMENTED *See* LAGER.

BROWN ALE Style of dark ale in various strengths, still most frequently associated with England but widely recognized in different lands and languages.

CALIFORNIA COMMON Originally the poor man's working beer (or vice versa) of San Francisco, made using adjuncts and lager yeast, without refrigeration. Nowadays applied to the much-improved style of beers that sprung from Anchor Steam Beer.

CASK-CONDITIONED A term first coined in the 1970s to describe beer that completes its fermentation in the pub cellar rather than at the brewery. *See also* REAL ALE.

COLD-CONDITIONING Slow conditioning in refrigerated tanks kept at 32–37°F for up to three months. *See also* LAGER.

CONDITIONING *See* SECONDARY FERMENTATION.

CONTRACT BREWING The process whereby a brewery produces one or more beers for a separate company that owns the brands and markets them as their own.

CRAFT BREWING or CRAFT BEER The opposite of INDUSTRIAL BREWING or INDUSTRIAL BEER. *See pp.29–30.*

DOPPELBOCK *See* BOCK.

DORTMUNDER A faux sub-style of German blond lager, unrecognized in its home country.

DOUBLE Term long applied in different languages to stronger brown ales, increasingly used to indicate a stronger, fuller-bodied version of any existing style. *See also* IMPERIAL.

DRY HOPPING The practice of adding hops to a beer during its fermentation or conditioning period.

DUBBEL A term associated with Belgian monastic brewing, originally coined for the use of double the MALT of standard beer, to create a moderately strong, usually dark, predominantly malty ale.

DUNKEL Dark lager of a style once native to Munich and the surrounding area. Sometimes referred to as *Münchner*.

ESB Short for Extra-Special Bitter and denoting a stronger, hoppier, maltier form of BITTER, typically over 5% ABV.

FILTERED Term used to denote beer from which YEAST and other particulate matter have been physically removed in some fashion.

FININGS Substances used to cause YEAST and proteins to drop as sediment in CASK-CONDITIONED ales. *See also* UNFINED.

FRUIT BEERS Wide-ranging classification referring to any beer fermented and/or conditioned with fruits or flavored by fruit juices, extracts, or syrups.

GALLON Traditional measure of both brew run and beer cask sizes. 1 US gallon = 3.79 liters; 1 imperial (UK) gallon = 4.55 liters.

GOLDEN ALE *See* BLOND(E) ALE

GOSE A tart variety of wheat beer seasoned with salt and coriander, originating in the German town of Goslar but popularized in Leipzig, hence sometimes *Leipziger Gose*.

GRAIN BILL The mix of MALTs and other grains used in the MASH that creates a beer.

GRAVITY DISPENSE Method of serving CASK-CONDITIONED or other beers tapped directly from the barrel.

GRODZIŠZ or GRODZISKIE A light beer brewed with oak-smoked malted wheat, mostly associated with Poland but also found as *Grätzer* in parts of northern Germany.

GRUIT (also *GRUT* or *GRUUT*) Historically, mixtures of dried herbs and spices for flavoring beer before the use of HOPS but nowadays a term occasionally used to describe a beer made without the use of hops.

G(U)EUZE A bottled beer made with lambic. When designated *oud(e)* or *vielle*, it must be blended from 100 percent lambic beers only.

HANDPUMP or HANDPULL The colloquial terms for what is correctly known as a beer engine, the most popular means of drawing a CASK-CONDITIONED ale mechanically from the pub cellar to the bar top.

HELLES Pale lager style originally associated with Munich and the surrounding areas. Sometimes referred to as *Münchner Helles*.

HIGH-GRAVITY BREWING Production method common to industrial brewing whereby a beer is fermented to a high percentage of alcohol and diluted with water to the desired final strength at the canning, bottling, or kegging stage.

HOPS The flowers or cones of the plant *Humulus lupulus*, first introduced to brewing on a grand scale in the Middle Ages and now considered an essential ingredient in all but a very small number of beers.

HOPS—AMERICAN American hop varieties that typically bestow on a beer an aggressive, often citrusy bitterness. Sometimes known collectively as "C-hops" (including Cascade, Centennial, Chinook, Citra, and Columbus) and "non-C" (Amarillo, Magnum, Simcoe, and others).

HOPS—CZECH The classic Czech hop is Saaz, also known as Žatec after the town around which it was originally cultivated. Strongly floral in character, it is used in SVĚTLÝ LEŽÁK and others. Now grown in many countries.

HOPS—ENGLISH English hop varieties are characteristically mild to moderate in their bitterness and aroma. East Kent or Kentish Goldings are perhaps best known, along with Styrian Golding, Fuggle, Target, Challenger, Northern Brewer, and others.

HOPS—GERMAN The best-known German hops are referred to as noble hops and include Hallertau, Hersbrucker, Tettnang, and Spalt, each possessing diverse characteristics.

HOPS—NEW ZEALAND Noted for their intensely aromatic qualities and tropical fruit notes, and featuring new varietals, such as Nelson Sauvin, Riwaka, and Motueka.

IMPERIAL Term originally used to denote a strong and intensely flavored style of

STOUT, now haphazardly employed to describe any unusually strong interpretation of a classic style. *See also* DOUBLE.

IPA (INDIA PALE ALE) Style of PALE ALE that derives its name from its popularity in India during the days of the Raj. Originally native to England, it is now recognized in American (very hoppy and moderately strong), British (less assertively hopped and lighter), double (stronger and hoppier), session (lower strength), rye (spicy from rye in the mash), black (deep brown but not roasty) forms, and others.

INDUSTRIAL BREWING or INDUSTRIAL BEER The production of beer on a massive scale, typically by multinational or global companies, using various cost-cutting techniques, such as HIGH-GRAVITY BREWING. *See p.28.*

KÖLSCH A style of light blond, TOP FERMENTED, COLD-CONDITIONED beer, confined by legislation in the European Union to the German city of Cologne (Köln) and its immediate area but still imitated elsewhere.

KRAUSENING The process of adding a small amount of vigorously fermenting WORT to an already fermented beer, typically LAGER, to encourage a SECONDARY FERMENTATION and cause natural carbonation.

KRIEK When designated *oud(e)* or *vielle*, a lambic refermented in the cask while whole cherries are steeped within it and subsequently BOTTLE-CONDITIONED. More commonly applied to cherry-flavored beers made with fruit juices or extracts and often sweetened.

KVASS A liquid form of lightly fermented bread and grain residue, popular in Eastern Europe.

LAGER Beer resulting from cool fermentation by YEAST of the *Saccharomyces pastorianus* family, such as the *carlsbergensis* strain, traditionally afforded a long COLD-CONDITIONING period. Sometimes referred to as BOTTOM-FERMENTED. In Germany, the word "lager" is confined to beers that have undergone some additional aging.

LAMBIC Collective name for the family of beers fermented by the action of wild YEAST and also the name given to the unblended draft form of such beers.

LICENSED BREWING *See* CONTRACT BREWING.

MALT Grain, usually barley, that after germination is kilned to stop the growth.

MÄRZEN Moderately strong style of German lager historically brewed in the month of March for cellaring and consumption during the nonbrewing summer season. Widely associated with fall festivals, such as Munich's Oktoberfest.

MASH or MASHING The mixing of ground malt with hot water, which begins the process of converting grain starch into fermentable sugars, resulting in WORT.

MICROBREWERY Term from the early 1980s used to distinguish new, small breweries set up to produce older styles of beer against the trend to industrialization. Now virtually meaningless.

MILD or MILD ALE Traditional British term originally used to describe immature beer but now a style term denoting ales light in alcohol, usually dark in color, and predominantly malty.

MÜNCHNER (incorrectly *MÜNCHENER*) *See* *HELLES* and *DUNKEL*.

OAK AGING The CONDITIONING of a beer in oak casks either dedicated to generations of ale or else recently used to age spirits, occasionally wines. Some brewers add oak staves or chips to mimic the effect with varying degrees of success.

OKTOBERFESTBIER See MÄRZEN.

ORIGINAL GRAVITY (OG) A measure of the concentration of fermentable sugars found in WORT relative to the density of water, which is given the base value of 1.000. It is usually expressed as a four-digit number without the decimal, for example 1050 rather than 1.050.

PALE ALE Hoppier ale that first appeared in Britain in the seventeenth century and classically featured English HOPS. Now recognized in a hop-forward American style. Sometimes synonymous in the UK with BITTER. More recent derivatives include New Zealand and Australian pale ale made with regional hops.

PASTEURIZATION A means of cleansing microorganisms from beer (or other consumables) by applying heat for a brief period of time, stopping short of sterilization.

PILSNER Pale lager first brewed in the Bohemian, now Czech, city of Plzeň (Pilsen), rendered meaningless as a style by the ruling of a Munich court in 1899 to allow its use for lesser beers.

PINT The traditional British unit of measurement for serving a draft beer, made up of 19.2 ounces. In the US and parts of Canada this can mean 16 ounces or almost any other volume.

PLATO or DEGREES PLATO An alternate way of expressing ORIGINAL GRAVITY, measured with a device known as a saccharometer, expressed in degrees Plato (°P) and used in some countries on beer labels to help denote style and strength.

PORTER A moderately bitter, deep-brown or black style of ale originating in London in the eighteenth century. In modern terms, similar to STOUT. Sometimes termed robust or Baltic to reference, respectively, strong and sweet versions.

PRIMARY FERMENTATION First stage of fermentation during which the bulk of fermentable sugars are converted to CO_2 and alcohol. It can last for up to 14 days but more frequently takes between three and seven.

QUADRUPEL The term invented by the Dutch Trappist brewery La Trappe in 1990 to distinguish its then new barley wine, increasingly adopted by craft brewers to denote a strong ABBEY ALE.

RAUCHBIER German style of LAGER made using a portion of MALTs that have been smoked over wood, typical of Bamberg and the surrounding area.

REAL ALE Term coined by the UK consumer group CAMRA to denote CASK-CONDITIONED and BOTTLE-CONDITIONED ales, often taken (incorrectly) to mean the former only.

REINHEITSGEBOT Bavarian beer purity law of 1516, ultimately adopted across the whole of Germany in 1919 until it was ruled a restriction of trade by the European Union in 1988.

RYE BEER Any beer in which malted or unmalted rye is substituted for malted barley.

SAHTI Traditional Finnish style of beer brewed from barley and rye, fermented with bread YEAST and filtered through juniper branches.

SAISON Belgian style of golden ale formerly brewed in the spring for cellaring and consumption during the nonbrewing summer months, now widely interpreted and misinterpreted.

SCHWARZBIER Type of black-hued, dominantly malty LAGER once typical of eastern Germany.

SCOTCH ALE or WEE HEAVY The term used outside the UK to denote sweet, malty, and strong ales originally widely brewed in Scotland, where they were termed Wee Heavy. Nowadays more common elsewhere, most notably in Belgium and North America.

SECONDARY FERMENTATION The slower, second stage of fermentation, also known as conditioning, in which residual sugars continue to ferment and flavors are allowed to meld. It can last anywhere from a week to several months.

STEINBIER Beer produced by the ancient practice of raising the temperature of the WORT through the addition of superheated stones. Examples remain in Austria, Germany, and the Faroe Islands.

STOUT A family of black or near-black ales originally derived from PORTER, including oatmeal, milk, oyster, Irish, dry, sweet, imperial, and others, ranging widely in strength, degree of sweetness, and hoppiness but always featuring some measure of roasty character.

SVĚTLÝ LEŽÁK The Czech name for the most accomplished expression of blond Bohemian lager.

TERTIARY FERMENTATION A protracted period of conditioning by slower YEAST strains, used particularly in old (oud) lambic and oak-aged ales, lasting anything up to three years.

TOP-FERMENTED See ALE.

TRAPPIST BEER Celebrated ales brewed under the direct supervision of monks, produced within a Trappist monastery. See also ABBEY ALE.

TRIPEL The strongest type of beer produced by monastic breweries and their imitators, originally dark and made with three times the MALT in standard beer but nowadays usually golden, after Westmalle Tripel from the Belgian Trappist abbey of that name, near Antwerp.

UNFILTERED Reference to beers left hazy by residual YEAST or grain haze, although not necessarily bottle-fermented (see LAGER).

UNFINED A cask ale to which no FININGS have been added to assist clarification.

UR- German prefix indicating "original," as in Ur-Typ Pilsner.

VIENNA LAGER or WIENER Style of amber-red or medium-brown lager, once associated with the city of Vienna but now more directly related to the use of a specific type of barley MALT known as Vienna malt.

WEISSBIER (also WEIZENBIER or HEFEWEIZEN) Titles denoting a style of wheat beer typical to southern Germany containing a large proportion of malted wheat and properly fermented with YEAST that produce banana and clove aromas and flavors during fermentation. When filtered termed Kristall.

WEIZENBOCK Strong and usually quite dark WEIZENBIER.

WHEAT BEER or WHEAT ALE General terms used to indicate that a sizable proportion of wheat has been added to barley in the GRAIN BILL of a beer.

WHITE BEER (also WIT or BIÈRE BLANCHE) A style of beer typical to Belgium, made with barley MALT and unmalted wheat, nowadays spiced with dried orange peel and coriander but sometimes other spices, too.

WORT The sugar-rich liquid that results from the MASH.

YEAST Microscopic, unicellular organisms that are essential to the production of alcohol and other aspects of beer making.

ZOIGL A twenty-first century remnant of the communal brewhouse tradition of Bohemia and Bavaria.

ZWICK(E)LBIER A draft beer drawn off soon after PRIMARY FERMENTATION, typically hazy and sometimes up-hopped to assist with longer shelf life.

ZYTHOLOGIST One who studies beer and beer making.

Overleaf: Brewing is both craft and science. Having a healthy understanding of mechanics doesn't hurt, either.

Recommended Reading & Resources

International
Pocket Beer Book, 2nd edition (Mitchell Beazley) by Stephen Beaumont and Tim Webb; www.ratebeer.com; www.beeradvocate.com; www.beerme.com; www.beerfestivals.org; www.booksaboutbeer.com; untapped

General
The Beer & Food Companion (Jacqui Small) by Stephen Beaumont; *The Oxford Companion to Beer* (Oxford Press) edited by Garrett Oliver; *The Handbook of Porters & Stouts* (Cider Mill Press) by Josh Christie & Chad Polenz; *Beer Pairing* (Voyageur Press) by Julia Herz & Gwen Conley; *Tasting Beer* (Storey Publishing) by Randy Mosher; *Boutique Beer* (Jacqui Small) by Ben McFarland; *For the Love of Hops* (Brewers Publications) by Stan Hieronymus; *Vintage Beer* (Storey) by Patrick Dawson

Argentina
GoBeer, Spanish language online magazine at www.revistagobeer.com

Australia
www.brewsnews.com.au; www.craftypint.com

Austria
Bier Guide (Medianet) by Conrad Seidl; www.bierig.org; www.bierguide.net

Belgium
Good Beer Guide Belgium (CAMRA Books) by Tim Webb & Joe Stange; *LambicLand* (Cogan & Mater) by Tim Webb, Chris Pollard & Siobhan McGinn; www.zythos.be; www.bierebel.com

Brazil
www.brejas.com.br

Canada
www.canadianbeernews.com; regional guides like *Good Beer Revolution* (Douglas & McIntyre) by Joe Wiebe; *The Ontario Craft Beer Guide* (Dundurn) by Robin LeBlanc & Jordan St. John; www.momandhops.ca; www.acbeerblog.ca; *Original Gravity* magazine

Chile
Cerveteca (Spanish language magazine, also online at www.cerveteca.cl)

Czechia
www.pratelepiva.cz; www.pivni.info

Denmark
www.ale.dk

Finland
Suomalaiset Pienpanimot (Kirjakaari) by Santtu Korpinen & Hannu Nikulainen; www.olutliitto.fi

France
Le Guide Hachette des Bières (Hachette) by Elisabeth Pierre; www.brasseries-france.info; www.jimsfrenchflanders.com

Germany
www.german-breweries.com; www.bier.by; *The Beer Drinker's Guide to Munich* (Freizeit Publishers) by Larry Hawthorne; *Around Berlin in 80 Beers* (Cogan & Mater) by Peter Sutcliff

Greece
www.beer-pedia.com

Hungary
www.budapestcraftbeer.com

Ireland
Sláinte (New Island Books) by Caroline Hennessey & Kirsten Jensen; beoir.org

Israel
www.beers.co.il; www.beerometer.co.il (both Hebrew only at present, although the latter is scheduled to be translated into English)

Italy
Guida alle Birre d'Italia (Slow Food) by Luca Giaccone & Eugenio Signoroni; *Italy Beer Country* (Dog Ear Publishing) by Paul Vismara & Bryan Jansing; www.microbirrifici.org

Japan
Craft Beer in Japan (Bright Wave) by Mark Meli; www.japanbeertimes.com

Lithuania
Lithuanian Beer: A Rough Guide by Lars Marius Grashol; www.garshol.priv.no

Netherlands
Beer in the Netherlands (Homewood Press) by Tim Skelton; pint.nl; www.cambrinus.nl; www.pinkgron.nl

New Zealand
www.beertourist.co.nz; www.brewersguild. org.nz

Norway
www.knutalbert.wordpress.com

Poland
www.bractwopiwni.pl; beerguide.pl

South Africa
Beer Safari (Lifestyle) by Lucy Corne; www.craftbru.com; www.brewmistress.co.za

Spain
Guia de Cerveses de Catalunya (Editorial Base) by Jordi Expósito Perez & Joan Villar-i-Marti (in Catalan)

Sweden
www.svenskaolframjandet.se

Switzerland
www.bov.ch

UK
www.camra.org.uk; *Britain's Beer Revolution* (CAMRA Books) by Roger Protz & Adrian Tierney-Jones; *Good Beer Guide* (CAMRA Books) edited by Roger Protz; *London's Best Beer, Pubs & Bars* (CAMRA Books) by Des de Moor; *Original Gravity* magazine

USA
State by state brewers guild listings at www.brewersassociation.org/guild; magazines like *DRAFT, Celebrator, All About Beer, Ale Street News, Imbibe*; regional guides like *Wisconsin's Best Beer Guide: A Travel Companion* (Thunder Bay Press) by Kevin Revolinski; *The San Diego Brewery Guide* (Georgian Bay Books) by Bruce Glassman; Craft *Beers of the Pacific Northwest* (Timber Press) by Lisa Morrison; *California Breweries North* (Stackpole Books) by Jay Brooks, and many others

Vietnam
Beer Guide to Vietnam & Neighbouring Countries by Jonathan Gharbi; www.beervn.com

Picture Credits

Acknowledgments

The authors wish to acknowledge the leadership and indispensible contributions of Michael Jackson (1942–2007), beer writing pioneer and friend, without whom much of what we have been able to describe in this book may never have existed.

We also wish to thank the following for their insights and generously offered advice, counsel, and knowledge while compiling this edition.

Rodolfo Andreu

Miguel Antoniucci

Luis Arce

Jason & Julie Radcliffe Atallah

Max Bahnson

Uno Bergmanis

Matt Bod

Matt Bonney

Frank Boon

Jay Brooks

Willard Brooks

Pete Brown & Liz Vater

André Brunnsberg

Lew Bryson

Phil Carmody & Anna Shefl

Annie Caya

Pierre Clermont

Greg Clow

Melissa Cole

Lucy Corne

Martyn Cornell

Jim Cornish

Lorenzo Dabove

Erik Dahl

Tom Dalldorf

Yvan De Baets

Des De Moor

Horst Dornbusch

John Duffy

Tim Eustace

Jeff Evans

Andreas Fält

Alfredo Luis Barcelos Ferreira

Christoph Flaskamp

Per Forsgren

Ludmil Fotev

Fran Gabarró

Alain Geoffroy

Jonathan Gharbi

Reuben Gray

Geoff Griggs

Simonas Gutautas

John Hansell & Amy Westlake

Brandon Hernández

Shachar Hertz

Stan Hieronymus

Gerry Hieter

Natasha Hong

Red Hunt

Bo Jensen

Julie Johnson

Andre Junqueira

Pekka Kääriäinen

Heikki Kähkönen

Carl Kins

Matt Kirkegaard

Fernanda Lazzari

Robin LeBlanc

Jan Lichota

Phil Lowry

Maurizio Maestrelli

Marduk

Catherine Maxwell-Stuart

Chris McDonald

Jennifer McLucas

Chris McNamara

Mark Meli

Juliano Borges Mendes

Anna-Mette Meyer Pedersen

Neil Miller

Navin Mittal

Ralph Morana

Lisa Morrison

Laurent Mousson

Matthias Neidhart

Luke Nicholas

German Orrantia

Josh Oakes & Sunshine Kessler

Garrett Oliver

Menno Olivier

Darin Oman

Charlie Papazian

Edu Passarelli

Ron Pattinson

Clare Pelino

Tom Peters

Cassio Piccolo

Elisabeth Pierre

Rob Pingatore

Chris Pollard & Siobhan McGinn

Roger Protz

Evan Rail

Andris Rasinš

Henri Reuchlin

Tom Rierson

Luis Enrique Huaroto Riojas

Scott Robertson

Jose Ruiz

Roger Ryman

Jordan St. John

Lucy Saunders

Martynas Savickis

Keith Schlabs

Ignacio Schwalb

Conrad Seidl

Hugh Shipman & Marlies Boink

Tim & Amanda Skelton

Joe Stange

Jan Šuráň

Dr Bill Sysak

Péter Takács

Martin Thibault

Steve Thomas

David Thornhill

Adrian Tierney-Jones

Rojita Tiwari

Joe Tucker

Peter van der Arend

Willem Verboom

Eduardo Villegas

Fred Waltman

Michelle Wang

Paul Peng Wang

Tracy Chenxi Wang

Polly Watts

Joe Wiebe

Pete Wiffin

Kathia Zanatta

Index